COPULAS

OXFORD STUDIES IN TYPOLOGY AND
LINGUISTIC THEORY

SERIES EDITORS: Ronnie Cann, *University of Edinburgh*, William Croft, *University of Manchester*, Anna Siewierska, *University of Lancaster*.

This series offers a forum for innovative work in language typology and linguistic universals. It aims to link theory and empirical research in mutually productive ways and at the same time to make available a wide range of cross-linguistic data.

Published:

Classifiers: A Typology of Noun Categorization Devices
by Alexandra Y. Aikhenvald

Subordination
by Sonia Cristofaro

The Paradigmatic Structure of Person Marking
by Michael Cysouw

Indefinite Pronouns
by Martin Haspelmath

Anaphora
by Yan Huang

Copulas
by Regina Pustet

The Noun Phrase
by Jan Rijkhoff

Intransitive Predication
by Leon Stassen

In Preparation:

Double Object Constructions
by Maria Polinsky

To be Published in Association with the Series

The World Atlas of Language Structures
edited by Matthew Dryer, Bernard Comrie, David Gil, and Martin Haspelmath

COPULAS

Universals in the Categorization of the Lexicon

REGINA PUSTET

OXFORD

UNIVERSITY PRESS

Great Clarendon Street, Oxford OX2 6DP

Oxford University Press is a department of the University of Oxford.
It furthers the University's objective of excellence in research, scholarship,
and education by publishing worldwide in

Oxford New York

Auckland Bangkok Buenos Aires Cape Town Chennai
Dar es Salaam Delhi Hong Kong Istanbul Karachi Kolkata
Kuala Lumpur Madrid Melbourne Mexico City Mumbai Nairobi
São Paulo Shanghai Singapore Taipei Tokyo Toronto

Oxford is a registered trade mark of Oxford University Press
in the UK and in certain other countries

Published in the United States
by Oxford University Press Inc., New York

© Regina Pustet 2003

A catalogue record for this title is available from the British Library.

Library of Congress Cataloging in Publication Data
(Data available)
ISBN 0 19 925850 3

1 3 5 7 9 10 8 6 4 2

Typeset by Newgen Imaging Systems (P) Ltd, Chennai, India
Printed in Great Britain
on acid-free paper by
T. J. International Ltd, Padstow

Dedication

For
Marianne Pustet

and
in memoriam
Eberhard Pustet (1924–2000)

Contents

Preface

The present investigation of copulas evolves around a vast amount of empirical data which have either been collected during field sessions with native speakers of various—mainly non-Indo-European—languages, or on the basis of grammatical descriptions. The empirical database is composed of two independent sections. As a first step, a cross-linguistic sample has been established that provides an overview of the typological variation encountered in the grammatical domain of copularization. Due to the considerable genetic and geographical stratification of this language sample, data from the descriptive literature, rather than field data compiled by the author, had to be used. However, the detailed investigation of the potential semantic motivation of copula usage, which follows the typologically-oriented part of the study, is exclusively based on field data. The information on the semantic content of individual lexemes required in this context is so specific that dictionaries and other descriptive materials could not be utilized as data sources. As is always the case when language data are collected by means of consultant work with native speakers, some variation in the responses to a given question may occur. This effect could be observed also in the surveys that were conducted for the purpose of the present study. Most languages were investigated in cooperation with more than just one native speaker. By and large, however, responses were surprisingly consistent from speaker to speaker. This part of the empirical study yielded about 1 600 pages of field data.

The general theoretical model of copularization that is derived from the empirical data compiled in this study is in line with recent functional-typological approaches to the parts-of-speech issue.

The field data this investigation is based on have been gathered both in discrete places in Germany and the United States, and on sporadic trips to Austria and Thailand. The project, as well as the extensive amount of travel connected with it, was generously supported by a grant from the Deutsche Forschungsgemeinschaft from 1998 through to 2001. The University of Colorado at Boulder and the University of Oregon at Eugene have hosted my research during this period. The manuscript was completed during a stay at the Research Centre for Linguistic Typology, La Trobe University, Melbourne, Australia, in 2001. I am indebted to Bob Dixon and Sasha Aikhenvald for making the Australian adventure possible for me.

I would like to express my gratitude to the following persons who mustered up the patience to provide me with data on their native languages in lengthy, exasperating, and presumably brain-wrecking field sessions: Hassan Adam, Neda Afrashi, May Au, Michael Bauer, Carlos Búa, Violet Catches, Olga Chapado,

Gwen Frishkoff, Sevim Genç, Eugen Hill, Mehmet Hacısalihoğlu, Makoto Hayashi, Joshi Ito, Budsakorn Jedkhuntod, Maria Jernej, Hamid Kante, Nedime Karakaplan, Hitomi Kashiwazaki, Akiko Kishimoto, Shou-Hue Kuo, Jennifer Kwong, Hsin-Yun Liu, Le-Ning Liu, Amina Manchano, Hiromi Miyata, Katalin Molnár, Yuna Morita, Kensuke Nakajo, Keiko Ono, Jong-Hee Pak, Kong Peng, Alon Raab, Bill Raymond, Florine Red Ear Horse, Namika Sagara, Chris Searles, Norio Shima, Magid Shirzadegan, Aaron Siu, Watcharee Srikham, Chayada Srithong, Suranchana Srithong, Neva Standing Bear, Isabelle Süthold-Ferchaud, Suraporn Suriyamonton, Akiko Takeyama, Kadri Tamm, Şebnem Uzunlar, Juliana Wijaya, and Than Than Win. Without their assistance, discipline, and continued cooperation this book would not have been written.

My thanks also go to Bernard Comrie, Tom Givón, Michael Noonan, and David Rood for valuable comments on some of my papers which are thematically related to the present book, and once again, to Bernard Comrie for commenting on an earlier draft of this work. Any errors are, of course, my responsibility. I am also indebted to two anonymous referees for the journal *Studies in Language* who encouraged me to expand the original version of this manuscript into a book. A preliminary version of this monograph was used as an Habilitations thesis at the University of Munich, Germany. I would also like to express my gratitude to my thesis advisor Wolfgang Schulze, as well as to Bernard Comrie, Daniel Jacob, and Dietmar Zaefferer, for acting as referees in the evaluation of the Habilitations thesis.

Regina Pustet
Munich, July 2002

List of Abbreviations

1, 2, 3	first, second, third person	MSC	masculine
ABS	absolutive	NEG	negative
AFX	affix	NM	nominalizer
AG	agent	NOM	nominative
ALL	allative	NPS	non-possessed
AUX	auxiliary	NPST	non-past
CL	class prefix	NTR	neuter
CLF	classifier	P	participle
CNT	continuative	PAT	patient
COP	copula	PL	plural
DAT	dative	PLT	polite
DCL	declarative	POR	possessor
DEF	definite	POS	positive
DIR	directional	POT	potential
EX	existential	PRD	predicator
FEM	feminine	PRF	perfective
FOC	focus	PRG	progressive
FUT	future	PRS	present
GER	gerund	PRT	particle
HAB	habitual	PSS	possessive
IDF	indefinite	PST	past
IN	inanimate	RED	reduplication
IND	indicative	RFL	reflexive
INS	instrumental	S	part of verb stem
IPF	imperfective	SBJ	subject
LOC	locative	SG	singular
LPR	locative predicator	TOP	topic

List of Figures

List of Tables

1 Copulas in Current Research

1.1. The copula paradox

Many languages have copulas. The grammatical inventory of such languages may comprise more than just one copula. In contrast, other languages do not employ copulas. Although such cross-linguistic divergences with respect to copula usage may be worth noting, they are unlikely to create a stir among scholars who are actively engaged in contemporary language typology. For one, there are few grammatical categories which are universally attested—such as, presumably, the categories of first, second, and third person. Thus, it comes as no surprise that the category of copula is not universal either. Further, within any grammatical domain, the degree of categorial differentiation may vary considerably from language to language. While many native American languages such as Hopi (Whorf 1950) distinguish few, if any, tense categories, Indo-European languages, such as Latin, usually have a broad spectrum of tense categories. Copula systems which comprise more than just one copula can be expected to occur as well. So, from this superficial perspective, there seems to be nothing particularly exciting about copulas. This impression is confirmed by the treatment that copulas have received in the theoretical and descriptive literature so far. Although the term 'copula' is encountered regularly both in the descriptive and in the theoretical literature, authors hardly ever bother to define it; nevertheless, they are readily understood by any reader who has mastered the basics of philology. The meaning of the term 'copula' is, apparently, so self-evident that rigid definitions become unnecessary. However, what is true for so many traditional grammatical categories that had not been considered problematic until they were made the subject of systematic cross-linguistic research, is also true for copulas: there is more to it than meets the eye. As with any linguistic element, a copula can be viewed from a variety of angles. Rewarding topics of investigation include the function of copulas, their morphosyntactic properties, their syntagmatic properties, such as their compatibility with different parts of speech, their historical origin, and their distribution in discourse. These issues are addressed in this book—and the comparative data presented should make it clear that copulas, with respect to any of these potential areas of investigation, show considerable diversity. But the most startling property of copulas is that they are thought to be meaningless, that is 'semantically empty' (Hengeveld 1992: 32). Of all the characteristics of copulas cited in the literature, this is the one that has met with the widest acceptance. This leads to one of the central questions the present study is concerned with: if the existence of copulas cannot be accounted for in terms of meaning, how can it be accounted for? Usually, the existence of linguistic items of whatever kind can be motivated through the meanings they carry. Moreover, the fact that copulas are lacking entirely in certain languages, such as Tagalog (see §2.3.4), indicates that languages can operate effectively without copulas. Nevertheless, languages which have copulas are more frequent than those that do not, as the cross-linguistic sample discussed in the next chapter reveals.

However, the fact that the function of a given linguistic element cannot be rendered in terms of meaning does not preclude the possibility that it fulfills some kind of function that lies outside the domain of semantics. Another characteristic shared by linguistic elements that are referred to as copulas is their usage in syntax. Copulas are encountered only in predicate position. Thus, it might be argued that copulas exist because they fulfill certain syntactic functions. The three most widely acknowledged syntactic functions which have been ascribed to copulas include:

(a) the function of a linker between subject and predicate;

(b) the function of a syntactic 'hitching post' to which verbal inflectional categories can be attached;

(c) the function of a predicator which is added to lexemes that do not form predicates on their own.

According to the linker hypothesis, 'copula' can be defined as 'a term used in grammatical description to refer to a linking verb . . . whose main function is to relate other elements of clause structure, especially subject and complement' (Crystal 1980: 93). This functional characterization of copulas, ultimately, does not motivate the existence of copulas any more convincingly than the observation that copulas are semantically empty does. The linker hypothesis, first of all, raises the basic question of why clause structure should be considered defective unless some kind of a connection between subject and predicate is established through a linking verb. The fact that there are languages which lack copulas underscores this point; Tagalog is one of the numerous examples. Tagalog clauses are certainly not incomplete because they do not contain a linking verb. A more vexing problem, however, is the fact that in most languages which have copulas only certain types of lexemes must be linked to the subject when they figure as the nucleus of a predicate phrase, while others do not require the insertion of a linking verb. Thus, in English, nouns and adjectives have to be combined with a copula in predicate position, while verbs are not compatible with a copula, as the following examples show.

1.1. this is a cup

1.2. this cup is full

1.3. this cup broke

In response to this, it might of course be argued that verbs, in contradistinction to nouns and adjectives, might be analyzed as having an intrinsic linking potential of their own. This, however, does not settle the question yet if data from a broader spectrum of languages are taken into account. In Mandarin and other varieties of Chinese only nouns receive a copula in predicate position, while verbs and adjectives do not, as examples 1.4 to 1.6 illustrate.

1.4. Dàmíng   shì   lǎoshī
    Da-Ming   COP   teacher
    'Da-Ming is a teacher' (author's field data)

1.5. Dàmíng   hěn   gāo
    Da-Ming   very   tall
    'Da-Ming is very tall' (author's field data)

1.6. Dàmíng   zài   pǎobù
    Da-Ming   IPF   run
    'Da-Ming is running' (author's field data)

Does this imply that only nouns lack a linking potential in Mandarin, while adjectives, unlike English adjectives, do not? Instead of getting lost in such considerations, one might as well abandon the linker hypothesis, and start looking for an alternative explanation for the existence of copulas, as well as for the seemingly idiosyncratic behavior of copulas with respect to compatibility with lexical items. Copulas are often portrayed as dummy elements whose sole purpose lies in carrying verbal morphology in predicate phrases whose nucleus consists of a lexeme which is incompatible with verbal morphology:

. . . the idea underlying the Dummy Hypothesis is that the copula is basically a 'hat-rack' for categories of verbal morphology.

(Stassen 1997: 66)

. . . the principal function of the copulative verb *to be* in Russian, Greek and Latin is to serve as the locus in surface structure for the marking of tense, mood and aspect.

(Lyons 1968: 322)

If, indeed, the sole reason for the existence of copulas is to be sought in their alleged syntactic 'hitching post' or 'hat-rack' function, certain structural constellations are unlikely to occur. First, there should be no copulas which never carry verbal inflectional categories. Secondly, a predicate in which verbal inflectional categories are coded in the lexical nucleus itself should never contain a copula. Neither one of these predictions made by the dummy hypothesis is substantiated by the empirical facts. For instance, the Mandarin copula *shì* cannot be combined with verbal morphology simply because Mandarin is an isolating language and thus lacks morphologically marked categories. In Turkish, categories of predicate inflection, such as person affixes, are directly attached to the predicate nucleus, regardless of the parts-of-speech membership of the latter. However, in addition, Turkish predicate phrases may contain the affix -*y*, which is analyzed as a copula by Kornfilt (1997):

1.7. (ben)   satıcı-y-ım
     1SG   seller-COP-1SG
     'I am a seller' (Kornfilt 1997: 77)

(For a more detailed discussion of the Turkish data, see §§2.3.1 and 2.3.3.)

Thus, as with the 'hitching post' model, the dummy hypothesis fails to provide a satisfactory account of the phenomenon of copula use.[1]

Further, examples such as 1.7 entail the question of why certain types of lexemes in particular languages should be incapable of carrying verbal inflectional categories at all, while their semantic counterparts in other languages are compatible with such categories. This picks up on the issue concerning cross-linguistic variation with respect to the lexical class membership of lexemes which combine with copulas, which has already been addressed above. As example 1.8 illustrates, there are languages, such as Classical Nahuatl, in which nouns can be inflected for categories of verbal morphology, such as person; no copula is needed.

1.8. ni-teūc-tli
     1SG.SBJ-lord-NPS.SG
     'I am a lord' (Andrews 1975: 147)

The verbal inflectional affix *ni-* 'first person singular subject' attaches directly to a nominal nucleus. The latter also carries the nominal suffix -*tli*, which indicates non-possessed status and singular number. Faced with such examples, one must conclude that the parts-of-speech class affiliation of a given lexeme should not interfere with its ability to combine with categories of predicate morphology. Although a Eurocentric outlook on language may foster the general expectation that nouns, and maybe adjectives as well, are not directly compatible with categories of predicate morphology, example 1.8 proves that such an a priori assumption does not live up to the facts. Thus, it is not quite clear why a syntactic 'hitching post' is needed at all in any language, even in those languages in which predicate categories are marked by morphologically bound elements.

Bypassing the controversial issues of the alleged linking and 'hitching post' functions of copulas, the motivation for the use of copulas may also be seen in the syntactic function of rendering certain types of lexemes eligible for predicate position:

A copula enables a non-verbal predicate to act as a main predicate in those languages and under those circumstances in which this non-verbal predicate could not fulfill this function on its own.

(Hengeveld 1992: 32)

---

[1] For a partly analogous but more explicit evaluation of the dummy hypothesis, see Stassen (1994, 1997: 65ff.).

Like the other potential functions of copulas which have been discussed so far, the predicator hypothesis leaves a central issue unresolved: why is it that lexical items that denote the same concept may behave differently with respect to compatibility with copulas in different languages? Why, for instance, does an English adjective such as *tall* require the insertion of a copula when functioning as a predicate nucleus, while the corresponding Mandarin adjective does not (see example 1.5)? Why does the English noun *lord* require the presence of a copula, while its semantic equivalent in Classical Nahuatl is capable of forming predicates on its own (see example 1.8)? Obviously, the traditional accounts of copula usage raise more questions than they answer.

Before dealing with the state of the art regarding copulas in the more comprehensive theoretical context of recent approaches to the parts-of-speech issue, the specific definition of 'copula' which provides the basis for the present study will be presented.

1.2. Definition of 'copula'

In accordance with traditional definitions which are essentially based on the criterion of the semantic emptiness of copulas (see for instance, Hengeveld 1992: 32 and Stassen 1997: 65), the notion of 'copula' can be defined as follows:

1.9. A copula is a linguistic element which co-occurs with certain
lexemes in certain languages when they function as predicate nucleus.
A copula does not add any semantic content to the predicate phrase it
is contained in.

In this context, two additional types of elements which participate in the formation of predicates, and are therefore related to copulas to some extent, must be addressed: semi-copulas—or quasi-copulas, as they are sometimes called— and auxiliaries. However, unlike copulas, both semi-copulas and auxiliaries add meaning to the predicate phrases in which they are contained. This semantic function, while not directly affecting the inner core of the predicate phrase, that is, its lexical nucleus, by altering the intrinsic semantic content of the latter, consists in 'importing' either grammatical categories or other meaning components into the predicate phrase.

English examples for semi-copulas include *to become*, *to feel*, *to look*, and *to remain*, to name just a few.

1.10. to become big

1.11. to feel good

1.12. to look nice

1.13. to remain intact

Semi-copulas occupy an intermediate position between copulas and full verbs in that they show similarities with both lexeme types. Thus, a squish can be posited between these three linguistic elements (M. Noonan, p.c.). Copulas are neither meaningful, nor can they function as predicates on their own.[2] Full verbs, on the other hand, are both meaningful and capable of forming predicates independently. Like copulas, semi-copulas cannot be used as predicates on their own. However, as has been pointed out above, semi-copulas can be differentiated from copulas in that they add meaning to the predicate phrase they are contained in. The semantic aspect of the distinction between copulas and semi-copulas is elaborated on by Hengeveld (1992: 35):

The main difference between constructions containing a copula and those containing a semi-copula is that the semi-copula can never be left out without changing or affecting the meaning of the resulting construction. In other words, the semi-copula adds an element of meaning to the construction in which it occurs, whereas the copula does not.

Hengeveld (1992: 36) further remarks that semi-copulas often express aspectual meanings, and cites the English verbs *to become* and *to remain* as examples. In many cases, auxiliaries also function to code aspectual categories. The English auxiliary *to have* is a well-known example of an auxiliary acting as an aspect marker. It is probably not too far-fetched to consider the possibility that semi-copulas and auxiliaries might be analyzed as members of a single grammatical category. Hengeveld (1992: 37) also alludes to this analytical alternative, which suggests itself on the grounds of the shared structural and semantic properties of semi-copulas and auxiliaries. Neither auxiliaries nor semi-copulas are semantically empty; neither auxiliaries nor semi-copulas are capable of forming predicates on their own. However, it should, in principle, be possible to draw a dividing line between auxiliaries and semi-copulas. From the usage of the two terms in the descriptive literature scanned for the purpose of the present study, one gains the impression that the label of auxiliary tends to be applied to linguistic items which code grammatical categories, while the label of semi-copula is preferably chosen for elements which convey meanings of a more lexical nature.

The definition given above is solely concerned with the question about the semantic scope of copulas at the level of the predicate phrase. The fact that copulas are not meaningful at this level of the organization of language, however, does not rule out the possibility that copula use may be sensitive to certain functions operating at other levels of language description. In some languages, copula usage is, in fact, controlled by pragmatic factors, more specifically, by style—colloquial *vs.* formal style, spoken *vs.* written style, and so on. For instance,

---

[2] If a copula is homonymous with a full verb (for examples, see §2.3.3), the functionally ambiguous linguistic element in question is capable of functioning as a predicate on its own, of course. However, the present study operates with a strict separation of copula functions and other potential functions a linguistic item may fulfill. Thus, a full verb which is homonymous with a copula is treated as an independent lexeme.

in colloquial Indonesian, the copula is not used; it occurs only in formal style (author's field data). In Burmese, the copula is missing in the spoken language; it is only used in the written language (author's field data).

Copulas are typically intransitive. However, the above definition does not preclude the existence of transitive copulas. Languages which have transitive copulas include Basque and Koasati (Kimball 1991: 90). The Basque copula *ukan*, which occurs in combination with transitive verbs, is homonymous with the full verb *ukan* 'to have' (author's field data). (For an in-depth discussion of the Basque data, see §§2.3.4 and 4.2.)

One more note on terminology is in order here. Henceforth, lexemes which co-occur with a copula in predicate position will be referred to as COPULARIZING lexemes. By way of analogy, the phenomenon of copula use will be referred to as COPULARIZATION. Neither the verb 'to copularize' nor the noun 'copularization' has a processual connotation. Thus, these terms should not be understood as denoting, for instance, a process in which a lexeme 'acquires' a copula when it is used as a predicate nucleus.[3]

The definition of copula given in 1.9 is based essentially on the assumption that copulas lack semantic content, and on the assumption that the occurrence of copulas is restricted to predicate position. The aim of the present study is developing a cross-linguistically viable approach to copularization. Thus, the definition of the elements under investigation, that is copulas, must be applicable at the cross-linguistic level as well. Since occurrence in predicate position is one of the defining criteria of copulas, definition 1.9 is applicable only in languages which have the function of predicate. However, serious arguments against the universality of the predicate function have never been proposed. Therefore, definition 1.9 is suited as a basis for cross-linguistic approaches to copularization.

1.3. The parts-of-speech issue

In §1.1, it is stated that there is considerable cross-linguistic variation with respect to the compatibility of copulas with lexical items. More specifically, in dealing with copulas in cross-linguistic perspective, one cannot help but notice that there is an intimate connection between patterns of copula usage and the division of the lexicon into the major parts of speech noun, verb, and adjective. In characterizing the syntagmatic distribution of copulas in individual languages, grammar writers notoriously resort to the lexical categories noun, verb, and adjective, which are more or less tacitly accepted as universally applicable descriptive primitives of lexical structure. However, the parts of speech themselves present a considerable challenge for language theory (Anward, Moravcsik, and Stassen 1997, Croft

---

[3] This is in sharp contrast with Hengeveld's (1992: 237ff.) and Stassen's (1997: 94ff.) usage of the term copularization, which refers to the grammaticalization process which turns full verbs or other non-copular elements into copulas.

1999, Vogel and Comrie 2000). Tackling the copula issue on the basis of the concepts noun, verb, and adjective inevitably leads to further complications because a comprehensive and satisfactory approach to the parts-of-speech issue is not available yet. Nevertheless, the topics of copula and parts of speech are inextricably interwoven for another reason as well. It has long been recognized that purely semantic definitions of the parts of speech are not viable (see §1.3.2). As a consequence, semantic definitions of the parts of speech have been replaced with, or at least supplemented with, formal definitions. This approach dates back, at least, to the era of American structuralism. Bloomfield emphasizes the necessity of providing form-based definitions of lexical classes which derive from their morphosyntactic properties:

> ...every lexical form is assigned always to the customary form-classes. To describe the grammar of a language, we have to state the form-classes of each lexical form, and to determine what characteristics make the speakers assign it to these form-classes.

> (Bloomfield 1933: 266)

In the same vein, Sapir states: 'A part of speech outside of the limitations of syntactic form is but a will o' the wisp' (Sapir 1921: 118f.).

Copula usage is regarded as one of the most important of the morphosyntactic criteria that accomplish a separation between language-specific parts-of-speech classes (see Stassen 1997: 62ff.). In this respect there seems to be a general consensus among contemporary scholars dealing with lexical categorization. Given the interconnectedness of the parts-of-speech issue and the phenomenon of copularization, the first step in approaching the latter is, of necessity, a detailed discussion of the parts-of-speech issue.

1.3.1. Parts-of-speech class indistinctions

Analysis into parts of speech dates back to antiquity. The major parts of speech that language theory has been operating with ever since are noun, verb, adjective, and adverb. This distinction may have shaped grammar writing more than any other linguistic concept. However, as linguistic research expands beyond the Indo-European language family, more and more grammatical categories long taken for granted lose their reliability. Contemporary approaches to lexical categorization cite evidence from a variety of languages that seems to challenge the universality of noun, verb, and adjective. Many languages collapse the lexical items that represent these parts of speech into less than three lexical classes. For instance, it is claimed that Nootka is either endowed with an extremely weak noun-verb-adjective distinction, or lacks it entirely (Schachter 1985: 11ff.); the lexicon of this language may be said to consist of a single lexeme class only. A division of the lexicon into two classes is appropriate for languages in which adjectives cannot be differentiated from either nouns or verbs (see Dixon 1977b, below). (Analogous facts concerning neutralizations of lexical class distinctions emerge in Chapter 2 in the attempt to determine what patterns of distribution of copularizing *vs.* non-copularizing items in the lexicon of individual languages are attested at the cross-linguistic level.)

However, potential reasons for disagreement on the parts-of-speech issue do not just lie in the hard facts of the grammatical structure of individual languages; considerations of a more fundamental nature, such as what the ingredients of a general theory of language should be, also play a role here. Parts of speech can be defined at several levels of language description, in particular, at the levels of semantics, syntax, and morphology. It should be kept in mind that typological variation with respect to the language-specific elaboration of lexical class distinctions is a phenomenon that is intimately connected with the formal level of language. In addition, theoretical approaches that emphasize distinctions pertaining to formal aspects of language, such as the surface-level distinction of grammatical categories, and purely semantic approaches to the lexicon do not necessarily come up with the same patterns of segmentation of the lexicon into lexical classes. Semantic approaches differentiate parts of speech on the basis of the distinction between object, property, and event concepts. Advocates of the morphosyntactic approach to lexical categorization include Bloomfield and other American structuralists:

The languages of the Indo-European family are peculiar in having many parts of speech. . . . Most languages show a smaller number. A distribution into three types is quite frequent (Semitic, Algonquian); usually one resembles our substantives and one our verbs. It is a mistake to suppose that our part-of-speech system represents universal features of human expression. If such classes as objects, actions, and qualities exist apart from our language, as realities either of physics or of human psychology, then, of course, they exist all over the world, but it would still be true that many languages lack corresponding parts of speech.

(Bloomfield 1933: 198f.)

Viewing the parts-of-speech issue from a purely semantic standpoint that excludes morphosyntax will not lead to the discovery of typological diversity because any language has lexemes that correspond to Indo-European nouns, verbs, and adjectives in their semantic content, as Bloomfield points out. All speakers of human languages are, presumably, familiar with concepts such as 'dog', 'water', 'moon', or 'to run', 'to speak', 'to eat', or 'black', 'big', and 'good'. Thus, if language X is said to lack adjectives on formal grounds, this does not mean that it has no lexemes expressing property concepts such as color, shape, or dimension. Rather, it means that the respective lexemes do not display any morphosyntactic features that justify the establishment of a separate lexical class. For example, in many languages, such as Dyirbal, lexemes expressing adjectival concepts can barely be differentiated from nouns with respect to their morphosyntactic behavior:

Dyirbal . . . has distinct sets of inflections for verbs, on the one hand, and nouns and adjectives, on the other. An adjective has exactly the same inflectional and derivational possibilities as a noun, and can comprise a complete NP, as can a noun. The two classes are distinguished in terms of their co-occurrence with article-like 'noun markers' ... A noun can only occur with a noun marker that agrees with it in noun class ('gender') whereas an adjective can occur with a noun marker inflected for any of the four genders.

(Dixon 1977b: 54)

Well-known examples of languages in which the adjective–verb distinction is almost non-existent include native American languages such as Lakota or East-Asian languages such as Mandarin. Grammatical descriptions of such languages treat adjectives as a subclass of verbs.

Languages which neutralize distinctions between the parts of speech noun, verb, and adjective to the point of collapsing them into a single form class are found particularly in the Americas and Oceania. However, some scholars claim that this kind of indistinction is never thorough, but rather, a matter of degree. Schachter (1985) assumes that a set of criteria differentiating between nouns and verbs, however restricted, can be identified in every language. But even if a language that provides no evidence of a formal distinction between nouns, verbs, and adjectives were to exist, this would not necessarily mean that there is no reality at all to the traditional segmentation of the lexicon into nouns, verbs, and adjectives at the semantic level. The observation that a given language may not overtly express functional distinctions which are marked overtly in another language is so trivial that examples do not have to be cited at this point. The fact that there are languages which distinguish between lexical classes, but which do not partition the lexicon exactly the way Indo-European languages do, is much more detrimental to the view that nouns, verbs, and adjectives are universally valid primitives of lexical categorization, than the existence of languages which neutralize distinctions between some or all of the traditional parts of speech. For instance, Stassen (1997: 200ff.) discusses several languages in which semantic-ally adjectival concepts do not behave uniformly with respect to their parts-of-speech affiliation.

1.3.2. Cluster definitions of noun, verb, and adjective

The traditional definition of parts of speech is a cluster concept that comprises semantic, pragmatic, and morphosyntactic criteria. Although it seems intuitively clear at first glance what is meant by the terms noun, verb and adjective, exact definitions turn out to be quite problematic.

The semantic subdefinition of the traditional parts of speech noun, verb, and adjective is as follows:

1.14. Subdefinition 1:
    Prototypical nouns designate things, entities, or concrete objects. Prototypical verbs designate actions, events, and processes. Prototypical adjectives designate properties.

The idea that the traditional labels of noun, verb, and adjective merely constitute loose semantic cover terms, or semantic prototypes, whose applicability to individual lexical items may vary from case to case, has been around for quite a while. It is clearly articulated in the following statement by Sapir (1921: 117):

> Our conventional classification of words into parts of speech is only a vague, wavering approximation to a consistently worked out inventory of experience. We imagine, to begin with, that all 'verbs' are inherently concerned with action as such, that a 'noun' is the name of some definite object or personality that can be pictured by the mind, that all qualities are necessarily expressed by a definite group of words to which we may appropriately apply the term 'adjective'. As soon as we test our vocabulary, we discover that the parts of speech are far from corresponding to so simple an analysis of reality.

In the more recent literature, Sapir's view is echoed, for instance, by Croft (1991: 65, 2001: 87f., 2001: 103) and Stassen (1997: 13f., 28f.). Croft and Stassen explicitly treat the traditional parts of speech as lexical prototypes.

The pragmatic subdefinition of nouns, verbs, and adjectives is based on the fact that in the clausal context, each of the latter parts of speech shows a preference for fulfilling a specific function.

1.15. Subdefinition 2:
Nouns tend to function as arguments. Verbs tend to function as predicates. Adjectives tend to function as attributes.

The functions of argument, predicate, and attribute are referred to as 'pragmatic functions' by Croft (1991: 37ff.). In the present study, this terminological label will, henceforth, be adopted.

Subdefinition 3 deals with the grammatical behavior of parts of speech in discourse. Cross-linguistically, specific lexeme types exhibit a pronounced inclination to attract specific grammatical categories. This is a direct consequence of the phenomenon of the preference for a specific pragmatic function, which is addressed in subdefinition 2.

1.16. Subdefinition 3:
In discourse, nouns tend to combine with grammatical categories that denote case, number, definiteness/indefiniteness, and gender/noun class; verbs tend to combine with grammatical categories that denote person, tense, aspect, modality, and voice; adjectives do not show such categorial preferences.[4]

However, with respect to categorial differentiation in grammar both language-internal and cross-linguistic variation are so pronounced that subdefinition 3 reflects no more than crude tendencies. On the one hand, language-specific grammatical inventories may differ drastically, since none of the above groups of categories is an obligatory component of language-specific grammars; the only

---

[4] For a possible explanation of this latter fact, see Thompson (1988).

exception to this may be the category of person. Needless to say, it is impossible to provide universal definitions of lexical classes by establishing an invariable list of grammatical categories that occur in every language. Moreover, the categorial 'equipment' of a lexeme co-varies with its pragmatic function. For instance, a verb will display its maximal potential of person and/or tense and/or aspect etc. marking in its prototypical function as a predicate. In other syntactic positions, however, it will carry a reduced set of these categories (Croft 1991, Hopper and Thompson 1984, 1985). In addition, defining lexical classes on the basis of formal criteria should pose considerable problems in languages whose grammatical inventories are extremely reduced, or which lack grammatical categories altogether. Candidates for this type of language are, in particular, the pidgin and creole languages.

It may be true that the majority of lexemes contained in language-specific lexeme inventories coincide with one of the categorial prototypes characterized by the definitions given above. However, when the above subdefinitions of the traditional parts of speech are combined, certain problems arise, which makes it clear that the traditional cluster definition of noun, verb, and adjective is only feasible for a rough first approximation to the parts-of-speech issue.

Even when the traditional cluster definition is applied to Indo-European languages, which are its historical foundation, some familiar conflicts arise between the subdefinitions. A 'morphosyntactic' noun can designate an event, for example, *explosion*; or a property, for example, *fool*. 'Morphosyntactic' verbs may denote properties rather than events, for instance, *to resemble*. Certain 'morphosyntactic' adjectives denote passing states rather than properties, such as *angry* or *dizzy*. Occasionally, 'semantic' adjectives cannot be used in their prototypical pragmatic function of attribute. This phenomenon is attested in many languages.

The situation in Tzotzil in this respect is complex in that there are both adjectives that cannot be used as attributes, as well as adjectives that cannot be used as predicates, as the following quotation suggests.

Some A[djectival, R.P.] stems function predicatively but not attributively. These include ... A stems which describe positions, like *chotol* 'seated' and *va7al* 'pronc', as well as *yox* 'green', *sak* 'white', *muk'* 'large', *7ep* 'much', *takin* 'dry', *nat* 'deep, long, tall'. Some of these are derivationally related to stems which function attributively but not predicatively, e.g. *yaxal* 'green', *sakil* 'white', *muk'ta* 'large', *7epal* 'many', *taki* 'dry', *natil* 'deep, long, tall'. It is not clear what lexical class the latter stems belong to: if they are A stems, then that class must contain a subclass whose members cannot function predicatively.

(Aissen 1987: 5f.)

In English, adjectives whose occurrence is exclusively restricted either to the attribute position, or to the predicate position, are found as well. Examples for these types of adjectives include *former* and *ready*, respectively. *Former* is not acceptable as a predicate, while *ready* cannot be used as an attribute.

1.17. the former president

1.18. *the president is former

1.19. the sandwich is ready

1.20. *the ready sandwich

(For additional examples from English, see Bolinger 1967, Quirk *et al*. 1972: 234.)

In the light of these facts, one cannot help but conclude that the traditional theoretical approach to the parts-of-speech issue is in need of revision and refinement. The traditional notions of noun, verb, and adjective are inaccurate as descriptive primitives of lexical categorization because the cluster definitions of these three parts of speech merely capture the features of the prototypical class members. But any theory of the lexicon that rests on the concepts noun, verb, and adjective will only be as satisfactory as are the definitions given for these basic notions. The concepts of noun, verb, and adjective are, for a variety of reasons, not viable at the cross-linguistic level and are, consequently, not adequate as a basis for typological approaches to the phenomenon of copularization. The most urgent task in research on lexical categorization is either developing clear-cut and universally applicable definitions of lexical categories, or, if this is impossible, exploring the factors responsible for the fuzziness of lexical categories in a systematic way.

Anticipating the methodological approach outlined in the following chapters, it can be stated at this point that abandoning the structurally-based subdefinitions 2 and 3 of the traditional cluster definition of nouns, verbs, and adjectives, and operating with the semantic subdefinition 1 alone—that is, with the triple distinction of object concepts *vs.* event concepts *vs.* property concepts—is a promising line of attack in the attempt to develop a universal theoretical model of copularization (for details, see §2.1.1). This is mainly because the notions of object concept, event concept, and property concept appear to be semantic primitives which recur in the lexicon of all languages; such conceptual invariants, however, are a prerequisite for tracking down any cross-linguistic regularities holding in the domain of lexical categorization in general, and the domain of copularization, in particular.

1.3.3. The hybrid status of adjectives

Recent functional-typological research in the area of lexical categorization has focused to a considerable extent on adjectives (see, for instance, Bhat 1994, Dixon 1977b, Pustet 1989, Wetzer 1996). Adjectives are of particular interest because they are hybrid with respect to their categorial affiliation. They show both nominal and verbal characteristics, as has been noted repeatedly in the literature.

... just as there are languages that make verbs of the great mass of adjectives, so there are others that make nouns of them.

(Sapir 1921: 118)

Other works which advocate an analysis of adjectives as a lexical class which is intermediate between nouns and verbs include, for instance, Croft (1991), Dixon (1977b), Pustet (1989), and Stassen (1997).

In this context, Dixon (1977b) presents an extensive, pioneering survey on the morphosyntax of adjectives that does a lot to clarify the situation with respect to nouns and verbs as well. Dixon shows that the size of the adjective class, as defined by morphosyntactic criteria, varies considerably from language to language. Bantu languages, for example, have very small adjective classes that comprise between ten and fifty items; the classes cannot be enlarged by derivation. On the other hand, there are languages such as English, with large adjective classes to which further items can be added by means of derivation. Finally, there are languages that lack a formally independent adjective class; adjectival lexemes formally coincide with either nominals or verbals. For instance, there is no formal distinction between adjective and noun in Dyirbal, and none between adjective and verb in Mandarin and other Chinese languages. However, the mapping of lexemes that correspond semantically to Indo-European adjectives onto morphosyntactically defined classes seems to be determined by universal semantic principles. The semantic classification Dixon operates with is as follows:

The seven semantic types that make up the word class Adjective are:

1. DIMENSION—big, large, little, small; long, short; wide, narrow; thick, fat, thin, and just a few more items.

2. PHYSICAL PROPERTY—hard, soft; heavy, light; rough, smooth; hot, cold; sweet, sour and many more items.

3. COLOUR—black, white, red and so on.

4. HUMAN PROPENSITY—jealous, happy, kind, clever, generous, gay, cruel, rude, proud, wicked, and very many more items.

5. AGE—new, young, old.

6. VALUE—good, bad and a few more items (including proper, perfect and perhaps pure, in addition to hyponyms of good and bad such as excellent, fine, delicious, atrocious, poor, etc.).

7. SPEED—fast, quick, slow and just a few more items.

(Dixon 1977b: 31)

The above semantic classification of adjectives is intended to capture the most basic semantic types of adjectives only, and ignores a multitude of concepts encountered in the adjectival domain of languages with large vocabularies, which are adapted to the communicative needs of Western civilization. Examples of adjective types which are not covered by Dixon's classification include, for instance, English lexemes such as *abstract*, *former*, *modern*, *remote*, and *welcome*. However, Dixon's semantic classification of adjectives is quite adequate for dealing with the less complex vocabularies of the non-Indo-European languages which make up the greater part of Dixon's language sample in this case.

Dixon's survey discloses universal rules that govern the morphosyntactic behavior of the above semantic classes.

The languages fall into two kinds: (a) those with a large open adjective class, consisting of all or most of the members of all seven semantic types . . . : and (b) those with a small closed adjective class, involving only some of the types . . . The AGE, DIMENSION, VALUE and COLOUR types are likely to belong to the adjective class, however small it is . . . The HUMAN PROPENSITY type is predominantly associated with the noun class for languages of kind (b). The PHYSICAL PROPERTY type is typically associated with the verb class for languages of kind (b). Where the adjective class is small, there are likely to be no physical property adjectives; as it gets larger—from language to language—we encounter some physical property adjectives. Overall, an adjective class of a given size is more likely to include some physical property adjectives than it is to include human propensity . . . if the PHYSICAL PROPERTY type is predominantly associated with the adjective class, then so will the speed type be; . . . if the PHYSICAL PROPERTY type is predominantly associated with the verb class, then the SPEED type will be associated with the adverb class.

(Dixon 1977b: 55f.)

The fundamental insight to be gained from Dixon's study is that lexical class distinctions imposed by subdefinitions 1 and 2 (see §1.3.2) are often neutralized at the morphosyntactic level, that is at the level of subdefinition 3. On the basis of language-specific morphosyntactic evidence only two major lexical classes, noun and verb, can be identified in many languages; semantically adjectival lexemes are absorbed by one of these major classes. This situation also holds for languages which have a very small class of morphosyntactically autonomous adjectives. Since there is only a restricted set of 'true' adjectives in such languages, the overwhelming majority of semantically adjectival concepts must materialize in a different part of the lexicon, that is, either in the nominal or in the verbal section of the lexicon. Thus, in morphosyntactic terms, adjectives can be affiliated either with nouns or with verbs. According to Croft, the intermediate status of adjectives is particularly evident in predicate position:

. . . adjectives . . . are . . . intermediate [between nouns and verbs, R.P.] in grammatical characteristics . . . Predicate adjectives fall between nouns and verbs in structural markedness: predicate nouns are more likely to be structurally marked (with a copula) than predicate adjectives . . . The most obvious evidence for the intermediate status of adjectives with respect to verbs and nouns is the sharing of morphological inflections with one or the other of those categories.

(Croft 1991: 130f.)

Similarly, Stassen argues:

Within the domain of intransitive predication, adjectives form an in-between category . . . Whatever the further features of an encoding pattern in a language may be, the encoding of the predicative adjectives will always be stipulated to be derivative, in that it will be aligned to the encoding of one or more of the other predicate categories in the pattern. In a manner of speaking, we can regard predicative adjectives as a kind of no man's land in the domain of intransitive predicate encoding. One might say that predicative adjectives constitute a 'battleground' for the other predicate categories, each of which may succeed in incorporating this 'adjectival area', or parts of it, into its own encoding options.

(Stassen 1997: 343)

On this basis, Stassen proposes the following language universal:

The Adjective-Nominal Universal

(a) If predicate nominals are encoded verbally, then predicate adjectives are encoded verbally.

(b) Alternative version: if predicate adjectives are encoded nonverbally, then predicate nominals are encoded nonverbally.

(Stassen 1997: 614)

The above observations regarding the hybrid status of adjectives can be schematically represented by means of the implicational hierarchy given in (1.21) (see also Croft 1995: 506).

1.21. NOUNS > ADJECTIVES > VERBS

An analogous implicational hierarchy is also proposed in Pustet (1989: 113) on the grounds of the morphosyntactic behavior of lexical items not only in predicate function, but in argument and attribute function as well.

It can be hypothesized that the structure given in 1.21 has the potential for providing an important building block for a general model of lexical class formation. In what follows, the implicational hierarchy 1.21 will be embedded into a more comprehensive theoretical context.

1.3.4. Towards a universal theory of lexical class formation

1.3.4.1. Implicational hierarchies

Scales like the implicational hierarchy 1.21, which condense language universals into typological superstructures, are frequently encountered in the functional-typological literature. The idea that linguistic typology is well-advised to work with theoretical constructs which describe cross-linguistic variation as being gradual, rather than in terms of binary all-or-nothing distinctions, is anything but new. Sapir already advocates this kind of procedure:

There is something irresistible about a method of classification that starts with two poles,... clusters what it conveniently can about these poles, and throws everything else into a 'transitional type'.

(Sapir 1921: 123)

The concept of the typological scale is akin to—and has certainly been inspired by—Wittgenstein's (1918) notion of family resemblance. In today's functionally-oriented language typology, such scales play a central role. Implicational hierarchies are empirically attested both at the formal or surface level and at the functional level of language. As a rule, a scalar structure at the formal level is coextensive with a scalar structure at the functional level. The existence of such combined form–function scales supports one of the most fundamental tenets of functionalism, which states that linguistic form co-varies with linguistic function.

1.3.4.2. Markedness

Current functional-typological research offers two independent approaches to the parts-of-speech issue that can be expected to provide a clue to the question about the deeper motivation of the scale NOUNS > ADJECTIVES > VERBS presented in 1.21. For one, a fundamental explanation for the empirical data discussed above can be found in the context of markedness theory, in particular, in Croft's model (see below) which accounts for the universal markedness relations which become visible when the morphosyntactic potential of the individual parts of speech in different syntactic environments is investigated in detail. Further, Givón's time-stability scale (see below) has been widely accepted as a semantic parameter that constitutes a driving force behind the pronounced inclination of grammatical systems to produce structural patterns that comply with the scale NOUNS > ADJECTIVES > VERBS.

Markedness theory has a venerable tradition in linguistics. Markedness is commonly acknowledged as one of the most powerful natural principles that shape language. Numerous scholars, among them Benveniste (1946), Givón (e.g. 1979, 1991, 1995), Greenberg (e.g. 1966), Jakobson (1971), and Trubetzkoy (1939), have documented markedness phenomena in a variety of linguistic domains. Two basic components which are crucial for defining the concept of markedness are the frequency principle and the quantity principle (see Givón 1991, Tomič 1989). In any linguistic domain in which manifestations of the markedness principle have been discovered, the following generalization holds: the more frequent member of a binary opposition tends to be structurally less complex; the less frequent member tends to be structurally more complex. The more frequent/less complex linguistic item within such oppositions is referred to as UNMARKED, the less frequent/more complex linguistic item is referred to as MARKED.

Croft (1991, 2001) utilizes the markedness principle to account for the differences in the morphosyntactic behavior of nouns, verbs, and adjectives, and proposes a general theoretical model of parts of speech distinctions. Croft's discourse analyses show that in (presumably) all languages, each of the three major parts of speech fulfills a specific prototypical pragmatic function: nouns usually function as arguments, verbs as predicates, and adjectives as attributes. Similarly, Hengeveld (1992: 32) states that 'a verb prototypically has a predicative function, an adjective an attributive function, and a noun the function of head of a term phrase'. Of course, all three parts of speech may fulfill any one of the two remaining non-prototypical functions, too, but they do so with significantly lower statistical frequency. Croft's investigations reveal a correlation between these frequency distributions and formal markedness patterns, as defined by the criterion of structural complexity. When lexical items figure in their prototypical pragmatic function the structural complexity of the grammatical constructions they are embedded in is low; in contrast, when they are used in the non-prototypical environments, the structural complexity of the respective grammatical constructions is high. These findings are summarized in table 1.1, which is taken from Croft (1991: 67); see also Croft (2001: 88) (for an analogous scheme, see Pustet 1989: 30).

This matrix accomplishes a systematic and innovative separation of the semantic categories of objects, properties, and actions, from the pragmatic functions of argument, attribute, and predicate. This separation is innovative because traditional grammar writing, in so far as it operates with a tripartite distinction of nouns, verbs, and adjectives, tends to deal only with three construction types, that is with the ones that are classed as unmarked in Croft's matrix: object concepts in argument function, property concepts in attribute function, and event concepts in predicate function. The remaining constellations usually receive a more or less superficial treatment only. In Pustet (1989) the morphosyntax of nouns, verbs, and adjectives in various languages is investigated on the basis of an analogous separation of semantic class membership and pragmatic function.

In Croft's matrix, various well-known construction types are listed which serve to code the respective combinations of semantic concepts and pragmatic functions.

TABLE 1.1. *Parts of speech and pragmatic functions*

	Reference [= argument function, R.P.]	Modification [= attribution, R.P.]	Predication
Objects	UNMARKED NOUNS	genitive, adjectivalizations, PPs on nouns	predicate nominals
Properties	deadjectival nouns	UNMARKED ADJECTIVES	predicate adjectives
Actions	action nominals, complements, infinitives, gerunds	participles, relative clauses	UNMARKED VERBS

Some combinations can be represented by more than a single construction type. Croft concludes:

The analysis of syntactic categories presented here predicts the existence of these constructions because they indicate the various combinations of lexical semantic class and pragmatic function. In addition, the analysis predicts the structural markedness of the constructions in the marked combinations of lexical class and pragmatic function: that is, that those constructions will be structurally more complex, or at least as complex, as the morphosyntax for the core category types.

(Croft 1991: 67)

Further, Croft replaces the pre-scientific terms of object, property, and event with bundles of semantic features, and thus increases the accuracy of the description of the semantic contrasts between the traditional parts of speech. The semantic parameters Croft uses are valence, stativity, persistence, and gradability (1991: 62ff.). The feature profiles he proposes are reproduced in table 1.2.

Croft's model is a selective synthesis of earlier attempts at tracking down semantic distinctions that correlate with lexical class distinctions (e.g. Dixon 1977b, Givón 1979, 1984, Langacker 1987, Wierzbicka 1986). However, Croft points out that the above feature profiles still define lexical prototypes only. They '...do not exhaustively classify the lexicon. For instance, mass nouns such as *syrup*, states such as *sick*, and nonrelational processes such as *rain* do not fall in any of the three categories...' (1991: 65).

Nonetheless, Croft's feature analysis establishes a connection between the hitherto monolithic concepts of object, property, and event, and thus adds considerable weight to the widely held assumption that cross-linguistic variation in lexical categorization correlates with specific semantic parameters.

The phenomenon of copularization can be regarded as one of the most conspicuous outgrowths of the markedness principle (Croft 1991: 68). A predicate that contains a copula is, of necessity, structurally more complex than a predicate that does not contain a copula. It can, therefore, be expected that copularization as an isolated phenomenon reflects the general markedness principle outlined in Croft's broader framework. Put differently, a cross-linguistic investigation of copula usage should also yield the implicational hierarchy NOUNS > ADJECTIVES > VERBS, which has been posited in 1.21 on the basis of previous research into the universal mechanisms underlying lexical class formation.

TABLE 1.2. *Parts of speech and their semantic feature profiles*

	Valency	Stativity	Persistence	Gradability
NOUN	0	state	persistent	nongradable
ADJECTIVE	1	state	persistent	gradable
VERB	1 or more	process	transitory	nongradable

The fact that there are prototypical constellations of the occurrence of the parts of speech in the syntactic slots of argument, attribute, and predicate has also given rise to the model of lexical class formation proposed by Hengeveld (1992), which will, however, not be explored in greater detail in the present study of copularization. A central component of Hengeveld's model is the typological opposition between 'specialized' and 'non-specialized' languages (Hengeveld 1992: 63ff.). Specialized languages differ from non-specialized languages in that the four parts of speech noun, verb, adjective, and adverb cannot be used in a pragmatic function other than the one prototypically associated with each of them 'without further measures being taken' (Hengeveld 1992: 58), that is, without the addition of further morphosyntactic material. Non-specialized languages, on the other hand, are characterized by the fact that individual parts of speech may occur in pragmatic functions other than the prototypical one without the addition of further morphosyntactic material.

1.3.4.3. Time-stability

As will become clear in the chapters to follow, Croft's markedness-based theory of lexical categorization will constitute a core element of the theoretical model developed in the present study. A more complete picture of the mechanisms at work in lexical categorization, however, will be gained when the markedness principle is supplemented with functional parameters which have turned out to be relevant for the distinction between the parts of speech noun, verb, and adjective. The inhomogeneous frequency distribution of nouns, verbs, and adjectives in the predicate slot should not just be taken as a fact—this phenomenon might be rooted in the specific semantic profiles of the individual parts of speech.

The time-stability scale, as proposed by Givón (1979, 1984) characterizes the semantic difference between the traditional parts of speech noun, verb, and adjective in terms of a single semantic parameter.

Experiences—or phenomenological clusters—which stay relatively STABLE over time, i.e. those which over repeated scans appear to be roughly 'the same', tend to be lexicalized in human language as NOUNS. The most prototypical nouns are those denoting CONCRETE, PHYSICAL, COMPACT entities made out of durable, solid matter, such as 'rock', 'tree', 'dog', 'person' etc. Their time-stability is obviously a matter of degree, since animates such as 'dog' or 'person' obviously are born, grow slowly, grow old and then die and cease to be. And they obviously change faster than 'tree', and 'tree' changes faster than 'rock'. But, relative to the ability of the human organism to perceive very subtle changes, and given scanning frequencies of every second, every minute, every hour or every day, such concrete entities obviously appear to remain 'the same' over time.

At the other extreme of the lexical-phenomenological scale, one finds experiential clusters denoting RAPID CHANGES in the state of the universe. These are prototypically *events* or *actions*, and languages tend to lexicalize them as verbs... within the verb category, members may be graded by their degree of time-stability. Thus, 'hit', 'shoot' or 'kick' are INSTANTANEOUS verbs, denoting an extremely rapid change. 'Sing', 'work', 'eat' or 'read' may denote a much slower process of change, and are character-istically ACTIVITY/PROCESS verbs. Finally, 'know', 'understand' or 'like' tend to denote long-lasting STATES, coding either no change or very slow change in the phenomenological universe.

The classes of noun and verb, the two prototypical extremes on our time-stability scale, are attested in the lexicon of all languages.

(Givón 1984: 51f.)

The most interesting lexical class . . . is one which is not universally attested, that of *adjectives* . . . percepts of *intermediate time-stability*, that is, those which depict states of varying degree of intermediate duration, lexicalize as adjectives [in languages which have a distinct class of adjectives, R.P.]. Among the latter, the more time-stable ('permanent') qualities have a higher chance of lexicalizing as nouns, while the less time-stable ('temporary') qualities tend more to lexicalize as verbs.

(Givón 1979: 321f.)

[Adjectives] most commonly . . . embrace at least the time-stable physical properties such as size, shape, color, texture, smell or taste . . .

The time-stability scale may be summarized as follows:

NOUNS - - - - - - - - - - - - - ADJECTIVES - - - - - - - - - - - - -VERBS

most time-stable   intermediate states   rapid change.

(Givón 1984: 52ff.)

The time-stability hypothesis may be criticized as inadequate or at least insuf-ficient because there are lexemes that refute it. According to their respective time-stability value, nouns like *explosion* have to be classed as verbs, verbs like *to last*, however, as nouns. But the amount of lexemes that contradict the hypothesis is extremely small if compared to the amount of those that support it. It would be premature to discard a hypothesis with high predictive power because there are some exceptions to it.

The time-stability hypothesis has had a tremendous impact on subsequent studies in lexical class distinctions. Time-stability is used as an explanatory parameter in virtually all of the more recent works dealing with the parts-of-speech issue within the functional-typological framework (for instance, Bhat 1994, Croft 1991, Hengeveld 1992, Stassen 1997).

Both markedness theory and the time-stability hypothesis independently account for the traditional segmentation of the lexicon into nouns, verbs, and adjectives, which entails the question of which model should be considered more appropriate. However, as an alternative, on the grounds of the functionalist tenet that semantics conditions linguistic form, at least to some degree, both models could be combined. More specifically, the inherent semantic content of indi-vidual lexemes or lexeme types could be interpreted as the motivation underlying the fact that individual lexemes favor certain pragmatic functions. This methodological step is taken in Croft (1991: 62ff.), where Givón's time-stability parameter is treated as a conflation of the semantic parameters of stativity and persistence. These two parameters, in turn, together with the additional semantic parameters of valence and gradability, are used to account for the structural markedness relations which become visible when the members of different lexical classes are compared to each other with respect to their behavior in different pragmatic functions.

Bhat (1994) also hints at a joint approach to the parts-of-speech issue in which the semantic properties of individual lexical items, which can be defined in terms of parameters such as time-stability, or relationality—a concept which corresponds to Croft's valence parameter—are held responsible for the higher frequency of occurrence of individual lexical items in specific pragmatic functions:

Nouns have to introduce, prototypically, entities that can participate in one or more events, and can therefore form the connecting link between several propositions. There is a need, therefore, for nouns to denote individualized and time-stable entities; verbs, on the other hand, have to denote, prototypically, actions or events in which one or more entities occur as participants; they are therefore primarily relational in nature and involve the notion of process or change as their basic semantic type. Adjectives..., being modifiers of nouns..., select certain specific single properties (involving permanence in the case of adjectives...) as their prototypical semantic types.

(Bhat 1994: 156)

If a synthesis of markedness theory and semantically-based theories of the lexicon provides a fruitful approach to lexical categorization, this should also be true for the more specific phenomenon of copularization, which can, according to what has been said in §1.3.4.2, be interpreted as one of the many structural facets of lexical categorization. In §3.4.3, this line of reasoning will be pursued further.

1.4. A possible theoretical approach to copularization

To sum up, the foregoing outline of the state of the art concerning the apparently interconnected issues of copularization and the division of the lexicon into parts of speech reveals a somewhat paradoxical situation. Although remarkably resistant to any attempts at motivating their existence through their semantic content or pragmatic function, copulas recur in languages all over the world with an astonishing regularity, and produce a colorful spectrum of cross-linguistic variation with regard to the division of lexical material into formal categories.

As unlikely as it may seem at this point, given the semantic vagueness of copulas, the conclusion that emerges from the present study of copulas in a cross-linguistic perspective is that, after all, semantics is to be held responsible for the cross-linguistic diversity in the distributional properties of copulas. In a nutshell, on the basis of complex analyses of empirical data, it will be argued that ultimately, a few theoretical concepts suffice to account not only for the considerable cross-linguistic variation regarding the compatibility of copulas with lexical items, but also for the more fundamental fact that copulas exist. These essential theoretical concepts are: the three semantic parameters valence, transience (the near-equivalent of Givón's time-stability), and dynamicity, all of which have been anticipated in Croft's (1991) model of lexical class formation and markedness theory. The approach developed in this study is aptly characterized by the following quotation:

> . . . the grammatical structure of languages may be partly, though not wholly, determined by semantic distinctions; and . . . semantic distinctions of the kind that are relevant to the definition of parts-of-speech expression-classes may be themselves determined by ontological distinctions that are, in part at least, independent of the structure of particular languages.

(Lyons 1977: 449)

The assumption that there is a causal relationship between semantics and grammatical form, that is, surface structure, is in sharp contrast with the general outlook on language advocated in contemporary mainstream linguistics. Today, linguistics is dominated by the Chomskian paradigm, which characterizes language as an organ or faculty innate to the human mind. This faculty generates utterances by means of an apparatus of rules that abides by its own laws. It neither reflects, nor responds to, external factors of whatever kind. Likewise, the different levels of linguistic description, such as morphology, syntax, semantics, and pragmatics, are seen as independent. No causal chains can therefore be established between these domains, which would be capable of explaining phenomena at one level of linguistic description through phenomena at another level.

However, in the past, before the rise of generativism, radically different approaches to language have been developed. One of the long-standing non-generative traditions in linguistics is functionalism. Scholars such as F. de Saussure, R. Jakobson, N. S. Trubetzkoy, and G. K. Zipf laid the foundations of functionalist thinking. At the core of the functional approach to language lies the tenet that language is not a self-contained mechanism that operates in total seclusion. On the contrary, language is conceived of as being shaped by external factors. Analogies from biology illustrate this: the morphology of an organism is influenced, or even dictated, by its habitat; body parts reflect the functions they fulfill. Language, too, is embedded in a system that is composed of physical, biological, cultural, social, intellectual, and such-like subsystems, and fulfills certain functions within it. Similarly to a living organism, language responds to system-internal pressures.

The present investigation is, basically, to be taken as a strictly empirical study that aims at a systematization of the distributional properties of copulas with respect to the lexicon. At that level, it should be considered theory-independent. The methodological approach used in this study, in which it will be argued that the compatibility of copulas with lexical items is determined by universal principles, can be outlined as follows. In Chapter 2, on the basis of a global sample that comprises 131 languages, universal rules that govern the usage of copulas are uncovered. These rules can be summarized by means of an implicational hierarchy that is equivalent to the scale NOUNS > ADJECTIVES > VERBS, which is proposed in §1.3.3 on the basis of the extant literature on the parts-of-speech issue: if any lexical class in this scale admits copula use in a given language, any lexical class to the left of it also admits copula use. Thus, the findings regarding copula distribution at the cross-linguistic level substantiate the hypotheses proposed in prior work on lexical categorization in general, such as Croft (1991), Pustet (1989), and Stassen (1997). Chapter 3 seeks to illuminate the putative semantic underpinnings of copula use in greater detail. The first analytical step taken in this regard consists in the compilation of descriptive data on the basis of consultant work with native speakers. In particular, relatively large samples of basic vocabulary were established for a variety of genetically diverse languages. The individual lexemes contained in these samples were then investigated with respect to their compatibility with copulas. The approach to the semantic motivation of copularization chosen in this study ultimately confirms Croft's predictions regarding the universal semantic principles governing lexical class formation. The semantic parameters which, in the analysis of the empirical data, turn out to be relevant in this respect are valence (labeled 'valency' in Croft 1991), transience (referred to by the notionally opposed term 'persistence' in Croft 1991), and dynamicity (referred to by the notionally opposed term 'stativity' in Croft 1991). In the present study, these three parameters are derived from the investigation of lexical minimal pairs of the type *similar* vs. *to resemble*. The members of such minimal pairs are more or less synonymous semantically, but their grammatical profiles differ with respect to the structural feature of copula use. Concerning the semantic relations among members of minimal pairs, a prospective language universal emerges, which is, at least, valid for the detailed lexical samples established: within minimal pairs, the lexical item that is compatible with a copula is always less transitive, less transient, and less dynamic than its counterpart which does not admit copula use, if the members of a given minimal pair diverge with respect to their semantic properties. The language samples investigated do not yield any exceptions to this formula. The languages which were analyzed with respect to lexical minimal pairs with the help of native speakers include Bambara, Burmese, Cantonese, English, Estonian, French, German, Hebrew, Hungarian, Indonesian, Japanese, Korean, Lakota, Mandarin, Persian, Sgaw Karen, Slovene, Spanish, Swahili, Thai, Turkish, and Vietnamese.

In defining the semantic parameters which become visible in the analysis of lexical minimal pairs, the strictly inductive theoretical approach developed in Chapter 3 relies heavily on semantic models of the lexicon by Croft (1991), Givón (1979, 1984), Langacker (1987, 1988), and Wierzbicka (1986, 1995).

Since the semantic parameters valence, transience, and dynamicity appear to be the decisive factors controlling copula distribution in the microcosm of lexical minimal pairs, the hypothesis that this might also be the case in the macrocosm of language-specific vocabularies as a whole is not too far-fetched. In order to test this hypothesis, as the second major analytical step taken in Chapter 3, statistical analyses of lexical samples which were compiled by means of consultant work with native speakers for ten genetically diverse languages, that is, Burmese, Cantonese, German, Hungarian, Indonesian, Japanese, Lakota, Swahili, Thai, and Turkish, are carried out. The language samples contain between, approximately, 500 and 850 lexical items each. In the analysis of the ten language samples, the share of lexical items whose behavior with respect to copularization is correctly predicted by each of the semantic parameters obtained by means of the minimal pair method is determined. The statistical results, for any of the ten sampled languages, reveal striking correlations between copula use and any of the semantic parameters investigated. Thus, the conclusion that copula distribution is controlled by these parameters seems warranted. At a more general theoretical level, these empirical data strongly support the functionalist tenet of the non-autonomy of linguistic form or surface structure.

In Chapter 4, it is shown that the semantic parameters relevant for a universally applicable theoretical model of copularization, which have so far been treated as independent motivations of copula distribution, can be combined in a unified multi-factor model of copularization. For a variety of reasons, the multi-factor approach to copularization must be regarded as superior to the single-factor analyses. Among other things, conflating the semantic parameters listed above in a multi-factor model of the lexicon yields a scalar structure which corresponds to the initial hierarchy NOUNS > ADJECTIVES > VERBS which is posited in 1.21 on the basis of current research into the parts-of-speech issue, and to an analogous scale derived from the cross-linguistic sample established for the purpose of determining the distribution of copularizing *vs.* non-copularizing lexemes in the lexicon of individual languages in Chapter 2. Thus, the overall result of the analysis of the data dealt with in Chapters 2, 3, and 4 is that linguistic form, in that case, presence *vs.* absence of copulas, can be motivated through linguistic function, in that case, through the inherent meaning of lexical items.

The multi-factor model of copularization introduced in Chapter 4 can, further, be integrated into current cognitive approaches to categorization—most notably, into the framework of prototype theory, as advocated by Rosch (e.g. Rosch 1973a, Rosch 1973b, Rosch 1975a, Rosch 1975b, Rosch 1978, Rosch and Mervis 1975, Rosch *et al.* 1976) and later, Lakoff (1987). In all ten languages for which large lexical samples have been compiled, three classes of lexical items, each of which can be characterized in terms of the three semantic parameters valence, transience, and dynamicity, make up the bulk of the lexical inventories under investigation. These three classes of lexemes can also be referred to by means of the semantic labels of entity concept, event concept, and property concept, respectively. On the basis of their quantitative dominance within language-specific vocabularies, these three conceptual classes can be interpreted as—possibly universal—lexical prototypes.

Taking the semantically-based model of copularization developed in this study as a point of departure, it is argued in the concluding Chapter 5, in which the parts-of-speech issue is picked up on again, that the controversial concepts of noun, verb, and adjective, which have served as descriptive primitives in grammar writing and in grammatical theory for so long, can be redefined in terms of the three semantic parameters valence, transience, and dynamicity. It is, further, hypothesized that the semantic profile of individual lexical items might not only determine their behavior with respect to copularization; lexical semantics might have an equally strong impact on the compatibility of lexical items with grammatical elements other than copulas. If this assumption is valid, the formal characteristics of lexical items which are commonly used for defining parts of speech in traditional approaches to the issue (see §1.3.2) derive from the semantic properties of the latter.

2 Copulas in Cross-linguistic Perspective

2.1. Scope of the investigation

As anyone familiar with language typology knows from experience, there may be considerable differences in the grammatical inventories of individual languages. In addition, individual grammatical categories in different languages which are, at first glance, equivalent, more often than not, do not overlap completely in their functional scope. These observations, of course, hold for the grammatical sub-domain of copula usage as well. Languages may have more than just a single copula. In §2.3, various language-specific copulas and copula systems are discussed to demonstrate that the cross-linguistic divergences in the functional scope of copulas, as well as in their morphosyntactic status, may be quite pronounced. Moreover, copulas participate in the formation of a vast spectrum of predicate types, as §2.1.2 reveals; the present study focuses only on a small subset of these. In §2.3.3, the diachronic sources of copulas are dealt with. In §2.3.4, generalizing hypotheses concerning the compatibility of copulas with lexical items will be proposed on the basis of a relatively large sample of languages. The basic question underlying this research is about the ways in which languages differ with respect to the use of copulas with various types of lexical items.

2.1.1. Basic methodological and terminological considerations

The main objective of this chapter is establishing a cross-linguistic sample which is complex enough to uncover universal rules governing the usage of copulas with lexical items. In the attempt to determine the most effective method of data compilation, a number of relevant factors have to be taken into consideration. Given the nature of the present project, the vocabulary of any language included in the sample should, ideally, be investigated in its entirety. Assuming, just for the purpose of illustrative calculations of the amount of work that would have to go into such a project, a hypothetical cross-linguistic sample size of 100 languages, and a language-specific vocabulary size of about 10 000 lexemes (only), the resulting research schedule would have to handle an overall sample of no less than 1 000 000 lexemes which have to be investigated with respect to their compatibility with copulas. Needless to say, working with a sample of this size renders the project unmanageable within reasonable time limits. But, apart from that, the mere process of the compilation of such data meets with serious difficulties already. Dictionaries are an insufficient source of data in this context because dictionaries do not usually specify lexemes with respect to the grammatical criterion of compatibility with copulas. The only alternative is consulting native speakers of the languages to be sampled within the project.

Given the range of problems which may arise in the context of doing fieldwork particularly on non-Indo-European languages, and the complexity of the task of investigating the entire lexical inventory of any language—or at least the hypothetical amount of 10 000 lexemes—with respect to copula use, it may take a fairly long time to complete the research program for a single language only. Consequently, the size of the overall sample must be reduced by resorting to the standard procedure of data compilation in contemporary typological research, that is, by using grammars and other descriptions of linguistic structure as the empirical basis for establishing data on copula use with lexical items. Working with grammars and other sources that offer condensed information on the language-specific patterns of compatibility of copulas and lexical items keeps the time spent on data compilation within limits.

Further, on the grounds of what is said about the problematic status of the traditional parts of speech noun, verb, and adjective in §1.3, such research should not operate with the cluster definitions which are commonly proposed for lexical categories; the latter do not provide universally applicable definitions. This is mainly because it is impossible to come to terms with the cross-linguistic variation in the morphosyntactic properties of lexical items.

However, since every language has lexemes that designate concepts belonging to the semantic macro-classes of entity, event, and property, using these semantic categories as cross-linguistically valid descriptive labels for types of lexical items is a viable alternative. As is argued in §1.3.2, entities, events, and properties constitute the semantic prototypes in terms of which the overwhelming majority of members of the traditional lexical classes noun, verb, and adjective, respectively, can be characterized. As a matter of fact, in the grammatical descriptions consulted for the purpose of this project, statements pertaining to the usage of copulas with lexical items are usually made in terms of the semantic prototypes entity, event, and property. This triple distinction of lexical items is also employed as the basis for deriving generalizing statements regarding the grammatical domain of intransitive predication in Stassen (1997), and it will play an equally important role throughout the present study. Henceforth, the terms NOMINAL, VERBAL, and ADJECTIVAL will be used to refer to these three semantic types of lexical items. A nominal is a lexical item that belongs to the semantic macro-class of entity concepts. A verbal is a lexical item that belongs to the semantic macro-class of event concepts. An adjectival is a lexical item that belongs to the semantic macro-class of property concepts. This choice of terminology is, of course, inspired by the traditional terms noun, verb, and adjective.

To emphasize this point once more, the difference between the first and second members of each of the terminological pairs noun *vs.* nominal, verb *vs.* verbal, and adjective *vs.* adjectival is that the first member of each pair, in line with the traditional cluster definition of the parts of speech dealt with in §1.3.2, not only is associated with one of the three semantic prototypes of object, event, and property, but also implies certain structural and behavioral features.

The second member of each pair of terminological labels, on the other hand, is exclusively defined in semantic terms. The sole purpose of the latter labels is assigning individual lexical items to one of the semantic macro-classes of entity, event, and property. Both sets of terms will be used in this study, although the occurrence of the labels of noun, verb, and adjective will be restricted, in particular, to references to lexical classes in languages which have been described within the traditional model of grammar writing, and to quotations.

The following discussion of copulas in cross-linguistic perspective is based on a sample of 154 languages. A subset of these, which comprises a total of twenty-three languages, merely serves the purpose of illustrating specific points which are relevant for a more thorough understanding of the phenomenon of copular-ization. The remaining 131 languages provide the empirical basis for the typo-logical generalizations regarding copula use with lexical items which are summarized in table 2.7. All 154 languages are listed in appendix A, together with their respective genetic affiliation. In the running text, genetic affiliations of individual languages are not specified.

2.1.2. *Copulas and predicate types*

Although one might feel tempted to associate copularizing predicates with predicates that contain a simple nominal or adjectival nucleus in the first place, such predicate types are by no means the only ones that may combine with copulas. A basic distinction within the domain of potentially copularizing predicates concerns the contrast between ASCRIPTIVE and IDENTIFICATIONAL predicates (Halliday 1994: 119ff.; Hengeveld 1992: 73ff.; Lyons 1977: 174ff.). The criterion that differentiates between these two predicate types is that of uniqueness *vs.* non-uniqueness of extra-linguistic referents of predicate phrases in the universe of discourse. An identificational predicate has only one possible referent in the specific universe of discourse it is embedded in. Thus, when an utterance like 2.1,

2.1. this is Sally

whose predicate nucleus consists of a proper name, occurs in discourse, the speaker implicitly instructs the hearer that there is only a single possible extra-linguistic referent to which the statement applies, and that can be unambiguously identified by the hearer. Proper names readily lend themselves to usage as nuclei of identificational predicates. So do linguistic items that denote ontologically unique entities, that is, entities that are unique not only in the universe of discourse, but in the universe *per se*, such as *Alpha Centauri*, the name of a fixed star.

2.2. this is Alpha Centauri

However, identificational predicates can also be built around other types of predicate nuclei. In fact, any predicable lexeme, regardless of its lexical class membership, yields identificational predicates. In examples 2.3 to 2.5, the noun *teacher*, the adjective *red*, and the verb *to buy* function as nuclei of identificational predicates.

2.3. he is the teacher

2.4. this is the red one

2.5. he is the one who bought my car

Ascriptive predicates, on the other hand, do not convey the notion of uniqueness in the universe of discourse. This predicate type can be regarded as less marked than the identificational predicate type in several respects. For one, it is semantically simpler in some sense because it merely predicates a certain state of affairs without the implicit instruction to the hearer to identify the single extra-linguistic referent in the universe of discourse that is denoted by the predicate of an identificational clause. Further, an identificational predicate is formed by means of more complex structural devices than a corresponding ascriptive predicate. Like identificational predicates, ascriptive predicates can be derived from any predicable lexeme. Consequently, the lexemes *teacher*, *red*, and *to buy*, which function as the nuclei of identificational predicates in examples 2.3 to 2.5, also yield ascriptive predicates.

2.6. he is a teacher

2.7. it is red

2.8. he bought the car

The comparison of the example triplets 2.3 to 2.5 *vs.* 2.6 to 2.8 shows that in English, ascriptive predicates are, in general, structurally less complex than identificational predicates, a tendency that is echoed in any one language investigated within the present study, if the data are explicit enough to allow any statements in this respect. For instance, identificational predicates with adjectival and verbal predicate nuclei are formed on the basis of the pronoun *one* in English, as in examples 2.4 and 2.5. Last but not least, the overall discourse frequency of ascriptive predicates is much higher than that of identificational predicates. Discourse frequency is one of the correlates of the complex notion of linguistic markedness (see §1.3.4.2).

Ascriptive predicates with a nominal nucleus establish membership in a class of items that are characterized by the concept that figures as predicate nucleus. Ascriptive predicates with an adjectival nucleus profile the clausal subject as having the property denoted by the predicate nucleus. Ascriptive predicates with a verbal nucleus prototypically feature events which extend over shorter periods in the life span of the extra-linguistic referent(s) of the argument(s) involved.

TABLE 2.1. *Subtypes of identificational and ascriptive predicates*

	NOMINAL	ADJECTIVAL	VERBAL
ascriptive	*he is a teacher* *this is a car*	*it is red*	*he bought my car* *he smokes*
identificational	*this is John*	*it is the red one*	*he is the one who* *bought my car*
	he is the teacher *this is Alpha Centauri*		*he is the one who smokes*

Table 2.1 summarizes the subtypes of identificational and ascriptive predicates discussed above.

The present study focuses mainly on the usage of lexemes as ascriptive predicates. Data on identificational predicates, as well as on the additional predicate types which are dealt with in what follows, have been collected as well. However, no attempt at systematizing these materials to the effect of extracting theoretical generalizations with respect to the usage of copulas within the domain of predication as a whole is made in the present monograph. Of course, the search for the patterns that emerge in this empirical context is also a very rewarding topic of investigation. For an in-depth treatise on these issues, the reader is referred to Stassen (1997).

Copulas are also frequently encountered as components of EXISTENTIAL PREDICATES. Examples include English constructions as in 2.9, or Spanish constructions as in 2.10. It is, however, not quite clear if the predicate markers occurring in such existential constructions are really devoid of meaning, or not. Only in the former case do they qualify as copulas.

2.9.   there is coffee in the kitchen

2.10. hay   mucha   gente
      EX   many   people
      'there are many people' (author's field data)

Another class of predicates which are formed by means of a copula in many languages are QUANTIFICATIONAL predicates. Quantificational predicates are either based on numerals, or on quantifiers such as English *all*, *few*, *many*, *much*, *some*. However, numerals and quantifiers are special in that they display a pronounced cross-linguistic tendency of being not directly predicable. Frequently, an existential construction, as in the English examples 2.11 and 2.12, must be used with quantificational predicates.

2.11. there are three

2.12. there are many

In fact, it seems to be the rule rather than the exception that the coding strategy used for quantificational predicates, if it involves copulas or copula-like elements, employs the copulas encountered in the formation of existential predicates, rather than copulas which combine with ascriptive predicates. This statement is based on the analysis of the cross-linguistic sample established for the purpose of the present study, which comprises 131 languages (see table 2.7). In English, as in many other languages which have copulas, the predicate structure represented by examples 2.13 and 2.14, in which a copula is simply added to a numeral or quantifier in predicate position, is not considered acceptable by native speakers.

2.13. ?? they are three

2.14. ?? they are many

However, there are in fact languages, such as Hungarian, in which predicate structures analogous to examples 2.13 and 2.14 are admissible. It should be noted, however, that the Hungarian examples 2.15 and 2.16 are not entirely parallel to the structures in examples 2.13 and 2.14 in that numerals and quantifiers in predicate position, at least in certain contexts, receive the 'curious -*an/en* suffix' (Kenesei, Vago, and Fenyvesi 1998: 61).

2.15. száz-an   volt-ak
       hundred-AFX   COP.PST-PL
       'there were a hundred' (author's field data)

2.16. sok-an   volt-ak
       many-AFX   COP.PST-PL
       'there were many' (author's field data)

Adverbials may also function as nuclei of predicate phrases. In many languages, the corresponding constructions employ a copula. The English clause 2.17 and the Hungarian clause 2.18 exemplify ADVERBIAL PREDICATES that contain a copula. (The element *jol* 'well' in example 2.18 is explicitly referred to as an adverb by Kenesei, Vago, and Fenyvesi (1998: 61).)

2.17. the key is here

2.18. a   lány-ok   jól   van-nak
       DEF   girl-PL   well   COP.PRS-PL
       'the girls are well' (Kenesei, Vago, and Fenyvesi 1998: 61)

Nominals which are combined with an oblique case marker may function as nuclei of predicate phrases as well. The term 'oblique case marker', in this context, is to be taken as covering all kinds of markers of semantic roles which do not code valence-bound arguments. The morphosyntactic status of these markers is not relevant here—an oblique case marker is simply defined here as a linguistic element that functions as a coding device for certain semantic roles. Thus, the term 'oblique case marker' includes not only case inflections, but adpositions as well. If an oblique case marker figures as part of a predicate phrase, and thus forms an OBLIQUE CASE PREDICATE, the use of a copula is mandatory in many languages. Numerous English examples of oblique case predicates involving prepositions can be cited. Needless to say, the range of meanings which can be expressed by such constructions is as varied as the semantic content of the oblique case markers which may be involved here. They include, among many others, the roles of locative (see example 2.19), comitative (see example 2.20), recipient (see example 2.21), and source/origin (see example 2.22).

2.19. he is in the kitchen

2.20. he is with her

2.21. the gift is for him

2.22. he is from Australia

Oblique case predicates containing copulas may also express possessive relations. An example comes from the Kölsch dialect of German. The possessor *Hannes* is marked by means of dative inflection of the definite article, which in that case results in the form *dem*, and figures as the predicate nucleus in the following example:

2.23. dat   Booch   is
      DEF.SG.NTR.NOM book   COP.3SG.PRS.IND
      dem   Hannes
      DEF.SG.MSC.DAT Hannes
      'the book belongs to Hannes' (author's field data)

Copulas are also frequently added to predicate nuclei that consist of time specifications. An example of a language in which such TEMPORAL PREDICATES receive a copula is English:

2.24. it is eight o'clock

The above list of potentially copularizing predicate types should be fairly comprehensive, but it is not exhaustive. A similar classification of predicate types that may employ copulas is provided by Hengeveld (1992: 73ff.).[1] It must be pointed out that a standardized checklist that summarizes such predicate types, and which could serve as a working basis for studies in copularization and related topics, is currently not available. This is at least in part responsible for the largely idiosyncratic and contradictory, if not to say chaotic, usage of terminological labels for the predicate types dealt with above both in the descriptive and theoretical literature.

---

[1] For very explicit and helpful discussions of focal as well as more marginal clause types in three individual languages, i.e. Gooniyandi, Manam, and Ndyuka, the reader is referred to Huttar and Huttar (1994) (on Ndyuka), Lichtenberk (1983) (on Manam), and McGregor (1990) (on Gooniyandi).

2.2. Copula dropping

A complicating factor, which in the worst case blocks the outlook on language-specific facts regarding copula usage, especially when descriptions are defective, is the phenomenon of COPULA DROPPING. In many languages which have a copula, the copula can be freely omitted. In other languages, the copula can or must be deleted in specific grammatical environments. Cantonese is an example of a language in which copula dropping is not limited to a particular context, but rather, may apply in any context. Thus, the Cantonese copula *haih*, which occurs with nominals only, not with adjectivals,[2] 'can be omitted without affecting the sense or structure of a sentence' (Matthews and Yip 1994: 129):

2.25. nī   go   haih   ngóh   sailóu   lèihge
      this   CLF   COP   1SG.POR   younger brother   PRT
      'this is my younger brother' (Matthews and Yip 1994: 129)

2.26. nī   go   ngóh   sailóu   lèihge
      this   CLF   1SG.POR   younger brother   PRT
      'this is my younger brother' (Matthews and Yip 1994: 129)

Likewise, the Turkish copula suffix *-DIr* is optional in all contexts (see examples 2.67 and 2.68).

Restricted copula dropping may be triggered by various grammatical categories. Usually, however, the phenomenon is tied to the grammatical context of the present tense. In Michoacán Nahuatl the copula *ka* is optional in the present tense:

2.27. ni-lakal
      1SG-man
      'I'm a man' (Sischo 1979: 319)

2.28. ti ka te   mičeros
      1PL-COP-PL   fishermen
      'we are fishermen' (Sischo 1979: 319)

In Russian, the copula *byl'* is obligatorily deleted in the present tense, as examples 2.31 and 2.32 show. *Byl'* regularly appears with nominals and adjectivals in combination with other tense/aspect/modality categories, as the past tense examples 2.29 and 2.30 demonstrate.

2.29. éto   by-l   dom
      this   COP-3SG.MSC.PST   house
      'this was a house' (author's field data)

---

[2] If the element *haih* is part of certain constructions which serve to express pragmatic categories *haih* is compatible with adjectives as well (see Matthews and Yip 1994: 129ff.).

2.30. dom   by-l   bol'šój
      house   COP-3SG.MSC.PST big
      'the house was big' (author's field data)

2.31. éto   dom
      this   house
      'this is a house' (author's field data)

2.32. dom   bol'šój
      house   big
      'the house is big' (author's field data)

In Hungarian, both nominals and adjectivals copularize, as the past tense examples 2.33 and 2.34 show. However, the copula *van* is obligatorily deleted in the third person present indicative both with nominals and adjectivals in predicate position, as examples 2.35 and 2.36 illustrate.

2.33. ez   egy   szék   volt
      this   IDF.SG chair   COP.PST.IND
      'this was a chair' (author's field data)

2.34. a   történet hosszú   volt
      DEF   story   long   COP.PST.IND
      'the story was long' (author's field data)

2.35. ez   egy   szék
      this   IDF.SG chair
      'this is a chair' (author's field data)

2.36. a   történet hosszú
      DEF   story   long
      'the story is long' (author's field data)

Aside from present tense, various additional grammatical categories can be identified which may trigger copula dropping, or at least team up with other grammatical categories in creating this effect. Third person is one of these categories (see Hungarian examples above). In some languages the copula can be skipped in the third person singular only.

In Tarma Quechua, the copula *ga-/ka-* 'is almost always omitted in the third person present tense form *gan/kan* and often so in the third person past tense form *gara/kara*' (Adelaar 1977: 178). Thus, past tense must also be included in the list of grammatical categories which may trigger copula dropping.

In Kenya Luo, the copula *ní* occurs with nominal subjects; it cannot be used with pronominal subjects:

2.37. nyíthíndo   ní   dúg·ê
      child.PL   COP naked
      'those children are naked' (Tucker 1993: 214)

2.38. gín   dúg·ê
      3PL   naked
      'they are naked' (Tucker 1993: 255)

The Swahili copula *ni* can be dropped in a similar set of contexts: 'If the subject is an independent pronoun or demonstrative, *ni* may be omitted' (Welmers 1973: 325).

In the following examples, the independent pronoun *mimi* '1SG' makes copula dropping admissible:

2.39. mimi   ni   Hassan
      1SG   COP   Hassan
      'I am Hassan' (author's field data)

2.40. mimi   Hassan
      1SG   Hassan
      'I am Hassan' (author's field data)

The copula *ni* can also be dropped when the subject '...is followed by a demonstrative or possessive' (Ashton 1944: 92):

2.41. m-ti   h-uu   m-bovu
      CL.SG-tree   this-CL.SG   CL.SG-rotten
      'this tree is rotten' (Ashton 1944: 93)

2.42. ki-su   changu   h-iki
      CL.SG-knife   1SG.POR   this-CL.SG
      'this is my knife' (Ashton 1944: 93)

In Punjabi, deletion of the copula *hoNaa* is 'virtually obligatory' (Bhatia 1993: 83) in the present negative. In all other contexts, the copula is either obligatory or optional.

Munro (1976: 50) quotes complexity of a clause as a factor which influences copula dropping in Mojave: 'In more complex sentences ... "be" is usually not omitted.' The same tendency can be observed in Mandarin (Hashimoto 1969: 84, Li and Thompson 1977: 422) and Indonesian. The Indonesian copulas *adalah* and *ialah* 'are most common in noun clauses where either the subject or predicate is long, in which case they break up a string of nouns and add a smoothness to the construction' (Sneddon 1996: 237).

The term copula dropping, as it stands, implies a process. Such a dynamic interpretation, however, is not intended here because it presupposes that the clause structures in question basically contain a copula, which disappears via some mechanism of deletion. There is, however, no evidence whatsoever for such a hierarchical relationship between the constructions in question. Nevertheless, the label copula dropping is convenient. It captures the intuition that in the respective contexts in which the copula is missing it should actually be expected to occur. This intuition is based on the fact that in any one language investigated which displays the phenomenon of copula dropping, the majority of grammatical categories never trigger copula dropping. Only with a very small subset of grammatical categories copulas are either optional or not admissible. Thus, the use of the term copula dropping is motivated by quantitative considerations based on the overall ratio of occurrence *vs.* non-occurrence of copulas with grammatical categories, rather than by the assumption that hypothetical deletion processes of some sort are taking place.

The cross-linguistic sample established for the purpose of the present study (see §2.3.4) suggests that languages in which nominals do not copularize, while at least one other lexical class does, might not exist. The sample contains only one potential candidate for such a language, namely Jacaltec, but it is actually not clear how Jacaltec should be analysed in this respect (see examples 2.163 to 2.166). On the assumption that this type of language does not exist, the following generalization can be proposed:

2.43. If any of the lexical classes of nominals, verbals, and adjectivals
        combines with a copula at all in a given language, it is the class
        of nominals.

These findings are in keeping with the results of parallel analyses carried out by Croft:

Predicate nouns are more likely to be structurally marked (with a copula) than predicate adjectives. In fact, the following implicational universal holds for the sample and probably holds more broadly: if the predicate nominal construction does not use a copula, the predicate adjective construction does not also.

(Croft 1991: 130)

The data further yield the following quasi-universal:

2.44. In any one language in which copula dropping occurs, it applies to
        nominals under the same conditions as to adjectivals.

The only exceptions to rule 2.44 found in the sample only confirm the findings concerning the higher susceptibility of nominals to copularization: in some languages in which both nominals and adjectivals may be combined with copulas, adjectivals are more prone to delete copulas than nominals are. The following compilation of quotations relating to Chalcatongo Mixtec and Shilluk demonstrate this.

Chalcatongo Mixtec:

Virtually all adjectives can appear with the copula.

(Macaulay 1996: 86)

All adjectives can appear with a zero copula.

(Macaulay 1996: 85)

...while nominal predicates require either an existential or the copula, adjectival predicates may occur alone.

(Macaulay 1996: 131)

Examples 2.45 and 2.46 illustrate the use of the copula and the existential with nominals:

2.45. ku   ɨ̃   čàà   ká̃ʔnũ
      COP.POT   one   man   big
      'he will be a big man' (Macaulay 1996: 131)

2.46. inì   kaxá   wã̃ã̃   žoo   tenànà
      insides   box   the   EX   tomato
      'in the box there are tomatoes' (Macaulay 1996: 129)

Adjectivals like *ñíʔní* 'hot' can form predicates either with the copula or with the existential, or with neither of these:

2.47. žó   ñíʔní
      EX   hot
      'it's hot' (Macaulay 1996: 87)

2.48. ka   ñíʔní
      COP   hot
      'it's hot' (Macaulay 1996: 86)

2.49. ñíʔní   nduča
      hot   water
      'the water is hot' (Macaulay 1996: 86)

Shilluk:

The Shilluk language has many words to express being, but each of them with a different value...*ba* expresses the essence of a being; it always requires a predicate, which is generally a noun.

(Kohnen 1933: 103)

2.50. ya   ba   yago
      1SG   COP   chief
      'I am the/a chief' (Kohnen 1933: 103)

'*bera* points out the quality of a being...Oftentimes the copula "to be" is omitted, **especially when a quality is denoted**' (Kohnen 1933: 104f.; boldfacing by R.P.).

2.51. yɔmo   bera   libo
      wind   COP   cold
      'the wind is cold' (Kohnen 1933: 105)

2.52. yɔmo   libo
      wind   cold
      'the wind is cold' (Kohnen 1933: 105)

2.3. The global sample

There are, of course, languages which do not have copulas, such as Tagalog (see examples 2.151 to 2.153), as well as many other Austronesian languages. Nevertheless, copularization is an extremely widespread phenomenon in human language, and it involves considerable cross-linguistic variation. This typological diversity manifests itself in several ways.

Above all, languages differ with respect to the number and the type of lexemes that are combined with a copula in predicate position. This issue has already been addressed in Chapter 1. No systematic attempt has been made so far to establish what the existing patterns of the distribution of copularizing *vs.* non-copularizing lexemes in the lexicon of individual languages are, and what patterns are missing. One of the major objectives of the present study is closing this gap in typological research. The results of the cross-linguistic survey conducted for this purpose are summarized in §2.3.4.

However, in dealing with cross-linguistic variation in the domain of copularization, at least two additional areas of investigation emerge. For one, linguistic elements that are referred to as copulas in the descriptive literature may differ considerably in their structural make-up. This creates problems in delimiting copulas from structurally and functionally similar elements, in particular, from certain types of predicate markers. Further, many languages have more than just a single copula. The question that arises with respect to such languages is how the respective copulas interact within the complex intra-linguistic system of copularization, and what rules, if any, govern this interaction.

2.3.1. Structural types of copulas

Linguistic elements that come to mind when examples of copulas are to be provided will, at least for native speakers of Indo-European languages, most likely be elements that can be grouped with the formal class of verbs in a given language on morphosyntactic grounds. But does a linguistic element necessarily have to be a morphosyntactic verb in order to qualify as a copula? Obviously not, since the descriptive literature abounds with linguistic items which are classed as copulas but which are not morphosyntactic verbs.

A basic criterion by which different structural types of copulas can be distinguished is that of syntactic autonomy. A copula may be a free or a bound morpheme. In the majority of cases, copulas are free morphemes. Depending on their respective degree of compatibility with categories of predicate formation, such as person, tense, aspect, and modality markers, syntactically autonomous copulas can be associated with specific lexical classes. The morphosyntactic potential of such copulas may be more or less identical with that of verbals in a given language. As a consequence, such copulas can be classed as morpho-syntactic verbs. However, very frequently, morphosyntactically verbal copulas display some kind of idiosyncratic behavior that sets them apart from verbs proper. For instance, verbal copulas tend to show irregular inflectional paradigms. This phenomenon is pervasive, and definitely not restricted to Indo-European languages. Further, the categorial inventory of verbal copulas, as compared to that of verbs proper, tends to show more or less pronounced reductions.

The inflectional paradigm of the German copula *sein* is, by and large, identical to that of intransitive verbs. The major categories of German predicate inflection are: person (agreement with the nominative phrase), number (singular, plural), tense (present, past, perfect, pluperfect, pluperfect 2, future 1, future 2), modality (indicative, subjunctive, imperative), voice (active, passive), infinitive, participle. *Sein* displays all of the grammatical categories listed above except the passive. Thus, the categorial inventory of *sein* can be considered almost non-defective.

The Japanese copula *da*, on the other hand, displays a more reduced set of inflectional categories which characterize verbals in this language. The major categories of Japanese predicate inflection are: tense (past, non-past), aspect (imperfective, perfective, resultative), modality (affirmative, negative, imperative, hortative, provisional, conditional, representative, presumptive, several types of honorifics), voice (active, two types of passive, causative), infinitive, and gerund. The copula *da* is compatible with all of the above categories except the infinitive, the imperative, both types of passive, resultative, causative, and potential.

The Mandarin copula *shì* is not a full-fledged morphosyntactic verb either, since it occurs only with a restricted set of the tense and modality markers associated with verbals (Li and Thompson 1981: 148). For example, unlike other morphosyntactic verbs, *shì* 'can be negated only by *bu*, not by *méi (yǒu)*' (Li and Thompson 1981: 148), and it lacks an imperative.

The Nuer copula *á* 'is a defective verb; it is invariable for all persons and tenses; it has but this one form' (Crazzolara 1933: 90). This kind of copula represents the maximum degree of reduction of inflectional possibilities with copulas.

The Kannada copula *iru* provides an interesting example of a reversal of the overwhelming cross-linguistic tendency of copulas to display a reduced cat-egorial inventory: '. . . unlike verbs proper, which show a two-fold past-nonpast tense distinction, the verb *iru* "to be" shows a three-fold past-present-future distinction' (Bhat 1994: 63).

In some languages, categorial distinctions encountered with verbals proper are neutralized with copulas. Telugu is a case in point: the verb *un* 'to be, to exist' 'has a special feature in that its past tense forms have both past and present meanings' (Krishnamurti and Gwynn 1985: 140).

Copulas which figure as full lexemes do not necessarily belong to the formal class of verbs, that is, to the class of lexemes that have the specific morpho-syntactic properties displayed by the lexical representations of event concepts. Copulas which have the morphosyntactic properties of the lexical representations of property concepts in a given language are also attested, as, for instance, in Korean: 'Taking into account the structural behavior of the copula as a free word, we may also treat the copular sentence as a subtype of adjectival sentence' (Chang 1996: 70).

Sohn (1994) is more explicit on this:

> Korean has the copula adjective *ita* 'be' whose basic function is to equate or identify the subject with its complement, or define or describe the subject as referred to by the complement.
>
> (Sohn 1994: 79)

The semantic class of adjectivals in Korean 'lacks the indicative mood suffix *-nun* that the verb…carries' (Sohn 1994: 95), and so does the copula *ita* (Sohn 1994: 95). Thus, 'the copula *ita* "be" is an adjective' (Sohn 1994: 95).

Similarly, in Navaho, 'verbs of being…are conjugated in the same… paradigm as the adjectivals' (Young and Morgan 1987: 190).

The Swahili copula *ni* is an example of a non-inflecting copula. *Ni* combines with nominals and adjectivals in predicate position, as examples 2.53 and 2.54 show, but not with verbals. Swahili verbals are inflected for a variety of categories, among them person and tense, as example 2.55 indicates. None of these categories can be attached to the particle *ni*.

2.53. h-uyu   ni   n-dege
      this-CL.SG   COP   CL.SG-bird
      'this is a bird' (author's field data)

2.54. ki-su   ni   ki-kali
      CL.SG-knife   COP   CL.SG-sharp
      'the knife is sharp' (author's field data)

2.55. simba   a-na-nguruma
      lion   3SG.SBJ-PRS-growl
      'the lion is growling' (author's field data)

Ni is used in the present indicative only. In combination with verbal inflectional categories other than present indicative, *ni* is replaced with the morphosyntactic verb *kuwa*, which is capable of carrying verbal inflectional affixes. In examples 2.56 *vs.* 2.57, present indicative is contrasted with past indicative, which is expressed by *li-*.

2.56. Ali   ni   m-wivu
      Ali   COP   CL.SG-jealous
      'Ali is jealous' (author's field data)

2.57. Ali   a-li-kuwa   m-wivu
      Ali   3SG.SBJ-PST-COP   CL.SG-jealous
      'Ali was jealous' (author's field data)

The set of syntactically non-autonomous copulas comprises affixal and suprasegmentally marked elements. Not everyone would consider grouping such elements with copulas—the alternative term predicate marker is frequently employed in referring to such linguistic items.

In Af Tunni, the element *-ów*, which is classed as a copula by Tosco (1997: 120), has affixal status:

2.58. ána   maʔállin-ów
      1SG   teacher-COP
      'I am a teacher' (Tosco 1997: 120)

Likewise, in Yagaria, the copula *-e′* attaches as a suffix to the predicate nucleus, as Renck (1975: 46) observes: '[*-e′*, R.P.] occurs mainly in non-verbal clauses and functions as a kind of copula which does not exist in Yagaria as a separate word.'

2.59. ima   yava   dalepa-e′
      there tree   casuarina-COP
      'that tree there is a casuarina' (Renck 1975: 47)

Parallel syntactic structures are found in Blackfoot:

2.60. nít-aakii-yi-hpinnaan
      1-woman-COP-1PL
      'we are women' (Frantz 1991: 23)

The element *-yi* might be classed as an affixal copula as well; examples 2.58, 2.59, and 2.60 are structually analogous. However, Frantz (1991: 23) prefers the term 'derivational suffix' in this case.

In Northern Paiute, elements which fulfill parallel functions of deriving the 'predicative form' (Snapp and Anderson 1982: 14) of adjectivals are found:

2.61. sawa-bi   odɨ-'yu
      sagebrush-NPS tall-PRD
      'the sagebrush is tall' (Snapp and Anderson 1982: 14)

In Arbore, there are similar predicators for nominals:

There is no one phonological form in Arbore which can be straightforwardly identified as the affirmative copula. Rather we find a heterogeneous collection of morphological processes which mark the terminal element of a noun phrase as functioning as a nominal predicate.

(Hayward 1984: 135)

2.62. w[áﬁạ]lo   kittiyyá-ḍa
this   bedbug-PRD
'this is a bedbug' (Hayward 1984: 135)

In Cubeo, there is a choice between the copula ʹbA-, which is used in example 2.63 and which has the same morphosyntactic status as lexemes expressing event concepts in this language, and the clitic -bU, which appears in example 2.64 (Morse and Maxwell 1999: 16):

2.63. bia   ʹbA-wɨ   di-E
hot pepper   COP-3   this-IN.PL.NM
'this is hot pepper' (Morse and Maxwell 1999: 16)

2.64. bia-bU   di-E
hot pepper-COP   this-IN.PL.NM
'this is hot pepper' (Morse and Maxwell 1999: 16)

The Persian copula *budæn* can be optionally cliticized in written style. In colloquial style cliticization is mandatory (author's field data). Thus, example 2.65 can be used in written style only, while example 2.66 is appropriate both in written and colloquial style.

2.65. gol   ğashang   ast
flower   beautiful   COP.3SG.PRS
'the flower is beautiful' (author's field data)

2.66. gol   ğashang-st
flower   beautiful-COP.3SG.PRS
'the flower is beautiful' (author's field data)

According to Kornfilt (1997: 78ff.), Turkish has two suffixal forms of the copula which both surface only in specific contexts. The copula -DIr occurs only in the third person present, and it is optional:

2.67. bu   fare-dir
this   mouse-COP.3SG
'this is a mouse' (author's field data)

2.68. bu   fare
this   mouse
'this is a mouse' (author's field data)

The occurrence of the copula -y is even more restricted. -y is encountered only in special phonological environments, that is, when the sound it follows is not a consonant.

2.69. (ben)   satıcı-y-ım
1SG   seller-COP-1SG
'I am a seller' (Kornfilt 1997: 77)

In all other contexts, -*y* is deleted:

2.70. (ben)   öğretmen-im
      1SG   teacher-1SG
      'I am a teacher' (Kornfilt 1997: 78)

It must, however, be added at this point that the status of -*y* as a copula is controversial; for a more detailed discussion, see §2.3.3.

The final stage of physical reduction of predicators is illustrated by Shona. In this language, tone distinguishes between basic and predicative forms of nominals:

> In a number of Bantu languages, identification is expressed by a tonal replacive accompanying the noun class prefix if it is a full syllable . . . In Shona, . . . nouns by themselves have prefixes with low tone . . . To express identification, high tone replaces low tone.
>
> (Welmers 1973: 322f.)

2.71. mùnhù
      person
      'person' (Welmers 1973: 323)

2.72. múnhù
      person.PRD
      'it is a person' (Welmers 1973: 323)

On the basis of the usage of terminology in the literature for such cases of affixal and suprasegmental copulatives, the latter might have been excluded from the range of phenomena investigated in the present study. The elements in question are usually referred to as predicative forms, predicate markers, predicators etc. rather than as copulas. However, a cross-linguistic approach to copularization, first of all, presupposes a clear-cut definition of the phenomenon under investigation that allows for an unequivocal separation of copulas and non-copulas. In applying the functional definition of copula given in §1.2 at the cross-linguistic level, it may, occasionally, be necessary to go against the intuitions of grammar writers concerning the status of the elements in question. According to this definition, predicators of the above type do qualify as copulas: they are semantically empty—although they may perhaps be credited with coding the abstract function of predication, but this is also true of copulas proper. Imposing the structural requirement that a copula must be a syntactically autonomous element upon a definition of copula seems a somewhat arbitrary step to take which, ultimately, reflects nothing but a bias that is rooted in over two millennia of grammar writing from an Indo-European perspective. However, the decision of whether to include this restriction in the definition of copula, or not, also depends on the type of the investigation one is conducting.

As Chapter 1 shows, the phenomenon of copularization is embedded in the larger theoretical context of linguistic markedness. Since the explanatory model offered in Chapter 4 relies heavily on the notion of markedness, the question of whether a given copular element is syntactically autonomous or not loses its relevance. In terms of markedness, both structural types of copulas are equivalent, at least when a contrast is made with predicate constructions in which copulas are lacking. This contrast, in turn, is the basic issue around which the present investigation of copulas in cross-linguistic perspective evolves. Thus, syntactically dependent copulas, alias predicators, are not excluded from the scope of the investigation. Such a decision is supported by the observation that in diachronic development, copulas are as susceptible to the general laws of phonetic reduction and loss of syntactic autonomy as any other linguistic element. Cases in which an erstwhile morphosyntactically verbal copula is transformed into an affix are documented, for instance, in Turkish (see §2.3.3). Thus, syntactically dependent copulas do indeed exist. Uniformly assigning the label of predicators, rather than the label of copulas, to such elements would gloss over relevant historical connections—at least in cases where it is clear that the origin of the elements in question is to be sought in independent copulas.

Using a somewhat different classification of the domain, Stassen (1997: 76ff.) distinguishes three types of copulas: verbal copulas, pronominal copulas, and particle copulas. The two latter types are subsumed under the rubric of non-verbal copulas. Verbal copulas constitute a self-evident category. Pronominal copulas can be delimited from other copular elements by virtue of the fact that pronouns are among the possible diachronic sources of copulas (see §2.3.3). Particle copulas 'have their origin in a variety of . . . markers of discourse-oriented categories such as topicalization, backgrounding, or contrastive focus for subjects or predicates' (Stassen 1997: 85). In the cross-linguistic sample established for the purpose of the present study, copulas which are in some way associated with markers for certain pragmatic categories are met with as well. For details, see §2.3.3, examples 2.143 to 2.150.

2.3.2. *Multiple copularization*

Languages which have more than just a single copula are not infrequent. It can be assumed that such categorial differentiation is concomitant with certain functional distinctions—that is, copulas which coexist within a given language should differ in their functional scope. And in fact, such a 'division of labor' between copulas takes place in many languages that display multiple copularization. The patterns of formal differentiation encountered here may, for instance, coincide with one or the other distinction among the various predicate types discussed in §2.1.2.

In Lakota, there are two copulas, *héc^ha* and *é*. *Héc^ha* occurs exclusively with ascriptive predicates. *É*, on the other hand, must be used with all types of identificational predicates listed in table 2.1, and is ungrammatical with ascriptive predicates.

2.73. akícita   hécʰa
soldier   COPa
'he is a soldier' (author's field data)

2.74. lé   Mary   é
this   Mary   COPb
'this is Mary' (author's field data)

In Nuer, verbals and adjectivals do not copularize, while nominals are combined with the copula *ɛ́* in predicate position (Crazzolara 1933: 89). In addition, there is a special copula *á* which occurs exclusively with predicates denoting place and time specifications (Crazzolara 1933: 90f.). The examples given in Crazzolara (1933) indicate that these place and time specifications fall under the scope of oblique case predicates, adverbial, and temporal predicates.

However, multiple copularization may not only be sensitive to certain distinctions between the predicate types listed in §2.1.2. Multiple copularization may operate at a more specialized level as well. There are languages in which ascriptive predicates show inhomogeneous behavior in that different types of lexemes require the use of different copulas in predicate position. A particularly striking example of a language in which this situation holds is Bambara. Bambara displays a multi-copula system that comprises four copulas. The copula *ye...ye* occurs with nominal predicates only; the copula *ka* combines with adjectival predicates only, and the copula *bɛ* is compatible with verbal predicates only. The fourth copula, *dòn*, functions to code quantificational, temporal, and participial predicates, among other things.

2.75. nìn   ye   námása   ye
this   COPa   banana   COP
'this is a banana' (author's field data)

2.76. so   ka   sùrun
house   COPb   small
'the house is small' (author's field data)

2.77. ne   bɛ   taa
1SG   COPc   leave
'I am leaving' (author's field data)

2.78. caman   dòn
many   COPd
'there are many' (author's field data)

Epena Pedee employs distinct copulas for nominal and adjectival predicates as well. In non-present tense, *pa* is used with nominal predicate nuclei, while adjectival predicate nuclei combine with *bɨ*.

2.79. úsa   pʰaimáa   pa-hí
dog   black   COPa-PST
'(it) was a black dog' (Harms 1994: 34)

2.80. pía   bɨ
    good   COPb
    'that is good' (Harms 1994: 23)

The same kind of differentiation is encountered in Shilluk, as examples 2.50 and 2.51 demonstrate. With nominals, the copula *ba* is used; with adjectivals, on the other hand, the copula *bera* is used.

Similarly, the copularization system in Chalcatongo Mixtec draws a formal distinction between nominals and adjectivals:

> The copula in Mixtec has two forms, depending on whether the predicate is nominal or adjectival. Before adjectival predicates, it is *kaa* in realis aspect and *kuú* in potential. Before nominal predicates, it is *kúu* in realis aspect and, as with adjectives, *kuú* in potential.

> (Macaulay 1996: 130)

In Thai, the distinction between the two copulas *khɨ:* and *pen* is, to some degree, sensitive to the semantic contrast between nominals *vs.* adjectivals as well, although copula usage in Thai is controlled by a variety of additional factors. As a rule, both copulas are encountered in combination with nominal predicates only. In this context, *khɨ:* and *pen* can, by and large, be used interchangeably. There is a difference in meaning involved here, 'but it is so subtle that native speakers cannot normally pinpoint what it is' (Kuno and Wongkhomthong 1981: 66f.). The unmarked choice of copulas with prototypical nominal predicates is *khɨ:*, as in example 2.81, rather than *pen*, although *pen* can be substituted for *khɨ:*, as in example 2.82.

2.81. nî: khɨ: nók'
    this   COPa   bird
    'this is a bird' (author's field data)

2.82. nî: pen   nók'
    this   COPb   bird
    'this is a bird' (author's field data)

However, *pen* is felt to be more acceptable than *khɨ:* with nominal predicates denoting occupations (see examples 2.83 *vs.* 2.84), and nationalities (see examples 2.85 *vs.* 2.86), and when the predicate nominal is possessed (see examples 2.87 *vs.* 2.88).

2.83. dìchán   pen   khru:
    1SG   COPb   teacher
    'I am a teacher' (author's field data)

2.84. ?? dìchán   khɨ: khru:
    1SG   COPa   teacher
    'I am a teacher' (author's field data)

2.85. dìchán   pen   khon   Thai
      1SG   COPb   person Thai
      'I am a Thai' (author's field data)

2.86. ?? dìchán   khɨ: khon   Thai
         1SG   COPa   person Thai
      'I am a Thai' (author's field data)

2.87. nî: pen   bâ:n   dìchán
      this   COPb   house   1SG.POR
      'this is my house' (author's field data)

2.88. ?? nî: khɨ: bâ:n   dìchán
         this   COPa   house   1SG.POR
      'this is my house' (author's field data)

With a specific group of lexemes, the *khɨ:* vs. *pen* contrast expresses a semantic distinction which is analogous to the distinction between nominals and adjectivals. Many lexemes which designate shape or material assume a different reading in terms of this distinction when they are combined with *pen* rather than with *khɨ:*. In this context, *khɨ:* is regularly associated with nominal status; *khɨ:* indicates that a given lexical item should be interpreted as belonging to the semantic class of object concepts, as in example 2.89. *Pen*, on the other hand, imposes adjectival status, that is a reading as a property concept, as in example 2.90. Thus, *sǎ:mlìa:m* 'triangle, triangular' is translated by the English noun 'triangle' in example 2.89, and by the English adjective 'triangular' in example 2.90.

2.89. nî: khɨ: sǎ:mlìa:m
      this   COPa   triangle
      'this is a triangle' (author's field data)

2.90. (kracok')   nî: pen   sǎ:mlìa:m
      mirror   this   COPb   triangular
      'this (mirror) is triangular' (author's field data)

Likewise, the copula *khɨ:* establishes reference to a substance in combination with certain lexemes which designate material, such as *lèk'* 'iron'. If, however, the copula *pen* is added to such lexemes instead, the resulting reading is best rendered by English adjectives which denote the substance an entity is composed of—such as *golden* or *wooden*—or by the phrase 'made of . . .'.

2.91. nî: khɨ: lèk'
      this   COPa   iron
      'this is iron' (author's field data)

2.92. (tó)   nî: pen   lèk'
      table   this   COPb   made of iron
      'this (table) is made of iron' (author's field data)

The *khɨ:* vs. *pen* contrast is also used for a systematic disambiguation between the nominal and adjectival readings of the lexeme *dèk'* 'child, childish':

2.93. Somsàk'   khɨ: dèk'
      Somsak   COPa   child
      'Somsak is a child' (author's field data)

2.94. Somsàk'   pen   dèk'
      Somsak   COPb   childish
      'Somsak is childish' (author's field data)

Spanish presumably has the most widely known and thoroughly studied multi-copula system. But the Spanish system differs from those met in the above languages. In those languages there is a fixed (i.e. lexicalized) relation between an individual lexeme and a specific copula, so that a given lexeme can be combined with a single copula only. In Spanish, on the other hand, many adjectivals are compatible both with the copula *ser* and with the copula *estar*. Nominal predicates select *ser* only:

2.95. ellos   son   aristócrata-s
      3PL.MSC   COPa.3PL.PRS.IND   aristocrat-PL
      'they are aristocrats' (Porroche Ballesteros 1988: 39)

Exclusive use of *estar* is observed with a restricted set of adjectivals which, for the most part, derive from participles, such as *contento* 'happy', *descalzo* 'barefoot', *descontento* 'unhappy', *desnudo* 'naked', *enfermo* 'sick', *fijo* 'solid', *florido* 'florid', *harto* 'weary of', *insatisfecho* 'dissatisfied', *lleno* 'full', *maltrecho* 'maltreated', *oculto* 'secret', *preso* 'captive', *satisfecho* 'satisfied', *suspenso* 'undecided', and *vacío* 'empty' (Porroche Ballesteros 1988: 56). In addition, lexicalized participles which originate in the resultative *estar* + participle construction are combined with *estar*. An example is *excitado* 'excited', which is derived from *excitar* 'to excite':

2.96. él   esta-ba   muy   excitad-o
      3SG.MSC   COPb-PST.IPF.IND   very   excited-SG.MSC
      'he was very excited' (Porroche Ballesteros 1988: 57)

The basic resultative construction which constitutes the diachronic source for such lexicalized participles is illustrated by example 2.97.

2.97. la   puerta   esta-ba   abiert-a
      DEF.SG.FEM   door   AUX-PST.IPF.IND   open-SG.FEM
      'the door was open' (Butt and Benjamin 1988: 302)

The alternation between *ser* and *estar* with lexemes admitting both copulas is almost always concomitant with a change in meaning. To the rare lexemes which freely substitute one copula for the other belong those which indicate marital status such as *casado* 'married', *divorciado* 'divorced', *soltero* 'single', and *viudo* 'widowed' (Butt and Benjamin 1988: 313).

2.98. soy   solter-o
      COPa.1SG.PRS.IND   single-SG.MSC
      'I am single' (author's field data)

2.99. est-oy   solter-o
      COPb-1SG.PRS.IND   single-SG.MSC
      'I am single' (author's field data)

If the alternation *ser* vs. *estar* causes a change in meaning, the latter can, by and large, be characterized in terms of the semantic parameters quality *vs.* state, or permanent *vs.* transitory, as the contrastive examples 2.100 *vs.* 2.101 and 2.102 *vs.* 2.103 show.

2.100. es   muy   guap-a
       COPa.3SG.PRS.IND   very   pretty-SG.FEM
       'she's very good-looking/a beauty' (Butt and Benjamin 1988: 314)

2.101. est-á   muy   guap-a
       COPb-3SG.PRS.IND   very   pretty-SG.FEM
       'she's looking very attractive (e.g., in a certain dress)'
       (Butt and Benjamin 1988: 314)

2.102. es   muy   joven
       COPa.3SG.PRS.IND   very   young
       'he's very young' (Butt and Benjamin 1988: 314)

2.103. est-á   muy   joven
       COPb-3SG.PRS.IND   very   young
       'he looks very young' (Butt and Benjamin 1988: 314)

With some lexemes the meaning change brought about by copula switching is more drastic; it affects semantics beyond the permanence *vs.* non-permanence opposition:

2.104. *ser atento* 'to be courteous' vs. *estar atento* 'to be attentive'
       (Butt and Benjamin 1988: 315)

2.105. *ser un enfermo* 'to be an invalid' vs. *estar enfermo* 'to be ill'
       (Butt and Benjamin 1988: 315)

2.106. *ser listo* 'to be clever' vs. *estar listo* 'to be ready'
       (Butt and Benjamin 1988: 315)

2.107. *ser un vivo* 'to be unscrupulous' vs. *ser vivo* 'to be sharp/alert'
       vs. *estar vivo* 'to be alive' (Butt and Benjamin 1988: 315)

Although the permanence *vs.* non-permanence distinction is to be regarded as the general principle underlying the copula alternation, there are a few lexemes which contradict this principle, such as *estar muerto* 'to be dead' (Butt and Benjamin 1988: 309). Moreover, *ser* occasionally shows up in contexts expressing transitory states. Thus, a transitory reading of *valiente* 'courageous', which is implied by the adverbial complement *esta tarde* 'this evening' in the following examples, is compatible with *ser* as well as with *estar*:

2.108. ha   esta-d-o   muy   valiente   est-a   tarde
       AUX.3SG.IND   COPb-P-SG.MSC   very   courageous   this-SG.FEM   evening
       'this evening he was very courageous' (Porroche Ballesteros 1988: 45)

2.109. ha   si-d-o   muy   valiente   est-a   tarde
       AUX.3SG.IND   COPa-P-SG.MSC   very   courageous   this-SG.FEM   evening
       'this evening he was very courageous' (Porroche Ballesteros 1988: 45)

The unexpected occurrence of *ser* in example 2.109 can be explained by assuming that the *ser*-version of the sentence in question does in fact have the connotation of permanence; it ascribes a personality feature. The adverbial complement *esta tarde* merely refers to the circumstances which led to the assigment of this trait (Porroche Ballesteros 1988: 44ff.).

An analogous semantic distinction is expressed by the use of different copulas in Barasano. In this language, the copula *yã* 'to be' conveys the notion of permanency (Jones and Jones 1991: 21), while the copula *bahi* 'to be, to be like' indicates 'temporary states and comparative constructions of manner and appearance' (Jones and Jones 1991: 22). There are lexical items which are compatible with both copulas, as examples 2.110 *vs.* 2.111 demonstrate.

2.110. riha-go   yã-a-bõ
       sick-SG.FEM   COPa-PRS-3SG.FEM
       'she is a sick person' (Jones and Jones 1991: 22)

2.111. riha-go   bahi-a-bõ
       sick-SG.FEM   COPb-PRS-3SG.FEM
       'she is sick' (Jones and Jones 1991: 22)

Of the two copulas *de* and *na* in Ndyuka, '*de* often suggests less permanence about the described state than does *na*' (Huttar and Huttar 1994: 137). A semantic distinction between two competing copulas in terms of permanence *vs.* non-permanence is also reported for Limbu (Van Driem 1987: 63), Maltese (Borg and Azzopardi-Alexander 1997: 34), and Nigerian Pidgin (Faraclas 1996: 48).

Multi-copula systems can be based on factors other than the permanence *vs.* non-permanence distinction. For instance, the inventory of copulas in Alacatlatzala Mixtec includes a special copula *sīvī* which is exclusively reserved for predicating terms of relationship (Zylstra 1991: 19).

2.112. ta   kāa   sīvī   yīvā   ún
      he   that.visible   COP.CNT   father   2SG.POR.SG
      'he is your father' (Zylstra 1991: 20)

A special copula for terms of relationship is also attested in Sgaw Karen (author's field data).

Aside from other copulas which fulfill more common functions, Ateso has two special copulas which express 'numerical quantity' (Hilders and Lawrence 1956: 6) and 'size or bulk' (Hilders and Lawrence 1956: 6), respectively.

In addition, multiple copularization may not only be sensitive to the intrinsic semantic content of the predicate nucleus, but to the semantic make-up of the clausal subject as well. Dumi has two copulas, *gɨnɨ* and *mɨnɨ*, which select inanimate *vs.* animate referents, respectively (Van Driem 1993: 168ff.):

2.113. khənɨkpa   go:-t-a
      beautiful   COPa-NPST-3SG
      'it's beautiful' (Van Driem 1993: 171)

2.114. khənɨkpa   mo:-t-a
      beautiful   COPb-NPST-3SG
      'he's beautiful' (Van Driem 1993: 171)

In Panyjima, the following situation holds:

The intransitive stance verbs *panti-Ø*, 'sit, stay', *karri-Ø*, 'stand' and *ngarri-Ø*, 'lie', may function as tense bearing copulas in essentially ascriptive predications…The unmarked copula is *panti-Ø*, 'sit, stay', while the choice of *ngarri-Ø*, 'lie', or *karri-Ø*, 'stand' depends partly on the physical dimensions of the object. Things seen as having a primarily horizontal extent may select the *ngarri-Ø* copula. Things with a primarily vertical orientation select the *karri-Ø* copula.

                                                              (Dench 1991: 184)

2.115. panti-wuru   marlpa   ngunha   pilakurta
      COP-HAB   man   that   carpenter
      'that man used to be a carpenter' (Dench 1991: 185)

Similar classificatory copulas are documented in Imonda. The copulas *lõh* and *ale* are homonymous with verbs of position, that is, with *lõh* 'to stand' and *ale* 'to sit'. The copula *lõh* 'occurs with many nouns whose referents are not intrinsically tall or erect' (Seiler 1985: 158), while *ale* is used 'with nouns whose referents may assume a sitting posture such as people or animals' (Seiler 1985: 158). However, when male humans function as the subject of a copularizing predicate, *lõh* is much more likely to be chosen than *ale*. When the predicate refers to females, *ale* is usually preferred.

2.116. Bob   kuii-l   lõh-f
      Bob   long-NM   COPa-PRS
      'Bob is tall' (Seiler 1985: 158)

2.117. Luise kuii-l   ale-f
      Luise long-NM   COPb-PRS
      'Luise is tall' (Seiler 1985: 158)

Canela-Krahó has a particularly selective copula *te* which is used only with the lexical item which designates the concept 'name': 'When the noun *haprỳ/japrỳ* 'name' is the subject, the form of the relator copula is *te* rather than *pê*' (Popjes and Popjes 1986: 134).

2.118. i-pê   capi
      1-COPa   Capi
      'I am Capi' (Popjes and Popjes 1986: 134)

2.119. haprỳ   te   capi
      name   COPb   Capi
      'his name is Capi' (Popjes and Popjes 1986: 134)

Further, the choice of copulas in multi-copula systems may be determined by grammatical factors. In Indonesian, there are two copulas, *adalah* and *ialah*. While the element *adalah* is used regardless of the grammatical context it is embedded in, *ialah* 'only occurs after third person subjects' (Sneddon 1996: 237).

Multiple copularization may also be sensitive to pragmatic distinctions. For instance, the contrast between the two Thai copulas *khɨ:* and *pen*, which is too multifaceted to be dealt with in detail here (see Kuno and Wongkhomthong 1981), can be used to convey subtle distinctions at the level of social interaction. Thus, examples 2.120 and 2.121 characterize the social relationship between the speaker and the person spoken about in different ways.

2.120. nî: khɨ: phî:an dìchán   khâ
      this COPa   friend 1SG.POR PLT
      'this is my friend' (Kuno and Wongkhomthong 1981: 88)

2.121. nî: pen   phî:an dìchán   khâ
      this COPb   friend 1SG.POR PLT
      'this is my friend' (Kuno and Wongkhomthong 1981: 88)

[2.120, R.P.] is the proper form to use for introducing one's friend to the addressee. In comparing [2.120, R.P.] and [2.121, R.P.], Thai speakers feel that [2.120, R.P.] implies that the person that is being introduced is an important friend of the speaker, and that the speaker is asking the addressee to treat him/her as such. On the other hand, if [2.121, R.P.] is used for introduction, it implies that the person being introduced is not an important friend of the speaker.

                                 (Kuno and Wongkhomthong 1981: 88)

2.3.3. The genesis of copulas

In diachronic perspective, copulas can be studied both with respect to their origins, as well as with regard to changes in their compatibility options with lexical items. The following discussion, which deals with the genesis and the possible development of copulas with respect to their distributional scope in the lexicon, rests on the essential tenets of grammaticalization theory (Heine, Claudi, and Hünnemeyer 1991, Hopper and Traugott 1993, Traugott and Heine 1991). Among these tenets are, for one, the assumption that grammatical items develop from lexical items; and, further, the assumption that the functional scope of linguistic items, as well as their distributional properties, may change over time.

The diachronic development of copulas from lexical or grammatical material has been dealt with quite explicitly in the extant literature. The main sources for copulas seem to be verbs and pronouns (see also Hengeveld 1992: 237ff., Stassen 1997: 90ff.). Frajzyngier (1986) argues that copulas may also develop from prepositions.

De-verbal copulas may derive from verbs expressing location, position, and existence, as well as from verbs denoting concepts such as ' "do/make/build", "happen/occur", "go/turn into/come/become", and "act (like)" ' (Stassen 1997: 92f.). The Thai copula *pen* originates in Proto-Tai *pen* 'to be alive' (Alec Coupe, p.c.). Copulas which are homonymous with verbs expressing existence are characteristic of Indo-European languages. Similarly, the Bambara copula *bɛ* is homonymous with the verb for 'to live, exist'. The Basque copula *izan* is homonymous with the verb for 'to exist', while the Basque copula *ukan* is homonymous with the verb for 'to have'. The Burmese copula $p^h j\imath ?$ is homonymous with the verb for 'to become'. The Spanish copula *estar* derives from Latin *stare* 'to stand' (Hengeveld 1992: 245).

Homonymies between copulas and stance verbs can be observed in a variety of languages. Thus, in Kawaiisu, 'the positional predicates *kari-* "to sit", *wɨnɨ-* "to stand", and *havi-* "to lie", are often used to express "be" ', (Munro 1990: 23).

2.122. ʔivoyo-pɨgadɨ   ʔuusɨsu   hiivoʔopiiči   kari-dɨ   ʔɨɨvi
        big-PRF   long ago   little   sit-NM   now
        'it used to be big, but now it's little' (Munro 1990: 23)

An analogous situation holds in Martuthunira:

> Martuthunira makes use of three intransitive stance verbs as copulas: *nyina-Ø* 'sit, stay, be', *karri-Ø* 'stand', and *wanti-Ø* 'lie'. Of these, only *nyina-Ø* can be said to function like a true dummy copula; both *karri-Ø* and *wanti-Ø* retain something of their core meaning in a copula construction.
>
> (Dench 1995: 210)

2.123. nyina-layi   pularna   mir.ta-rru   panyu
        COP-FUT   3PL   not-now   good
        'they aren't going to be good' (Dench 1995: 210)

Languages in which there are homonymies between stance verbs and copulas, which indicate that grammaticalization processes are or have been at work, also include Guugu Yimidhirr (Haviland 1979: 115f.), Imonda (see examples 2.116 and 2.117), Lango (Noonan 1992: 145), Panyjima (see example 2.115), and Sranan (Arends 1986: 119).

A curious source for a verbal copula can be identified in Hua:

[The verb *ro-*, R.P.], whose principal lexical meaning is 'burn', functions as the perfective auxiliary. It also occurs as the copula with a small number of complements, all of them pejorative and expressive of physical decrepitude or stuntedness: among them are *Kosita* 'old' (man), *tava* 'old' (inanimate object), *Kagia* 'bald', *KeBiri*, *Keva* 'stunted' (animal or vegetable), and *fuipa'* 'stunted' (vegetable).

(Haiman 1980: 265)

Copulas originating in pronouns are also widely documented in the literature. This type of copula is met with, for instance, in Tok Pisin:

In Tok Pisin, a nonverbal copula has now for some time been developing from the pick-up pronoun *em*.

(Verhaar 1995: 81)

2.124. em   Praim Minista
       COP   Prime Minister
       'that is the Prime Minister' (Verhaar 1995: 83)

The most widely known instantiation of a pronoun developing into a copula is the case of Mandarin *shì*. According to Li and Thompson (1977), in Archaic Chinese (11th–3rd centuries BC) the demonstrative pronoun *shì* could be used as an anaphoric pronoun in a specific construction type which is illustrated by example 2.125.

2.125. jì   yú   qí   shēng   yòu   yù   qí   sǐ   ,
       already   wish   3SG   live   also   wish   3SG   die   ,
       shí   huò   yě
       this   indecision   DCL
       'wishing him to live while wishing him to die, that is indecision'
       (Li and Thompson 1977: 424)

This construction type gave rise to the reanalysis of *shì* as a copula:

2.126. cǐ   bái   wù   shì   hé   děng?
       this   white   thing   COP   what   kind
       'what kind of stuff is this white thing?' (Li and Thompson 1977: 425)

In today's Mandarin, the demonstrative meaning of *shì* has been lost; only the copular function remains. According to Li and Thompson (1977), analogous processes of the grammaticalization of pronouns into copulas have taken place in Hebrew and Palestinian Arabic.

Homonymies between copulas and pronouns, which are indicative of such grammaticalization processes, can, for instance, be observed in Kenya Luo (Tucker 1993: 308), Lango (Noonan 1992: 145f.), Logbara (Crazzolara 1960: 67), Maltese (Borg and Azzopardi-Alexander 1997: 49ff.), and Nuer (Crazzolara 1933: 89). In Kenya Luo, 'a third person pronoun may optionally be used as a copula' (Tucker 1993: 308):

2.127. dhákó   e'n   béˆr
       woman   COP   goodness
       'woman she is goodness' (Tucker 1993: 308)

2.128. dhákó   béˆr
       woman   goodness
       'woman she is goodness' (Tucker 1993: 308)

In Lango, which is closely related to Kenya Luo, the grammaticalization of the third person singular pronoun *én* into a copula has reached a stage in which the original pronominal function is not transparent any more. The copula *én* occurs not only with third person singular subjects, as example 2.129 illustrates.

2.129. án   én   à-dáktâl
       1SG   COP   1SG-doctor.HAB
       'I am the doctor' (Noonan 1992: 146)

Copulas derived from pronouns may develop into verbal copulas. The Lakota copula *héc^{h}a* is etymologically based on the demonstrative pronoun *hé* 'this' and the element *c^{h}a* 'such'. Neither *hé* nor *c^{h}a* are compatible with verbal inflectional categories; *héc^{h}a*, however, can be inflected like a stative intransitive verb (see examples 2.170 and 2.172).

Verbal copulas, further, may evolve into affixes. In Modern Turkish, there exist two copular affixes. Both of these occur in a very restricted set of contexts only. The distributional scope of at least one of these copulas, the verb *i-* 'to be', which originates in the stem *er-* 'to be', which was 'abraded in the course of time' (Lewis 1967: 96), was higher in the recent past. This verb lost its syntactic autonomy and developed into an affix. As an affix, it was exposed to phonological reduction processes. As a consequence, this element, in its current phonetic form *-y*, can be used in specific phonological contexts only in Modern Turkish. The copula *-y* occurs only after non-consonants, as examples 2.69 and 2.70, which are repeated here for convenience, show.

2.130. (ben)   satıcı-y-ım
       1SG   seller-COP-1SG
       'I am a seller' (Kornfilt 1997: 77)

2.131. (ben)   öğretmen-im
       1SG   teacher-1SG
       'I am a teacher' (Kornfilt 1997: 78)

The historical process which led to this synchronic state of affairs is illuminated by Kornfilt (1997: 80):

> Until as recently as the early years of the Republic, the tense and agreement suffixes in copular sentences were 'carried' by the free morpheme *i* in the past tenses…In a change that first affected colloquial levels and then more formal stylistic levels (including the written language), these inflected copular forms became postclitics, attaching themselves onto the preceding word, and with the copular *i* turning into the glide *y*; where the *y* was preceded by a consonant, it dropped. The free inflected copular forms are found, albeit rarely, in current written Turkish, too.
>
> (Kornfilt 1997: 80)

In examples 2.132 and 2.133 the copula *i* figures as a free morpheme:

2.132. (ben)   satıcı   i-di-m
      1SG   seller   COP-PST-1SG
      'I was a seller' (Kornfilt 1997: 80)

2.133. (ben)   öğretmen   i-di-m
      1SG   teacher   COP-PST-1SG
      'I was a teacher' (Kornfilt 1997: 80)

The corresponding, decidedly more common, reduced forms are:

2.134. (ben)   satıcı-y-di-m
      1SG   seller-COP-PST-1SG
      'I was a seller' (Kornfilt 1997: 79)

2.135. (ben)   öğretmen-di-m
      1SG   teacher-PST-1SG
      'I was a teacher' (Kornfilt 1997: 79)

It must be added at this point that the preceding discussion of the element *i* in Turkish relies heavily on Kornfilt's (1997) analysis, which is innovative but somewhat controversial. There exist alternative hypotheses which deny Kornfilt's claim that *i* has copular status, at least in cases in which this element figures as the affix *-y*. Instead, *-y* is analyzed as a linking consonant that appears in specific phonological contexts (e.g. Jansky 1986: 19). The impression to be gained from dealing with the extant literature on the subject is that the solution of this analytical problem requires an in-depth assessment of the historical developments that have taken place in this area of Turkish grammar since the emergence of the copular verb *i*.

The second (undeniably) copular element in Turkish, the suffix *-DIr*, is characterized as a 'suppletive form for the copula' by Kornfilt (1997: 81). The historical source of *-DIr* is a stance verb; in this context, Lewis (1967: 96) cites the form *turur* 'he stands'. The copula *-DIr* is used in the third person present only, and it is always optional, as the comparison of examples 2.136 and 2.137 shows (see also Kornfilt 1997: 81f.).

2.136. bu   cadde-dir
       this   road-COP.3PRS
       'this is a road' (author's field data)

2.137. bu   cadde
       this   road
       'this is a road' (author's field data)

The Turkish data on copularization are exclusively based on the distribution of the element *-DIr*. The copula *-y* has not been investigated because it is impossible to provide a coherent account of the semantic motivation of copula usage for a copula whose realization depends on phonological factors. It seems safe to conclude, however, that the distributional scope of *-y* in the lexicon coincides with that of *-DIr*:

> The copula that shows up with adjectival complements has exactly the same properties as the copula that is used with nominal complements—in its regular form, in the distribution of *-y*, and in its suppletive forms *ol* [for future tense, R.P.] and *-DIr*.
>
> (Kornfilt 1997: 82)

The Turkish case is very instructive because it appears that both *-y* and *-DIr* have independently developed from syntactically autonomous verbs to copular affixes.

On the basis of data from Mojave, Munro (1977) argues that existential constructions ('there is') should also be included in the set of possible diachronic sources for copulas (see also Hengeveld 1992: 254). This assumption is supported by data from Chalcatongo Mixtec:

> Mixtec also allows a construction in which the existential is used with an adjective. This construction...apparently has the same meaning as the normal copula + adjective construction.
>
> (Macaulay 1996: 87)

In example 2.138, the predicate is formed with the 'normal' copula *kaa·*

2.138. Xʷã   ka   lúlí
       Juan   COP   small
       'Juan is small/short' (Macaulay 1996: 130)

In example 2.139, the existential marker *žóó* 'there is' functions as a copula. The existential usage of *žóó* 'there is' is illustrated by example 2.140.

2.139. kìsì   žóó   xáá
       pot   EX   new
       'the pot is new/there is a new pot' (lit. 'as for the pot, it exists new')
       (Macaulay 1996: 130)

2.140. inì   kaxá   wã̃ã   žoo   tenànà
       insides box   the   EX   tomato
       'in the box there are tomatoes' (Macaulay 1996: 129)

For further data on Chalcatongo Mixtec, see examples 2.45 to 2.49.

As another possible source of copulas, adpositions may be taken into consideration. In Gbeya, the copula *né* 'resembles the preposition *né* in several respects' (Samarin 1966: 76). The copula *né* is peculiar in that it is used in combination with other copular elements: it 'seems to occur exclusively with the verbs *ɔ* and *ya*, the singular and plural verbs "to be"' (Samarin 1966: 75).

2.141. wa   yá   né   wéey
     3PL   COP.PL   COP   man
     'they are men' (Samarin 1966: 77)

2.142. téa   ɔ́   né   búu
     tree   COP.SG   COP   white
     'the tree is white' (Samarin 1966: 77)

For the preposition *né*, a variety of meanings are given: '(a) accompaniment (translated "accompanied by, with", etc.), (b) instrument (translated "by means of, out of, with", etc.), (c) object (translated "into, resulting in, against, about, concerning", etc.), and (d) location (both of time and place, translated "at, on", etc.)' (Samarin 1966: 75).

Another hint at the origin of copulas lies in the fact that copulas are sometimes homonymous with elements conveying certain pragmatic notions, such as emphasis. In this connection, the Turkish data must be addressed once more. The element *-DIr*, which is identified as a copula in the preceding sections, can also be used to express 'emphatic, official certainty' (Kornfilt 1997: 82). A third function of *-DIr* is marking of 'inference' (Kornfilt 1997: 82). An example such as 2.143, in which *-DIr* is, due to vowel harmony, realized as *-tur*, has two possible readings.

2.143. bölüm   başkanı   dekan   ol-muş-tur
     department   head   dean   become-PST-?
     'the department head has become a dean' (Kornfilt 1997: 81)

[The suffix *-DIr*, R.P.] has two functions: 1. used at a formal, even official, stylistic level, to express emphatic certainty; 2. used at all levels (but perhaps preferred colloquially), to express inferred probability . . . If this example [2.143, R.P.] is found, for example, in an administrative bulletin or is uttered by a university official, this would be an example for the first usage just described. However, if no such news has been announced, but if a colleague has found the department's chair office empty and has seen the person settled in the dean's office instead, that colleague is likely to utter the same example, which would then illustrate the second usage. Examples like [2.143, R.P.], then, are systematically ambiguous between the two functions just discussed . . . (It should also be noted that, in both these usages, the suffix *-DIr* can show up with all persons, but it is preferred for third person, singular as well as plural.) . . . However, where a copular sentence is in the present tense and has a third person subject, the *-DIr* suffix takes on a third function, namely that of the copula.

(Kornfilt 1997: 81f.)

This latter usage is demonstrated in example 2.144:

2.144. bölüm   başkanı   aynı   zaman-da   dekan-dır
       department   head   same   time-LOC   dean-?
       'the department head is, at the same time, a dean' (Kornfilt 1997: 82)

While the 'emphatic, official certainty' reading and the 'inference' reading are available
here [i.e. for 2.144, R.P.), too, the main reading is that of a simple declarative.

(Kornfilt 1997: 82)

Likewise, the Mandarin copula *shì* is homonymous with elements which fulfill
certain pragmatic functions. One of these is the formation of the so-called illogical
copula construction (Hashimoto 1969: 86ff., Li and Thompson 1981: 150ff.). The
illogical copula construction 'allows a very loose linkage or connection between
the referential subject noun phrase and the nonreferential noun phrase following
the copula' (Li and Thompson 1981: 150). Thus, example 2.145, which would
normally be rendered by 'I am chicken-rice', is more appropriately interpreted as
conveying the meaning expressed by the more elaborate version 2.146.

2.145. wo   shi   jifan
       1SG   COP   chicken-rice
       'what I ordered is chicken-rice' (Hashimoto 1969: 88)

2.146. wo   jiao   de   shi   jifan
       1SG   order   NM   COP   chicken-rice
       'what I ordered is chicken-rice' (Hashimoto 1969: 88)

Another pragmatic function of the element *shì* is expressing special affirmation
(Li and Thompson 1981: 151ff.):

2.147. tā   méi   qián
       3SG   NEG.exist   money
       's/he doesn't have any money' (Li and Thompson 1981: 151)

2.148. tā   shì   méi   qián
       3SG   COP   NEG.exist   money
       'it's true that s/he doesn't have any money'
       (Li and Thompson 1981: 151)

Example 2.147 'is essentially neutral and could be used in volunteering information or in answering a question' (Li and Thompson 1981: 151), whereas example
2.148 'could be used only to affirm what had been said earlier or what had
been suspected or inferred by the speaker and the hearer' (Li and Thompson
1981: 151).

The Japanese construction type referred to as propredication (Martin 1986:
239ff.) in the literature involves an element which is homonymous with the

copula *da*. This construction, which is highly reminiscent of the illogical copula construction in Mandarin, allows for the omission of almost any syntactic constituent.

> In a propredicational sentence the copula is used to mark an ellipsis of some specific predicate either alone or together with any number of its adjuncts. This is a device that lets you be as vague, or unexplicit, as you like about the verbal element; usually you can prune the sentence back to any degree, revealing less and less of the situation, provided only that you retain at least ONE nominal element, for the copula will not normally stand alone.
>
> (Martin 1986: 239)

Thus, instead of the explicit utterance 2.149, the propredicational version 2.150 is possible.

2.149. yama   ni   yuki   ga   ar-u
       mountain   LOC   snow   NOM   LPR.IN-NPST
       'the mountain has snow on it' (author's field data)

2.150. yama   wa   yuki   da
       mountain   TOP   snow   COP.NPST
       'the mountain has snow on it' (Martin 1986: 242)

However, copulas which are homonymous with markers of pragmatic categories do not necessarily have to be regarded as historically derived from these markers of pragmatic categories. The assumption that both copular and pragmatic functions may develop simultaneously and independently from a common source is equally plausible. This issue is in need of some systematic cross-linguistic research.

The fundamental question to be raised at this point is whether the diachronic origin of a given copula influences its distributional scope in language-specific vocabularies. For instance, it could be tested whether pronoun-based and verb-based copulas show divergent statistical preferences for the major distributional patterns AN and AV. However, in this respect, the available data are too scant to allow for extensive and reliable statistical analyses.

2.3.4. Distribution of copularizing vs. non-copularizing lexemes in the lexicon of individual languages

In describing copula distribution, grammars often confine themselves to over-simplifying statements such as 'the copula occurs with nominals and adjectivals but not with verbals', which can be taken as characterizing the situation in English. Of course, in many languages the actual state of affairs is more intricate than such crude formulations imply. Thus, even closely related languages such as English and German may display copularization shifts. For instance, *to be angry* is the semantic equivalent of German *sich ärgern*. *Angry* copularizes, whereas *sich ärgern* does not; the concept 'angry' lexicalizes as an adjective in English, but as a verb in German. The overall difference in the scope of copularization in English and German, however, is minimal when compared with the other languages surveyed in this study. This kind of variation poses a particular challenge for language typology. A rewarding task in typological research is assessing what distributional patterns of copularizing *vs.* non-copularizing lexemes in the lexicon can be found in the languages of the world, and what patterns do not exist. Subsequently, universal principles that govern copula distribution can be derived from these empirical facts. Developing such a theoretical model, more specifically, a semantically-based model of copula distribution, is the major objective of the present study of copularization.

In what follows the results of a survey of grammatical descriptions which includes 131 languages will be presented. This survey should be comprehensive enough to be representative of the global inventory of possible and impossible distributional patterns of copularizing *vs.* non-copularizing lexemes in individual languages. In establishing a reliable data corpus for this purpose, a number of difficulties must be overcome. For a first analytical approximation, the semantic macro-classes of entity concepts, event concepts, and property concepts, alias nominals, verbals, and adjectivals (see §2.1.1) can be used as descriptive primitives by means of which the patterns governing copula usage in individual languages can be characterized with a satisfactory degree of accuracy. A main source of frustration in the attempt to obtain data on copularization and lexeme types is the quality of the available language descriptions, which is, more often than not, unsatisfactory. Many grammars do not contain any statements pertaining to the compatibility of individual lexical classes with copulas at all. Sporadic examples of copularizing structures which are—sometimes—given, nevertheless, are not particularly helpful because it would be empirically irresponsible to ascribe a language to a distributional type on the basis of two or three examples only. There is too much potential variation in the coding options even for a single lexical class, as the discussion of copula dropping and multiple copularization in §§2.2 and 2.3.2 shows, to name just one example. The ad hoc assumption that the available examples are representative of the set of copularization patterns employed by a given language inevitably produces unreliable databases. The lack of explicitness in the descriptions of copula usage in a given language can, to some extent, be blamed on the fact that clauses containing either (semantically) nominal or adjectival predicates, the main loci of copula constructions, constitute minor sentence types in any one language.

Grammarians, either consciously or unconsciously, tend to be influenced by the silent assumption that semantic nounhood is to be equaled with argument function, and semantically adjectival status with attribute function. In this view, nominal and adjectival predicates are not of particular interest, and are, as a consequence, either ignored or, at best, included under the rubric of 'minor sentence types' in many grammatical descriptions. The division of sentence types into major and minor types, of course, is grounded in universal patterns of frequency distribution of predicate types in discourse (see Chapter 1), and is therefore certainly not an arbitrary and artificial one. Nevertheless, the impression remains that the current treatment of such minor sentence types in the descriptive literature leaves a lot to be desired.

Since one of the strict requirements imposed on the database established is descriptive accuracy, language descriptions had to meet relatively high standards in order to be included in the database. Ideally, a description of copula usage in a given language contains a statement such as the following, which characterizes the situation in Warí:

> Copular sentences do not exist. This notion is expressed by what would be the nominal, adjectival, or adverbial complement of a copular appearing as the verb of the sentence... to say, for example, 'the baby is a man (male)', 'the house is small', or 'the boy is fast', one says, 'the baby mans (males)', 'the house smalls', and 'the boy fasts'.
>
> (Everett and Kern 1997: 117)

Copula usage in Persian is also clearly circumscribed by the following quotation taken from Mahootian (1997: 44ff.): 'A copula is obligatory in sentences with a nominal complement... A copula is obligatory in sentences with an adjectival complement.'

Unfortunately, statements like the two reproduced above, which set an example with respect to explicitness and clarity, were found only in about half a dozen of several hundreds of grammars that were scanned for the purpose of obtaining cross-linguistic data on copularization.

Moreover, the availability of a relatively large amount of data on a given language does not guarantee a sufficient degree of descriptive accuracy. Despite the fact that thousands of pages of data on Navaho could be compiled, the language had to be excluded from the sample because the descriptions did not yield the information required. Only a total of about 200 grammars were retained in the sample after the initial process of data selection. A subsequent evaluation of these materials led to the exclusion of about seventy more languages. The final sample, from which more or less justifiable cross-linguistic generalizations could be derived, comprises 131 languages (see table 2.7). Of these, a total of twenty-two languages, namely Bambara, Burmese, Cantonese, English, Estonian, French, German, Hebrew, Hungarian, Indonesian, Japanese, Korean, Lakota, Mandarin, Persian, Sgaw Karen, Slovene, Spanish, Swahili, Thai, Turkish, and Vietnamese, were investigated with the help of native speakers, particularly for the purpose of obtaining some insights into the semantic motivation of copularization. These data are discussed in detail in Chapter 3.

Eight logical patterns, reproduced in table 2.2, can be established using the three semantic macro-classes for which the respective terminological labels of nominals, verbals, and adjectivals have been introduced in §2.1.1 as heuristics for determining the distribution of copularizing *vs.* non-copularizing lexemes in the

TABLE 2.2. *Basic patterns of copula distribution*

	NOMINALS	ADJECTIVALS	VERBALS
Tagalog	−	−	−
Burmese	+	−	−
German	+	+	−
Bambara	+	+	+
?	−	+	+
?	−	−	+
?	−	+	−
?	+	−	+

(+ = copula used in predicate position; − = copula not used in predicate position)

lexicon of a given language. However, only four of these patterns are attested in the sample. They are exemplified by Tagalog, Burmese, German, and Bambara, respectively.

In what follows, examples of the ascriptive predicate constructions found in these languages are given. For Bambara, examples 2.75 to 2.77 are repeated here once more.

Tagalog:

nominal predicate:

2.151. maestro   ang   lalaki
      teacher   FOC   man
      'the man is a teacher' (Schachter and Otanes 1972: 97)

adjectival predicate:

2.152. bagu   ang   bahay
      new   FOC   house
      'the house is new' (Schachter and Otanes 1972: 64)

verbal predicate:

2.153. nag-hi-hi-lik   ang   lolo
      AG.FOC-S-RED.IPF-snore   FOC   grandfather
      'grandfather is snoring' (Schachter and Otanes 1972: 69)

Burmese:

nominal predicate:

2.154. i   əja   gà   eĩ   pʰjɪʔ   pa   ði
      this   thing   TOP   house   COP   PLT   POS
      'this thing is a house' (author's field data)

adjectival predicate:

2.155. i   ẽĩ   gà   ŋɛ   ba   ði
      this   house   TOP   small   PLT   POS
      'this house is small' (author's field data)

verbal predicate:

2.156. θu   gà   ji   ne   ba   ði
      3SG   TOP   laugh   PRG   PLT   POS
      's/he is laughing' (author's field data)

German:

nominal predicate:

2.157. das   ist   ein   Haus
      this.NOM   COP.3SG.PRS.IND   IDF.SG.NTR.NOM   house
      'this is a house' (author's field data)

adjectival predicate:

2.158. das   Haus   ist   klein
      DEF.SG.NTR.NOM   house   COP.3SG.PRS.IND   small
      'the house is small' (author's field data)

verbal predicate:

2.159. er   lach-t
      3SG.MSC.NOM   laugh-3SG.PRS.IND
      'he is laughing' (author's field data)

Bambara:

nominal predicate:

2.160. nìn   ye   námása   ye
      this   COP   banana   COP
      'this is a banana' (author's field data)

adjectival predicate:

2.161. so   ka   sùrun
      house   COP   small
      'the house is small' (author's field data)

verbal predicate:

2.162. ne   bɛ   taa
      1SG   COP   leave
      'I am leaving' (author's field data)

Stassen contrasts languages of the Tagalog type with those of the Burmese and German type. Languages which employ 'verbal' (Stassen 1997: 141) coding strategies with all types of predicates, which are characterized, among other things, by the absence of a copula, 'are opposed to what might be called "lexicon-oriented" languages, in which the lexical category of the predicative item (and, by prototypical connection, the semantic function expressed by the item) is, at least to some degree, the determinant factor in the choice of the morphosyntactic encoding strategy' (Stassen 1997: 142).

The hypothetical language type in which nominals and verbals do not copularize, while adjectivals do, deserves some closer scrutiny. The sample contains one language in which this pattern might be claimed to exist, namely Jacaltec.[3]

> The copula *-eyi* 'to be in a certain way or condition' expresses a state which either is a transient state of health or mood or is the result of an action.
>
> (Craig 1977: 22f.)

Craig's translation 'to be in a certain way or condition', however, seems to imply that the 'copula' *-eyi* might not be entirely devoid of meaning. If *-eyi* is meaningful, however, this element does not qualify as a copula according to the definition employed for the purpose of the present study (see §1.2).

Some Jacaltec adjectivals can be used both with and without the element *-eyi*. This contrast co-varies with a meaning distinction in terms of permanence:

2.163. c'ul   ix
       good   CLF.she
       'she is good/a good person' (Craig 1977: 23)

2.164. c'ul   ye   ix
       good   COP(?) CLF.she
       'she is fine/in good health' (Craig 1977: 23)

Although 'most adjectives never take a copula' (Craig 1977: 24), 'certain adjectives require the use of the copula *-eyi*' (Craig 1977: 24). These are 'the adjectives expressing emotional and affective states' (Craig 1977: 24), such as *tzalalal* 'happy'.

2.165. tzalalal   ye   naj
       happy   COP(?) CLF.he
       'he is happy' (Craig 1977: 24)

---

[3] Dumi has been considered as an example of a language in which adjectives copularize, while nouns and verbs do not. But the issue could not be resolved on the basis of the available data. The uncertainty stems mainly from the fact that, despite the author's claim that nominal predicates are formed without a copula (Van Driem 1993: 173), an example is given in the same paragraph that contains a nominal predicate and a copula.

However, the element -*eyi* also occurs with nominals. In this context, it 'denotes the appearance or resemblance of one thing to something else' (Craig 1977: 25).

2.166. añ   ye   te '   cape
      medicine   COP(?)   CLF.the   coffee
      'the coffee tastes like medicine' (Craig 1977: 25)

The decision of whether Jacaltec should be considered a language of the type that copularizes with adjectivals but not with nominals hinges on the semantic analysis of the element -*eyi*. The semantic essence of -*eyi* could be captured in terms of the notion of non-innateness. Goodness as a personality feature is an innate property, while the good health is not, since bodily states are subject to change. Likewise, happiness is not innate. The translation 'tastes like' in example 2.166 for -*eyi* evokes an association with non-innateness at a different level. The subject 'coffee' in example 2.166 is merely compared to medicine; it is not actually medicine, although a semantic configuration expressing the state of affairs 'the coffee is medicine' is plausible as well. The latter state of affairs features 'medicine-ness' as an innate property, while the semantic configuration 'the coffee tastes like medicine' does not. Thus, if the element -*eyi* is meaningful in all contexts in which it occurs, as Craig's translation 'to be in a certain way or condition' suggests, it is a semi-copula and not a copula proper according to the definition given in §1.2. This interpretation would disqualify Jacaltec as a language that employs a copula with adjectival predicates only. If, however, -*eyi* is classed as a semi-copula with nominals, but as a full copula with adjectivals like *tzalalal* 'happy' requiring the presence of -*eyi* in predicate position, this group of adjectivals must be regarded as the only copularizing lexeme class in Jacaltec. This issue can only be resolved with the help of additional information on whether native speakers feel that -*eyi* conveys the explicit semantic content of 'being in a certain way or condition' in combination with adjectivals that require the presence of this element in predicate position.

To the distributional types given in table 2.2 (see above) three more, statistically less common, patterns can be added, which are exemplified by Basque, Japanese, and Lakota in table 2.3:

TABLE 2.3. *Less common patterns of copula distribution*

	NOMINALS	ADJECTIVALS	VERBALS
Lakota	+/−	−	−
Japanese	+	+/−	−
Basque	+	+	+/−

(+ = copula used in predicate position; − = copula not used in predicate position)

In these languages, the cut-off point between copularizing and non-copularizing items in the lexicon is not in line with the conceptual boundaries between traditional parts of speech, but rather, cuts across the latter. Thus, Lakota nominals, Japanese adjectivals, and Basque verbals are divided into two classes, respectively, depending on whether copularization is admissible or not.

It must be pointed out that the assignment of Lakota to the language type that displays partial copularization with nominals is not uncontroversial. The situation holding in Lakota with respect to copularization is quite complex. For one, the copula *héc^{h}a* can be omitted in the third person present. Further, any nominal is compatible with *héc^{h}a*, while verbals and adjectivals are not:

2.167. lé   wašícu   héc^{h}a
        this   white man   COP
        'this is a white man' (author's field data)

2.168. c^{h}icá   ki   škáta-he
        child   DEF   play-PRG
        'the child is playing' (author's field data)

2.169. ógle   ki   sápe
        shirt the   black
        'the shirt is black' (author's field data)

Nominals may be directly combined with categories of predicate inflection, to the effect that number, tense, and polarity affixes are attached to the nominal itself, instead of being coded on the copula. Many nominals also admit direct affixation of person markers. An example of this type of nominal is *wašícu* 'white man'. However, with a limited set of nominals comprising mostly designations of animals, occupations, and tribal names, *héc^{h}a* is obligatory in all categories of person inflection except for the third person singular present. The nominal *P^{h}uláŋl* 'Pawnee Indian' belongs to this class of lexemes. Person affixes cannot be attached to nominals of this type. The contrast between the two types of nominal is illustrated in examples 2.170 to 2.174. In order to make the rules governing copula usage in these cases explicit, the predicates are inflected for the first person singular. Any stative predicate, that is any nominal, adjectival, or stative verbal in predicate position, receives the patientive or object form of the person affixes, that is the prefix or infix *ma-*, in the first person singular.

2.170. wašícu   he-má-c^{h}a
        white man   S-1SG.PAT-COP
        'I am a white man' (author's field data)

2.171. wa-má-šicu
        S-1SG.PAT-white man
        'I am a white man' (author's field data)

2.172. Pʰaláni   he-má-cʰa
       Pawnee Indian   S-1SG.PAT-COP
       'I am a Pawnee Indian' (author's field data)

2.173. *ma-Pʰálani
       1SG.PAT-Pawnee Indian
       'I am a Pawnee Indian' (author's field data)

2.174. *Pʰa-má-lani
       S-1SG.PAT-Pawnee Indian
       'I am a Pawnee Indian' (author's field data)

The question that poses itself at that point is whether any lexeme that optionally combines with the copula *hécʰa* in the first and second person, such as *wašícu* 'white man', should count as copularizing, or if only those lexemes that require the addition of the copula in the first and second person, such as *Pʰaláni* 'Pawnee Indian', should be classed as copularizing. The answer to this question decides on whether Lakota is to be assigned to the type of language exemplified by Burmese, or constitutes an example of the SPLIT-NOMINAL (henceforth, SPLIT-N) type. Lakota is the only language in the sample that can be used for an approximate illustration of this language type. However, the general procedure followed in the present study is classing lexemes as copularizing even if they are only optionally compatible with a copula. Thus, Lakota appears as a member of the Burmese type of language in the overall sample (see table 2.6, p. 74ff.).

Japanese provides an example of the SPLIT-ADJECTIVAL (henceforth, SPLIT-A) pattern of copula usage. In Japanese, nominal predicates receive a copula, while verbal predicates do not, as examples 2.175 and 2.176 show.

2.175. Hokkaido   wa   sima   da
       Hokkaido   TOP   island   COP.NPST
       'Hokkaido is an island' (author's field data)

2.176. Taroo   wa   tabe-ru
       Taro   TOP   eat-NPST
       'Taro is eating' (author's field data)

There are two types of adjectival, which are, among other things, distinguishable in terms of the presence *vs.* absence of the copula *da* in predicate position. *Taka-* 'high' does not copularize, while *koohuku* 'happy' does.

2.177. Yooko   wa   koohuku   da
       Yoko   TOP   happy   COP.NPST
       'Yoko is happy' (author's field data)

2.178. yama   wa   taka-i
       mountain   TOP   high-NPST
       'the mountain is high' (author's field data)

Basque illustrates the SPLIT-VERBAL (henceforth, SPLIT-V) pattern of copula distribution. Nominal as well as adjectival and verbal predicates copularize, with the sole exception of a small group of verbals. According to Bouda (1933), 39 of a total of 1006 verbals investigated do not copularize. These verbals are commonly referred to as 'synthetically inflecting'. These verbals may also combine with linguistic items which are structurally identical to the two Basque copulas *izan* and *ukan* when certain categories of predicate inflection are to be formed, but in these cases the elements *izan* and *ukan* have to be regarded as auxiliaries and not as copulas. The copula *izan*, which is homonymous with the full verb *izan* 'to exist', is obligatory with all types of intransitive predicates, that is when nominals, adjectivals, and intransitive verbals function as predicate nuclei. The copula *ukan*, which is homonymous with the full verb *ukan* 'to have', must be used with transitive verbals in all categories of predicate inflection—except with synthetically inflecting transitive verbals, of course. Some intransitive verbals combine with *ukan* rather than with *izan* (Saltarelli 1988: 64f.). Examples 2.179 and 2.180 represent nominal and adjectival predicates, respectively. Example 2.181 features a copularizing verbal in predicate position, while example 2.182 contains a synthetically inflecting, that is non-copularizing, verbal.

2.179. hura   gizon-a   d-a
       3SG.ABS   man-SG.ABS   3ABS-COP.PRS
       'he is a man' (Saltarelli 1988: 150)

2.180. mutil-a   haundi-a   d-a
       boy-SG.ABS   big-SG.ABS   3ABS-COP.PRS
       'the boy is big' (Saltarelli 1988: 150)

2.181. bi   ordu   barru   itzuli-ko   n-a-iz
       two   hour   inside   return-FUT   1SG.ABS-PRS-COP
       'I will return in two hours' (Saltarelli 1988: 191)

2.182. laku-ra   n-oa
       lake-ALL   1SG.ABS-PRS.go
       'I am going to the lake' (Saltarelli 1988: 22)

Although split systems are only marginally attested, they are, of course, relevant from a theoretical point of view. The existence of such languages provides one more piece of evidence in support of the insight that the segmentation of the lexicon into noun, verb, and adjective, on the basis of the situation holding in Indo-European languages, is an insufficient descriptive tool in the search for the universal mechanisms governing copularization (see §1.3.2).

The above discussion shows that there are extreme fluctuations with respect to the ratio of copularizing *vs.* non-copularizing lexemes in individual languages. Complete absence of copularization is documented by Tagalog. The opposite extreme, namely copularization with all lexeme types, including verbals, is

TABLE 2.4. *Typology of copularization patterns*

	NOMINALS	ADJECTIVALS	VERBALS
Tagalog			
Lakota			
Burmese			
Japanese			
German			
Basque			
Bambara			

(dark shading: copula used in predicate position; light shading: copula not used
in predicate position)

TABLE 2.5. *Typology of copularization patterns: quantitative distribution in the sample*

	number of occurrences	%	NOMINALS	ADJECTIVALS	VERBALS
non-copularizing	41	31.5%			
split-N	0	0.0%			
AV	27	20.8%			
split-A	6	4.6%			
AN	54	41.2%			
split-V	1	0.8%			
fully copularizing	2	1.5%			

(dark shading: copula used in predicate position; light shading: copula not used in predicate position)

exemplified by Bambara. Between the two typological extremes of Tagalog and
Bambara, the remaining languages in the sample, whose lexicon is composed of
both copularizing as well as non-copularizing lexemes, can be ranked according
to their overall inclination towards copularization. This yields the typological scale presented in table 2.4.

The respective percentages of language types occurring in the sample are given
in table 2.5. For languages that treat the semantic classes nominal, verbal, and
adjectival uniformly with respect to copularization, the terminological labels
NON-COPULARIZING (Tagalog), FULLY COPULARIZING (Bambara), AN (German), and

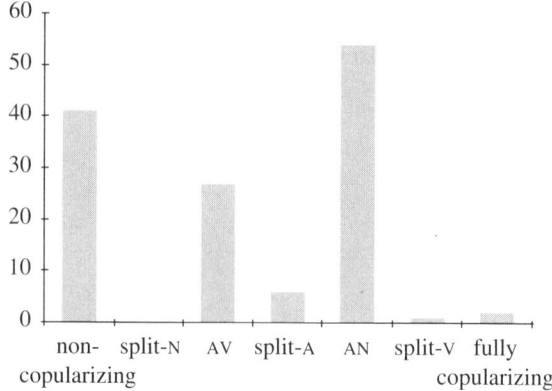

FIG. 2.1. *Quantitative distribution of language types in the cross-linguistic sample*

AV (Burmese) are introduced at this point. AN symbolizes parallelism in the treatment of nominals and adjectivals in a given language with respect to copularization, and AV signifies parallelism in the treatment of adjectivals and verbals.

The percentages of the individual types in the overall sample can be schematized by means of Fig. 2.1.

The global distribution of the individual language types shows a non-random pattern in that some types are considerably more frequent than others. The dominant types are AV, AN, and the non-copularizing type. Split-N, split-A, split-V, and the fully copularizing type are about equally marginal. These findings call for an explanation, which will be offered in Chapter 4 as part of a comprehensive functional-typological model of copularization.

In the language sample investigated, no really convincing example of the split-N type has been found, and Basque figures as the only representative of the split-V type. The split-A type is, obviously, slightly more frequent than the latter types, since it is represented by six of the languages contained in the sample. They are Copala Trique, Koromfe, Maasai, Tarma Quechua, and Yoruba, in addition to Japanese. The sample includes one more member of the fully copularizing language type in addition to Bambara, namely Iraqw. Depending on whether one chooses to analyze the linguistic element in question as a copula or as a marker for indicative modality, Mundari might also be considered a fully copularizing language (Bhat 1994: 18). There is some evidence that Burushaski has developed from an erstwhile fully copularizing system to an AN system (Berger 1998, W. Schulze, p.c.).

In sum, both the fact that not all of the logically possible types of distribution of copularizing *vs.* non-copularizing lexemes in the lexicon, and the fact that the existing types show a skewed frequency distribution in the global sample, suggest that copularization is controlled by some organizing principle that blocks the development of some logically possible distributional patterns, fosters the emergence of other patterns, and reduces the occurrence of a third group of patterns to a minimum. In Chapter 3 an attempt at uncovering these factors is made, which are to be sought in the domain of lexical semantics. At this point, it already seems safe to say that a theoretical model that explains the above distributional facts will draw on the segmentation of the lexicon into the semantic prototypes of nominals, verbals, and adjectivals. In the overwhelming majority of the sampled languages, the cut-off point between copularizing *vs.* non-copularizing lexemes in the lexicon obviously coincides with one of the cut-off points imposed by the division of the lexicon in terms of these semantic macro-classes.

The existing distributional patterns can be subsumed in the following implicational hierarchy:

2.183. NOMINALS > ADJECTIVALS > VERBALS

Any lexeme that is located to the left of the cut-off point between copularizing and non-copularizing lexemes in the lexicon of a given language receives a copula; any lexeme that is located to the right of this cut-off point does not combine with a copula. In other words, copularization is unidirectional: if any class of lexemes copularizes in a given language, the class of nominals does; if any lexical class other than nominals copularizes, the adjectival class does; only if both nominals and adjectivals copularize, verbals may also copularize.

2.3.5. *Global distribution of copulas*

Table 2.6 admits some interesting generalizations with respect to the global distribution of copulas. The impression to be gained from the data is that the geographic setting of a given language tends to determine its behavior with respect to copula usage. In Europe and the Near East the AN type predominates. Southeast Asia is the area which displays the greatest density of AV languages. Both Africa and the Americas show a very inhomogeneous picture; all of the major types, that is AN, AV, and the non-copularizing type, as well as some of the minor types, most notably the split-A type, are present. The same basic situation is also encountered in Australia, although the split types seem to be missing here. In Oceania, the non-copularizing type prevails.

2.4. A universal hierarchy of copularization

The findings reported in §2.3.4 show, for one, that only some of the logically possible patterns of the distribution of copularizing *vs.* non-copularizing lexemes in the lexicon of individual languages are realized in a comprehensive sample of 131 languages (see table 2.6). This is *per se* a remarkable fact which calls for

TABLE 2.6. *Copularization patterns: the global sample*

Language	Genetic affiliation	Type	Sources
Abkhaz	Caucasian	AV	Hewitt 1979
Acehnese	Austronesian	non-copularizing	Durie 1985
Acooli	Nilo-Saharan	non-copularizing	Crazzolara 1938
Af Tunni	Cushitic	AV	Tosco 1997
Ainu	Japanese-Korean	AV	Dettmer 1989; Refsing 1986; Shibatani 1990
Alamblak	Indo-Pacific	AV	Bruce 1984
Alyawarra	Pama-Nyungan	AN	Yallop 1977
Arabana-Wangkangurru	Pama-Nyungan	AV	Hercus 1994
Arabic	Semitic	AN	Gary and Gamal-Eldin 1982
Arbore	Cushitic	AN	Hayward 1984
Athpare	Tibeto-Burman	AN	Ebert 1997
Awtuw	Indo-Pacific	non-copularizing	Feldman 1986
Ayacucho Quechua	Andean	AN	Parker 1969
Bambara	Niger-Congo	fully copularizing	Kastenholz 1998; Long, Koita, and Konaré 1970/71; author's field data
Bari	Nilo-Saharan	AN	Spagnolo 1933
Basque	isolate	split-v	Saltarelli 1988; Tovar 1957; Umandi 1976
Belizean Creole	(pidgins and creoles)	AV	Greene 1999
Berbice Dutch Creole	(pidgins and creoles)	AV	Kouwenberg 1994
Blackfoot	Almosan-Keresiouan	AV	Frantz 1991
Boumaa Fijian	Austronesian	non-copularizing	Dixon 1988
Buriat	Mongolian-Tungus	AN	Poppe 1960
Burmese	Tibeto-Burman	AV	Okell 1969; author's field data
Canela-Krahó	Ge-Pano-Carib	AV	Popjes and Popjes 1986
Cantonese	Sinitic	AV	Matthews and Yip 1994; author's field data
Chalcatongo Mixtec	Oto-Manguean	AN	Macaulay 1996
Chamorro	Austronesian	non-copularizing	Topping 1973
Copala Trique	Oto-Manguean	split-A	Hollenbach 1992
Desano	Equatorial-Tucanoan	AN	Miller 1999
Diyari	Pama-Nyungan	AN	Austin 1981
Djapu	Pama-Nyungan	non-copularizing	Morphy 1983
English	Indo-European	AN	author's field data
Epena Pedee	Chibchan-Paezan	AN	Harms 1994
Estonian	Uralic-Yukaghir	AN	Oinas 1966; author's field data

TABLE 2.6. *(Contd)*

Language	Genetic affiliation	Type	Sources
Finnish	Uralic-Yukaghir	AN	Lehtinen 1963; Sulkala and Karjalainen 1992
French	Indo-European	AN	author's field data
Fulfulde	Niger-Congo	AN	Breedveld 1995
German	Indo-European	AN	Eisenberg 1986; Heidolph *et al.* 1981; author's field data
Gooniyandi	isolate	non-copularizing	McGregor 1990
Guugu Yimidhirr	Pama-Nyungan	AV	Haviland 1979
Halkomelem Salish	Almosan-Keresiouan	non-copularizing	Galloway 1993; Geerdts 1988
Hausa	Chadic	AN	Howeidy 1953; Kraft and Kraft 1973; Migeod 1914; Newman 2000; Robinson 1953; Schön 1862; Taylor 1959
Hebrew	Semitic	AN	Glinert 1989; author's field data
Hindi	Indo-European	AN	McGregor 1977
Hixkaryana	Ge-Pano-Carib	AN	Derbyshire 1979
Hungarian	Uralic-Yukaghir	AN	Kenesei, Vago, and Fenyvesi 1998; author's field data
Ila	Niger-Congo	AN	Smith 1907
Imonda	Indo-Pacific	AN	Seiler 1985
Indonesian	Austronesian	AV	Macdonald and Darjowidjojo 1967; Sneddon 1996; author's field data
Iraqw	Cushitic	fully copularizing	Mous 1993
Japanese	Japanese-Korean	split-A	Hinds 1986; Martin 1975; Shibatani 1990; author's field data
Kabardian	Caucasian	non-copularizing	Colarusso 1992
Kambera	Austronesian	non-copularizing	Klamer 1994
Kannada	Dravidian	AN	Bhat 1994; Schiffman 1983; Sridhar 1990
Karo Batak	Austronesian	non-copularizing	Woollams 1996
Kayardild	Pama-Nyungan	non-copularizing	Evans 1995
Kenya Luo	Nilo-Saharan	AV	Tucker 1993
Kilivila	Austronesian	non-copularizing	Senft 1986
Kisi	Niger-Congo	AN	Childs 1995
Koasati	Penutian	AV	Kimball 1991
Kobon	Indo-Pacific	AN	Davies 1981

TABLE 2.6. *(Contd)*

Language	Genetic affiliation	Type	Sources
Korean	Japanese-Korean	AV	Chang 1996; Lee 1989; Sohn 1994; author's field data
Koromfe	Niger-Congo	split-A	Rennison 1997
Koyra Chiini	isolate	AV	Heath 1999
Kriyol	(pidgins and creoles)	AN	Khim 1994
Kwaio	Austronesian	non-copularizing	Keesing 1985
Ladakhi	Tibeto-Burman	AN	Koshal 1979; Misra 1979
Lakota	Almosan-Keresiouan	AV	Boas and Deloria 1941; Buechel 1939; author's field data
Lango	Nilo-Saharan	AN	Noonan 1992
Lezgian	Caucasian	AN	Haspelmath 1993
Loniu	Austronesian	non-copularizing	Hamel 1994
Maasai	Nilo-Saharan	split-A	Tucker and Mpaayei 1955
Malayalam	Dravidian	AN	Asher and Kumari 1997
Maltese	Semitic	AN	Borg and Azzopardi-Alexander 1997
Mam	Penutian	non-copularizing	England 1983
Mandarin	Sinitic	AV	Hengeveld 1990; Li and Thompson 1981; author's field data
Manipuri	Tibeto-Burman	AV	Bhat and Ningomba 1997
Maori	Austronesian	non-copularizing	Bauer 1993
Margi	Chadic	non-copularizing	Hoffmann 1963
Martuthunira	Pama-Nyungan	AN	Dench 1995
Michoacán Nahuatl	Uto-Aztecan	AN	Sischo 1979
Misantla Totonac	Penutian	non-copularizing	MacKay 1999
Mojave	Hokan	AV	Munro 1976
Mokilese	Austronesian	non-copularizing	Harrison and Albert 1976
Nandi	Nilo-Saharan	non-copularizing	Creider and Creider 1993
Ndyuka	(pidgins and creoles)	AN	Huttar and Huttar 1994
Ngankikurungkurr	Non-Pama-Nyungan	non-copularizing	Hoddinott and Kofod 1988
Ngiti	Nilo-Saharan	AN	Kutsch Lojenga 1994
Nigerian Pidgin	(pidgins and creoles)	AV	Faraclas 1996
Nuer	Nilo-Saharan	AV	Crazzolara 1933
Nung	Daic	non-copularizing	Saul and Wilson 1980
Palauan	Austronesian	non-copularizing	Josephs 1973
Panyjima	Pama-Nyungan	AN	Dench 1991
Papago	Uto-Aztecan	AV	Zepeda 1988
Pero	Chadic	non-copularizing	Frajzyngier 1989
Persian	Indo-European	AN	Mahootian 1997; author's field data
Ponapean	Austronesian	non-copularizing	Rehg 1981
Punjabi	Indo-European	AN	Bhatia 1993
Rapanui	Austronesian	non-copularizing	Du Feu 1996
Retuarã	Equatorial-Tucanoan	AN	Strom 1992

TABLE 2.6. *(Contd)*

Language	Genetic affiliation	Type	Sources
Rotuman	Austronesian	non-copularizing	Churchward 1940
Russian	Indo-European	AN	Pulkina 1978
Samoan	Austronesian	non-copularizing	Churchward 1926; Mosel and Hovdhaugen 1992
Sgaw Karen	Tibeto-Burman	AV	author's field data
Shilluk	Nilo-Saharan	AN	Kohnen 1933
Slovene	Indo-European	AN	author's field data
So	Nilo-Saharan	non-copularizing	Carlin 1993
Somali	Cushitic	AN	Bell 1953; Saeed 1987
Spanish	Indo-European	AN	Butt and Benjamin 1988; Hengeveld 1986; Porroche Ballesteros 1988; author's field data
Squamish	Almosan-Keresiouan	non-copularizing	Kuipers 1967
Swahili	Niger-Congo	AN	Ashton 1944; Closs 1967; author's field data
Tagalog	Austronesian	non-copularizing	Schachter and Otanes 1972
Tamil	Dravidian	AN	Asher 1982, Schiffman 1999
Tarma Quechua	Andean	split-A	Adelaar 1977
Thai	Daic	AV	Kuno and Wongkhomthong 1981; Noss 1964; author's field data
Tok Pisin	(pidgins and creoles)	AN	Verhaar 1995
Tswana	Niger-Congo	non-copularizing	Cole 1955
Turkish	Turkic	AN	Kornfilt 1997; Lewis 1967; author's field data
Tzutujil	Penutian	non-copularizing	Dayley 1985
Uzbek	Turkic	AN	Sjoberg 1963
Vietnamese	Mon-Khmer	AV	Thompson 1987; author's field data
Wambaya	Non-Pama-Nyungan	non-copularizing	Nordlinger 1998
Warí	Equatorial-Tucanoan	non-copularizing	Everett and Kern 1997
West Futuna-Aniwa	Austronesian	non-copularizing	Dougherty 1983
Woleaian	Austronesian	non-copularizing	Sohn 1975
Written Mongolian	Mongolian-Tungus	AN	Poppe 1991
Yagaria	Indo-Pacific	AN	Renck 1975
Yapese	Austronesian	non-copularizing	Jensen 1977
Yidiɲ	Pama-Nyungan	non-copularizing	Dixon 1977a
Yimas	Indo-Pacific	AN	Foley 1991
Yoruba	Niger-Congo	split-A	Ward 1952
Yucatec Maya	Penutian	non-copularizing	Andrade 1955; Blair and Vermont-Salas 1965/1967

The genetic classification used in this table is based on Ruhlen (1987).

an explanation. A fundamental building block for a possible answer to the question of why such restrictions should hold is obtained when the existing distributional patterns are viewed in conjunction. A coherent structure emerges that can be captured in terms of the scale NOMINALS > ADJECTIVALS > VERBALS (see 2.183 (p. 73)). Obviously, distributional patterns that deviate from this structure are strictly avoided.

On this basis, a number of language universals can be proposed. Only those semantic macro-classes which are adjacent to each other in the scale in 2.183 may show uniform behavior with respect to copularization in a language that displays a distinction between copularizing and non-copularizing lexemes, and which treats any one of the basic semantic classes nominal, verbal, and adjectival uniformly with respect to copularization. An important generalization which can be derived from the scale in 2.183 concerns the unidirectionality of copulariza-tion: if a language has a copula which combines with only one of the three semantic macro-classes, this copula will combine with the class of nominals; if a language has a copula which combines with two of the three semantic macro-classes, this copula will combine with the classes of nominals and adjectivals; only if a given copula combines with all three of the basic semantic macro-classes, will it also combine with verbals. Languages in which verbals copularize, but nominals and adjectivals do not, are not documented in the sample. Lan-guages in which verbals and adjectivals copularize, but not nominals, apparently do not exist either. Put differently, copularization 'starts' at the left-hand pole of scale 2.183 and 'proceeds' to the right, but never vice versa. On the basis of the implicational hierarchy 2.183 a language which differentiates between copular-izing and non-copularizing lexemes, and which treats all members of a given semantic macro-class alike with respect to copula usage, fulfills the following criteria: nominals always copularize, while verbals never do; adjectivals may or may not copularize; if adjectivals do not copularize, verbals do not copularize either; if adjectivals copularize, nominals copularize as well.

2.5. The copularization scale and contemporary research on lexical categorization

The research on intransitive predication carried out by Stassen (1997) parallels the cross-linguistic investigation of copula distribution with respect to the lexicon which is the subject of the preceding sections. The present analysis, however, should not be interpreted as a mere replication of Stassen's investigations because the two approaches rest on methodological assumptions which diverge in at least one crucial point, which concerns the way in which absence of copulas in predicate position is handled.

In the model developed in this chapter, in particular, in §2.2, a distinction is drawn between two types of structural configurations which do not contain a copula: first, the case in which a given class of lexical items in a given language never combines with a copula, and second, the case in which a given class of lexical items does, in principle, occur with a copula, which is, however, omitted in specific grammatical contexts, such as present tense. The latter phenomenon is referred to as copula dropping in this study. Lexical items which exhibit copula dropping are treated as copularizing in the present approach.

Stassen (1997), however, differentiates between two other types of absence of copula: the structural configuration of 'non-supported' coding (Stassen 1997: 41), and the so-called 'zero copula' (Stassen 1997: 62ff.) construction. Non-supported coding constitutes one of the three criteria that must be fulfilled if a predicate construction is to be rated as an instance of a structural configuration that Stassen (1997) labels 'verbal encoding'. In order to be classed as an instance of the opposing structural configuration of 'nominal encoding', a predicate construction has to exhibit either a materially present copula or a zero copula. Structurally speaking, there is no difference between non-supported coding and a zero copula construction. Both construction types are characterized by the absence of a copular element. The analytical approach outlined in §§2.3.4 and 2.4 does not operate with the distinction between non-supported coding and zero copula, which is central to Stassen's approach, because it lacks a structural background. Since Stassen's empirical results are, of necessity, shaped by the strict separation of the zero copula construction and non-supported coding, Stassen's data could not be used as the empirical basis for the present study. Consequently, an independent cross-linguistic sample had to be established.

These discrepancies in the basic approach notwithstanding, Stassen (1997) and the cross-linguistic survey conducted in §2.3.4 arrive at analogous conclusions regarding the possible patterns of distribution of copularizing *vs.* non-copularizing lexemes in the lexicon of individual languages:

If predicate nominals are encoded verbally, then predicative adjectives are encoded verbally … if predicate adjectives are encoded nonverbally, then predicate nominals are encoded nonverbally.

(Stassen 1997: 126)

Stassen's term 'verbal encoding' implies absence of copulas, while the term 'nominal encoding' indicates that a copula can be present. Thus, the above quotation by Stassen captures part of the generalizations made at the end of §2.4, which are derived from the copularization scale given in 2.183.

In chapter 1, in the context of the discussion of Croft's work on the parts-of-speech issue, the possibility that the phenomenon of copularization could be explained in terms of Croft's model had been envisaged. Now that the copularization scale 2.183 has been proposed as a putative universal that describes the distribution of copularizing *vs.* non-copularizing lexemes in the lexicon of any one language, the more specific question of how this scale can be fitted into Croft's model arises. The crucial concept, in this respect, is the notion of markedness, which lies at the core of Croft's model. As stated in §1.3.4.2, markedness provides an explanation for the fact that the global inventory of patterns of copula distribution comprises only the structural types included in table 2.5. But, conversely, it could, of course, also be argued that the empirical research on copularization carried out in the present project bears out part of the predictions made by Croft's model.

The phenomenon of markedness is, essentially, defined in terms of the dimensions of discourse frequency and structural complexity (see §1.3.4.2). As Croft's text counts in a variety of languages reveal, there is a gradual cline between the frequencies of nominals, adjectivals, and verbals in predicate position (Croft 1991: 87ff.). Verbals are more frequent by far in this syntactic position than adjectivals, but adjectivals are still decidedly more likely to occur as predicates than are nominals. Thus, in terms of the frequency dimension of markedness, nominals, adjectivals, and verbals can be arranged in a scale, which corresponds to the scale NOMINALS > ADJECTIVALS > VERBALS posited above. In other words, the overall frequency of adjectival predicates is not on a par with that of nominal and adjectival predicates, but rather, shows values which are intermediate between those of the latter predicate types. Because of the hybrid status of adjectivals, the latter might be co-categorized with nominals as well as with verbals in terms of discourse frequency. Since the markedness principle, in turn, requires that the relative discourse frequency of linguistic items is mirrored by the degree of their structural complexity, adjectivals should also behave as a category that is intermediate between nominals and verbals with respect to their formal alignment with any one of these categories. More specifically, it can be predicted that not every language groups adjectivals with nominals in terms of the formal criterion of copularization, as is the case in Indo-European languages such as English or German. A pattern that co-categorizes adjectivals with verbals is equally plausible, and is, in fact, realized in numerous East-Asian languages, such as Burmese and Cantonese, and in many other languages as well.

The language types characterized either by the complete absence of copulas (for instance, Tagalog), or by thorough copularization with all types of ascriptive predicates (for instance, Bambara) is not problematic in the context of the model proposed by Croft, since such a model does not require that predicate constructions in a given language differ with respect to their degree of structural markedness at all.

Thus, it appears that the specific architecture of the scale NOMINALS > ADJECTIVALS > VERBALS, which governs copularization at the cross-linguistic level, can be exhaustively explained by means of the markedness model of lexical class distinctions. In sum, the overall picture that emerges is as follows. Copularization is tied to the pragmatic function of predicate, and lexical items differ with respect to their inclination to function as predicates. Verbals are more likely to occur as predicates than adjectivals are, and adjectivals are more widely used as predicates than nominals are. Further, as a general rule of language, discourse frequency is inversely proportional to morphosyntactic complexity: the higher the frequency rate of a linguistic configuration, the lower its morphosyntactic complexity, and vice versa. Copulas are semantically empty. Semantic function, therefore, cannot be invoked in order to account for their existence. But copulas comply with the markedness principle. For one, they increase the morphosyntactic complexity of predicate constructions. Further, copularizing predicates are less frequent in discourse than non-copularizing predicates (see §4.6). Copulas usually combine only with the more marginal ascriptive predicate types, either only with those containing a nominal nucleus, or with those containing either a nominal or an adjectival nucleus. On these grounds, it might be argued that the sole reason for the existence and distributional properties of copulas is to be sought in the markedness principle.

At this point, it seems that the model contains all the elements required for motivating the existence and distributional properties of copulas. But the above observations entail an additional question: what is responsible for the predilection of lexical items for a specific syntactic slot? What is it that makes a nominal most appropriate for argument function, a verbal most appropriate for predicate function, and an adjectival most appropriate for attribute function? In §1.3.4.3, Givón's time-stability hypothesis is discussed, which, via the semantic parameter of permanence, arranges the semantic macro-classes of nominals, verbals, and adjectivals in a scale. By and large, nominals are more time-stable than adjectivals, and adjectivals are more time-stable than verbals. At least with respect to the association of verbals with predicate function, a plausible connection with the time-stability parameter can be established. Arguments generally function as the given points of reference in a clause, whereas the predicate typically specifies distinctions pertaining to variation in time, such as tense and aspect. By virtue of their intrinsic semantic content, which usually includes the feature [-time-stable], which can in turn be associated with potential presence of variation in time, verbals are predestined for predicate position. Thus, the 'predicate worthiness' of individual lexemes may be interpreted as a function of their time-stability value. (For a more elaborate discussion of the possible interconnections between lexical semantics and pragmatic function, see §5.1.)

However, as tempting as it may appear at this point, time-stability effects, in conjunction with the markedness principle, should not be taken as the ultimate answer to the initial question about the motivation of copularization. In Croft's model, time-stability, in the terminological guise of the persistence and stativity parameters (Croft 1991: 63), provides two of the four semantic parameters by means of which the three basic semantic classes of nominals, verbals, and adjectivals can be differentiated. The remaining two parameters are valence and gradability (see §1.3.4.2). Simply ignoring the possibility that these two parameters might also play a crucial role in the markedness-based model of copularization, because an account based on time-stability alone appears satisfactory at first glance, might result in missing important theoretical insights. As the following chapter reveals, there is some additional evidence in favor of the hypothesis that time-stability is a crucial component of the complex mechanism which partitions lexical inventories into copularizing and non-copularizing items. But, as it turns out, time-stability is, in fact, not the only semantic parameter which is operative in this domain of grammar.

Be that as it may, the above considerations regarding time-stability suggest that semantic models of lexical categorization can be fruitfully integrated into the markedness model. Unfortunately, at this point, the methodological approach pursued so far, which operates with a relatively large cross-linguistic sample derived from grammatical descriptions, faces its limits. The model, at its present stage, establishes the scale NOMINALS > ADJECTIVALS > VERBALS as a first approximation to the universal regularities underlying the distribution of copulas with respect to the lexicon. Time-stability might be the semantic denominator that orders nominals, adjectivals, and verbals, alias entity, event, and property concepts, in a scale that runs parallel to this form-based scale, but, as the next chapter will show, the semantic classification of the lexicon in terms of the triple distinction of entity *vs.* event *vs.* property leaves a lot of room for alternative semantic theories. The division of the lexicon into entity, event, and property concepts is too crude to provide a conclusive answer to the question about the type and number of the semantic parameters governing copula use.

In Chapter 3, the putative connection between copularization and lexical semantics will be explored in greater detail. For this purpose, a different sampling method is employed. To allow a more refined semantic analysis that discloses the semantic forces underlying the phenomenon of copularization, the grammar-based method of data compilation is abandoned. Instead, extensive lexical samples are established by means of consultant work with native speakers for ten languages which have been selected on the basis of genetic diversity and accessibility. Due to the complexity of the language-specific samples required, in the next analytical step to be taken, cross-linguistic variation in the sample has to be reduced in order to increase analytic accuracy within individual languages.

3 Copularization and Lexical Semantics

As the preceding chapter has shown, the global patterns of distribution of copularizing *vs.* non-copularizing in language-specific vocabularies can be subsumed by means of the implicational hierarchy NOMINALS > ADJECTIVALS > VERBALS, which arranges lexical items in a scale with respect to their inclination to appear with a copula in predicate position. This inclination is most pronounced with nominals, and least pronounced with verbals. Regarding the possible semantic motivation of copularization, it can be surmised that the scale NOMINALS > ADJECTIVALS > VERBALS is structured by the semantic principle of time-stability. In this chapter, an attempt at uncovering additional semantic principles underlying the distributional behavior of copulas will be made. As a point of departure, more detailed empirical evidence will be presented in support of the hypothesis that the syntactic feature of presence *vs.* absence of copulas indeed correlates with the semantic parameter of time-stability, which figures so prominently in current works on lexical categorization (e.g. Hengeveld 1992, Pustet 1989, Stassen 1997). But, as §§3.2 to 3.4 will reveal, the semantic parameters of dynamicity, transitivity, and dependency are equally important in motivating the influence of lexical semantics on copula distribution.

3.1. Copularization and time-stability: a pilot study

In the pilot study (Pustet 2001), potential correlations between copularization and the time-stability parameter are explored by means of statistical analyses of complex language-specific samples from five languages: German, Japanese, Lakota, Mandarin, and Spanish. The results of this survey will be briefly summarized in the following.

Each of the language-specific lexical samples, which were compiled and analyzed with the help of native speakers, contains between 1 300 and 2 400 lexemes. In order to make generalizing statements about copula distribution in the sampled languages possible at all, a division into semantic classes is imposed upon the extensive corpus of data. For the purpose of this pilot study, the array of classes given in appendix B proved to be most effective. The semantic classification used does not pay any respect to the division of the lexicon into the semantic macro-classes of nominals, verbals and adjectivals—coherent semantic classes may cut across the traditional parts of speech, as pairings such as *fool* vs. *foolish* and *different* vs. *to differ* in English illustrate. Thus, some classes are composed of concepts associated with more than one of the traditional parts of speech. According to their overall affiliation with the semantic macro-classes of nominals, adjectivals, and verbals, the classes included in appendix B are specified as nominal, nominal/adjectival, adjectival, adjectival/verbal, or verbal. Polysemous lexemes are given separate entries in the respective classes for which they qualify. The members of antonym pairs are, of course, grouped in a single class. This classification is certainly not the one that would be chosen if structuring semantic domains as an end in itself were at issue, partly because it does not account for inclusive relationships among classes. However, it suits the purpose for which it was developed, namely covering the bulk of language-specific lexical inventories, and disclosing interactions of the factor time-stability with copularization.

The task of classifying language-specific lexemes involves certain pitfalls. In order to avoid these, class membership must be determined on the basis of language-internal usage and not on the basis of translations. Polysemy in the meta-language easily lures the investigator into wrong classifications.

After assigning individual lexemes to the appropriate semantic classes, the class-internal copularization rates are calculated for each language. On the basis of the proportion of copularizing lexemes they contain, the semantic classes are arranged in language-specific scales, which are then compared. The language samples do not usually contain the same number of lexical classes because not every language has all the lexical classes listed in appendix B. The result of the pilot study is that the sampled languages arrange semantic classes in extremely similar scales. In order to make the language-specific hierarchies comparable in detail, the following method has been devised. For each language the position of each semantic class relative to each other semantic class in the hierarchy is entered into a chart. The three possible values are higher, lower, or equal in rank. For instance, in German, the class artifact (e.g. *Hammer* 'hammer') ranks above the class emotion (e.g. *fürchten* 'to fear', *glücklich* 'happy') because the former shows thorough copularization, while the latter is mixed with respect to copularization. The classes of artifact and toponym (e.g. *Hügel* 'hill'), on the other hand, are equal in rank in German because they both contain copularizing lexemes only. The resulting charts can then be checked cross-linguistically for matches and mismatches of these values. Only the pairing higher–lower, which reverses hierarchies, counts as a mismatch, not the pairings higher–equal and lower–equal, since these relations simply mean that language X does not make a distinction between classes, while language Y does. Thus, the pairings higher–higher, lower–lower, and equal–equal are treated as matches; higher–equal and lower–equal are considered neutral values that do not supply any information as to the mutual similarity of language-specific hierarchies. For instance, both in German and in Spanish the class of artifact ranks above the class emotion. This combination of classes in the two languages is therefore assigned the value equal–equal. The rates obtained by this method are as shown in table 3.1.

TABLE **3.1.** *Ranking of semantic classes with respect to copula use: comparing German, Japanese, Lakota, Mandarin, and Spanish*

	Total of comparable positions	Matches	Mismatches	Neutral values
Mandarin–German	741	381 = 51.4%	17 = 2.3%	343 = 46.3%
Mandarin–Japanese	780	548 = 70.3%	11 = 1.4%	221 = 28.3%
Mandarin–Lakota	666	568 = 85.3%	13 = 2.0%	85 = 12.8%
Mandarin–Spanish	735	359 = 48.9%	0 = 0.0%	376 = 51.2%
German–Lakota	583	227 = 38.9%	24 = 4.1%	332 = 57.0%
German–Japanese	823	560 = 68.0%	60 = 7.3%	203 = 24.7%
German–Spanish	693	619 = 89.3%	10 = 1.4%	64 = 9.2%
Japanese–Lakota	692	391 = 56.5%	22 = 3.2%	279 = 40.3%
Japanese–Spanish	772	508 = 65.8%	24 = 3.1%	240 = 31.1%
Lakota–Spanish	617	239 = 38.7%	0 = 0.0%	378 = 61.3%

Thus, the similarities between the language-specific hierarchies range far above chance values. As a first rough generalization about the interaction of copularization and lexicon, it can be stated that nominals outrank adjectivals, and that these in turn outrank verbals, as the language-specific copularization hierarchies, which are reproduced in appendix C, show. These findings corroborate the above working hypothesis which states that the semantic parameter of time-stability has a direct impact on the compatibility of individual lexical items with copulas, so that the following universal can be proposed on the basis of the pilot study (Pustet 2001):

3.1. The higher the time-stability value of a given semantic class, the higher the percentage of copularizing lexemes within this semantic class.

However, particularly the statistical data on Japanese adjectivals, which were taken from Pustet (2001) and reanalyzed separately for the purpose of the present study, allow for more subtle conclusions with respect to the time-stability hypothesis. Japanese is an extremely interesting language in this context because it belongs to the split-A type (see §2.3.4), which is characterized by the fact that regarding compatibility with copulas, the members of the semantic macro-class of adjectivals exhibit inhomogeneous behavior. Although the time-stability hypothesis, in its original version, has been established by using the semantic macro-classes of nominals, alias entity concepts, verbals, alias event concepts, and adjectivals, alias property concepts, as basic descriptive units, the time-stability scale might, at least theoretically, be thought of as directly motivating copularization patterns at a deeper semantic level at which the differentiation of the semantic macro-classes nominals, verbals, and adjectivals is not relevant.

Stassen (1997) takes this possibility into consideration, but finally rejects it on the grounds of the behavior of adjectivals in a variety of languages (Stassen 1997: 168). For instance, the distinction between copularizing *vs.* non-copularizing adjectivals in Japanese, in Stassen's opinion, does not point to regular correspondences between formal class membership and time-stability because 'both sets of adjectival items contain predicates from all the major semantic subclasses' (Stassen 1997: 564). However, certain types of form-function correlations may have to be sought at a more subtle level, and will have to be made visible with the help of larger databases than Stassen had at hand. As the following section reveals, the analysis of Japanese adjectivals clearly indicates that time-stable adjectivals tend more strongly to combine with copulas than adjectivals which denote transitory states of affairs.

The semantic class of adjectivals, which is uniformly characterized as being 'of intermediate time-stability' by Givón (1979: 321), can in fact be subdivided into concepts whose time stability value corresponds to that of nominals, others whose time stability value corresponds to that of verbals, and a third subclass whose time stability value is indeterminate. The latter group includes prototypical adjectival concepts, which cover semantic domains such as dimension, color, and evaluation.

These are the concepts Givón had in mind in assigning an intermediate time-stability value to adjectivals. However, it can be assumed that any language also has adjectival lexemes which express a degree of time-stability that is comparable to that of nominals. Such adjectivals are found in the classes of body feature, material, personality feature, and sex. Examples include the English adjectives *color-blind*, *wooden*, *egotistical*, and *male* (for further examples, see appendix B). These concepts imply a degree of time-stability that is similar to, or identical with, that of nominals; states of affairs expressed by such lexemes are, as a rule, non-terminable. Prototypical adjectivals such as *good* or *red*, on the other hand, are indeterminate with respect to time-stability. Property concepts, however, may also display a time-stability value that equals that of verbals. Many of these are members of the semantic classes of bodily state/experience and emotion (see appendix B). Examples include the English adjectives *asleep*, *hungry*, *dizzy*, and *furious*.

Like typical verbals, and unlike typical nominals and other types of adjectivals, such concepts imply an endpoint. The overall ratio of copularizing *vs.* non-copularizing adjectivals in the Japanese sample is 54.3% : 45.7%. In the time-stable semantic classes 'personality feature' (example: 'stingy') and 'material' (example: 'golden') the percentage of copularizing adjectivals is significantly higher than in the overall sample: the respective ratios are 80.0% : 20.0% and 100% : 0.0%. Within classes characterized by low time-stability, on the other hand, the percentage of copularizing adjectivals drops: the ratios for the classes emotion (example: 'angry'), temperature (example: 'hot'), and weather (example: 'stormy') are 40.0% : 60.0%, 0.0% : 100%, and 16.7% : 83.3%, respectively. Thus, the data on Japanese adjectivals suggest that copularization is directly sensitive to the semantic parameter of time-stability: time-stable adjectivals are more likely to copularize than those whose time-stability value is indeterminate; adjectivals which express transitory concepts are less likely to copularize than adjectivals whose time-stability value is indeterminate.

In sum, on the basis of the pilot study (Pustet 2001), it can be hypothesized that the time-stability scale provides an implicational hierarchy of universal validity that helps to predict the behavior of lexemes with respect to copularization in any one language. If a given semantic class in a given language copularizes to some extent, the more time-stable classes can be expected to copularize to an equal or higher degree; the less time-stable classes should copularize either to an equal or to a lesser degree.

3.2. Copularization and lexical semantics: method of investigation

Since the pilot study on time-stability and copularization dealt with in the preceding section yields encouraging results, it can be concluded that attempting to identify additional semantic parameters that govern the distribution of copularizing *vs.* non-copularizing lexemes in individual languages should be a fruitful research program. The question to be raised at that point, however, is whether there is a need to resort to elaborate statistical analyses such as those conducted in the pilot study (Pustet 2001) to uncover other potentially relevant semantic factors, or whether there are more economical and straightforward methods of tackling the problem. Fortunately, such methods are in fact available. Statistical analyses of the kind described in §3.1 are concerned with the 'macrocosm' of form–function correlations in the lexicon—they represent a holistic approach to the problem. But there is a 'microcosm' of lexical class distinctions as well. For instance, in all the languages that were investigated with the help of native speakers for the present project lexemes could be identified which differ with respect to their morphosyntactic features—among other things, with respect to copula usage—but not so much with respect to their semantic content. Such lexical minimal pairs are exemplified by English verbal–adjectival pairs such as *to sleep* vs. *asleep* (see Pustet 2000): the adjective *asleep* copularizes, while the verb *to sleep* does not.

It can be expected that an in-depth investigation of such minimal pairs will lead to deeper insights regarding the semantic motivation of the segmentation of language-specific vocabularies into copularizing *vs.* non-copularizing sections. If a sufficient amount of global regularities are detected here, a general semantic approach to copularization might be derived from such data. The advantage of such a discovery procedure is that it is strictly inductive and thus entirely independent of potential biases pertaining to the parts-of-speech issue which are inherited from a long history of grammar writing from an Indo-European perspective. Traditional categories of grammar writing may be helpful for a first approximation to certain issues in universal grammar, but they should always be taken *cum grano salis* and with an eye on the well-known fact that contemporary language typology has already dismissed too many of them as not being universal. What is more, it must be kept in mind that any aspiring language universal will only be worth as much as the descriptive primitives it is based on. Unclear definitions of these primitives inevitably produce less-than-substantial theories. The consequence of the widespread sanction of inaccurate methodology is that functional typology remains vulnerable to the formalist objection of lacking scientific rigidity. If, for instance, providing feasible definitions for the notions of noun, verb, and adjective turns out to be impossible, as the discussion in §1.3 suggests, it is advisable to exclude these concepts from the set of admissible heuristics. This is what is done in the present study. The interaction of copularization and lexical semantics will be investigated by means of the minimal pair method instead. In bypassing the parts-of-speech issue and directly targeting the semantic principles governing one of its major formal symptoms, that is, copularization, the model developed here, ultimately, attempts to contribute to a better understanding of the elusive parts of speech.

As the following sections will show, the minimal pair approach yields semantic parameters that co-vary with copula usage language-internally as well as cross-linguistically. Not at all unexpectedly, the assumption that the time-stability parameter is effective in the separation of copularizing and non-copularizing lexemes is confirmed by the minimal pair method. But this method discloses additional semantic parameters which are equally relevant in this respect. Most importantly, statistical analyses of large lexical samples based on these additional semantic parameters uncover non-random form–function correlations with respect to copula usage (see §3.4). In what follows, the methodological foundation of the semantics-based model of copularization developed in this study will be outlined in greater detail.

Both the minimal pair method as well as the subsequent statistical analyses operate with large lexical samples obtained through consultant work with native speakers. By means of a questionnaire which comprises 622 basic concepts, that is, concepts which can be expected to have a lexical realization in any one language, extensive lexical samples ranging from about 530 to 850 items per language were established. The questionnaire (see appendix D) was obtained by scanning an English dictionary for concepts which satisfy the following criteria:

(a) semantic universality
This requirement aims mainly at the exclusion of culture-specific terms—particularly artifact terms peculiar to Western civilization —and abstract nouns from the lexical samples. These lexeme types are eliminated from the lexeme lists because it is advantageous to keep the semantic scope of the latter homogeneous across languages to make sure that they are directly comparable with respect to

the statistics described in §3.4. For instance, there is some evidence that abstract nouns are not universal; at least there are considerable cross-linguistic discrepancies with respect to the relative percentage of abstract nouns in language-specific vocabularies.

(b) predicability

The nature of the present investigation makes it necessary to restrict the samples to lexemes which, due to their semantic content, qualify as potential predicate nuclei. The questionnaire contains solely nominal, verbal and adjectival concepts. For instance, adverbials are usually not predicable (for some exceptions, see examples 2.17 and 2.18) and have, for this reason, not been included in the questionnaire. The fact that non-predicable adjectivals are also found in a variety of languages has already been addressed in §1.3.2.

The native speakers who participated in the project were instructed to handle the questionnaire flexibly. The finding of synonyms and semantic cognates was encouraged, and concepts lacking in a native equivalent were to be replaced with another concept for which a lexemic representation was available. For each lexemic entry in the lists, a detailed translation was provided, and at least one simple clause was formed in which the lexeme in question functioned as the predicate nucleus. Potential minimal pairs, which were in any case discussed with native speakers, were also obtained by scanning dictionaries of the target languages. The languages investigated by means of this method were English, Estonian, French, Hebrew, Korean, Mandarin, Persian, Sgaw Karen, Slovene, Spanish, and Vietnamese. For the remaining languages which were sampled in detail in cooperation with native speakers, lexeme lists based on the questionnaire reproduced in appendix D were established instead. These languages include Bambara, Burmese, Cantonese, German, Hungarian, Indonesian, Japanese, Lakota, Swahili, Thai, and Turkish. This sample of languages should be stratified enough to refute the potential speculation that the reason behind the observed correlations between copula usage and semantic parameters is to be sought in an areal and/or genetic coherence of the languages investigated.

The sizes of the language samples compiled by this method vary considerably: the Japanese sample, which is the largest of the ten samples, comprises 854 lexemes, while the Burmese sample, which is the smallest of the ten samples, contains only 527 lexemes. Inhomogeneity of sample sizes is, in part, due to the selectional criterion of predicability, which has been addressed above. Since copulas, by definition (see §1.2), occur in predicate position only, a given lexeme, in order to be eligible for combination with a copula at all, must be predicable.

There is, however, considerable cross-linguistic variation with respect to the predicability criterion. To cite just one of the numerous instances of such variation encountered in the lexical samples established for the purpose of the present study, the Indonesian lexeme *mendadak* 'sudden' is predicable, while its German counterpart *plötzlich* 'sudden' is not. The most important reason for fluctuations in the sizes of the ten lexical samples, however, is the fact that the sizes of language-specific lexical inventories in general are subject to extreme cross-linguistic variation. Japanese, for instance, has a much richer vocabulary than Burmese. Since, as has been pointed out above, the native speakers who participated in the project were instructed to provide more than just a single translation for each concept listed in the questionnaire, the size of the final sample reflects the size of the overall vocabulary of a given language. The Lakota sample has to be set apart from the other language samples in some sense because it was compiled on the basis of a dictionary (Buechel 1970) rather than with the help of the questionnaire used for the other languages. This is because work on copularization in Lakota had been completed before the questionnaire employed for the present project had been established. But since the basic selectional criteria which determine inclusion of individual lexical items in the language samples were applied to Lakota as well, the Lakota sample does not diverge too much from the other samples in conceptual content.

The empirical approach developed here depends on detailed information on the intrinsic semantic content of lexemes that is not provided by grammars or dictionaries, as the remainder of this chapter will show.

3.2.1. Lexical minimal pairs

In many, if not all, languages, pairs of lexemes can be found which can be considered synonyms or at least near-synonyms, but which belong to different parts-of-speech classes. Wierzbicka (1986, 1995) cites numerous examples of both nominal-adjectival and verbal-adjectival minimal pairs. She concludes that there are regular semantic differences between the members of the pairs. Wierzbicka's findings are discussed in greater detail in §§3.3.1 and 3.3.3. Minimal pairs whose members differ with respect to their parts-of-speech class status are relevant for tracking down the semantic contrast between copularizing and non-copularizing lexemes because differences in lexical class membership are often concomitant with a distinction in terms of presence *vs.* absence of copulas.

The minimal pair approach used for the purpose of the present study is based on the following sampling procedure. Basically, two lexemes which differ with respect to copula usage, but which are semantically similar, constitute a lexical minimal pair if it is possible to substitute one lexeme for the other in at least one linguistic context. The semantic 'threshold' which separates lexical minimal pairs from lexeme pairs which are not lexical minimal pairs can be defined as follows:

3.2. Two lexemes form a lexical minimal pair if their mutual substitution produces utterances which, according to native speakers' intuitions, can be used to describe the same real-world situation.

Needless to say, if lexemes are mutually substitutable, they do not necessarily overlap completely with respect to their semantic content. The English lexeme pair *to sleep* and *asleep* passes the substitution test. Native speakers of English feel that the utterances given in examples 3.3 and 3.4 are semantically equivalent.

3.3. the dog is sleeping

3.4. the dog is asleep

Frequently, mutual substitution is possible only in a subset of contexts in which members of a lexical minimal pair may occur. Thus, *to smell* and *smelly* are interchangeable in examples 3.5 and 3.6, but they are not interchangeable in examples 3.7 and 3.8.

3.5. this cheese smells

3.6. this cheese is smelly

3.7. this cheese smells of garlic

3.8. *this cheese is smelly of garlic

It goes without saying that synonymy relations holding between members of minimal pairs are subject to the same restrictions as any synonymy relation: as many semanticists have argued, there is probably no such thing as true synonymy at all. Even if two linguistic items do not differ with respect to their semantic content at first glance, they may still diverge in terms of distinct preferences for certain discourse environments or stylistic levels (e.g. Geeraerts 1988). The observation that there may be more or less subtle fluctuations in the semantic scope of members of minimal pairs is the essential building block of the minimal pair approach to copularization. Cases in which there is only a partial overlap in meaning, as with *to smell* and *smelly*, are more significant for a semantic model of copularization than cases in which there is no noticeable semantic difference, as with *to sleep* and *asleep*. The line of reasoning pursued here is as follows: if specific semantic differences between members of partial minimal pairs recur with a sufficient degree of regularity across languages, these differences can be interpreted as semantic primitives governing copularization at the cross-linguistic level. If such universal semantic parameters can be identified in the microcosm of lexical minimal pairs, they can further be applied as features in the statistical analyses of large lexical samples—that is, they can be utilized in exploring the macrocosm of lexical categorization. It can be expected that semantic features which correlate with copula usage in lexical minimal pairs also correlate with the distinction between copularizing and non-copularizing lexemes in the lexicon of individual languages as a whole.

In addition to minimal pairs which are based on the concept of synonymy, there is another type of minimal pair which can be used as a heuristic in the search for semantic parameters governing copularization. In these monolexemic minimal pairs, a single lexical form may occur as a predicate nucleus in both copularizing and non-copularizing predicate constructions. Presence *vs.* absence of copulas is concomitant with a regular meaning change in this case. Thus, for instance, when the copula is combined with a specific set of lexemes in Indonesian, such as *perak* 'silver, made of silver', a mass noun reading is obtained, as in example 3.9. If, however, the copula is missing, the respective lexeme must be interpreted as a property concept, as in example 3.10.

3.9. ini   adalah   perak
      this   COP   silver
      'this is silver' (author's field data)

3.10. ini   perak
      this silver
      'this is made of silver' (author's field data)

The answer to the question of whether a viable universal semantic model of copularization can be derived from lexical minimal pairs hinges on the following considerations:

(a) Are the semantic differences between the members of partial or monolexemic minimal pairs in a given language of a random, or of a regular, nature?

(b) If there are regular semantic differences between the members of partial or monolexemic minimal pairs in a given language, are these regularities language-specific or universal?

As it turns out, the distinction between copularizing and non-copularizing lexemes in partial and monolexemic minimal pairs can in fact be characterized by just a handful of semantic parameters which are, obviously, effective at the cross-linguistic level. The parameters which could be identified are DYNAMICITY, TRANSIENCE, TRANSITIVITY, and DEPENDENCY. Exact definitions of these parameters are provided in §§3.3.1 to 3.3.4 on the basis of a more detailed discussion of language-specific data. The dynamicity parameter is to some extent akin to Langacker's notion of processuality (Langacker 1987); transience largely coincides with Givón's time-stability principle; the term transitivity is more or less self-explanatory; and the notion of dependency is one facet of Croft's concept of relationality (Croft 1991: 63).

3.2.2. *Semantic features and statistics*

After semantic parameters that might be relevant for a semantic model of copularization have been established inductively via the minimal pair method, their respective predictive power and applicability to large lexical samples is tested. For this purpose, each entry in the language-specific lexeme lists compiled by means of the questionnaire described in §3.2 is classified with respect to the four semantic features dynamicity, transience, transitivity, and dependency, again in cooperation with native speakers. Subsequently, the statistical correlation of individual features with the formal criterion of compatibility *vs.*

non-compatibility with copulas is calculated. As the details in §3.4.1 show, some of these correlations are extremely high. Some features in some languages provide predictions of the occurrence of copulas which are close to the 100 per cent mark. Finally, for each language investigated, the feature that produces the best predictions is determined on statistical grounds. The results further raise the question of whether the most successful feature in each language is the same across languages, or if different features are dominant in different languages.

The basic hypothesis to be formulated and evaluated in the present monograph concerns the interconnection of the formal criterion of copularization and the intrinsic semantic content of lexemes. In §3.1 some empirical data that point to the existence of such a relationship have been discussed already. However, if copularization is sensitive to lexical semantics, why should there not be an interdependence between copularization and the semantics of grammatical categories as well? The dividing line between lexicon and grammar is a blurred and artificial one anyway—there are linguistic items, such as adpositions and auxiliaries, which cannot be unequivocally assigned to either linguistic domain. And, in fact, sensitivities of copula usage to certain grammatical categories are attested in many languages. Such phenomena are addressed under the rubric of copula dropping in §2.2. It is, however, not quite clear at that point whether copula dropping is a function of the semantic content of certain grammatical categories, or if the phenomenon is triggered by some other properties associated with the respective grammatical categories. The issue will be picked up on in §5.1.

Predicting the occurrence of copulas on the basis of sensitivities to the presence of certain grammatical categories is *per se* not very problematic. The enigmatic mechanisms underlying copula usage which cannot be stated in terms of clear-cut grammatical categories present a far greater challenge for a cross-linguistic approach to copularization. Until today, this area of investigation has, by and large, been uncharted territory in linguistic typology. As has been pointed out above, the results of the minimal pair method confirm the suspicion which was formulated in Chapter 1: the presence *vs.* absence of copulas as components of predicate phrases is, above all, conditioned by the intrinsic semantic content of the lexemes functioning as predicate nucleus. In order to separate both groups of factors which potentially trigger copula usage, and to make sure that grammatical factors did not interfere with the discovery procedure for conditioning factors in lexical semantics, the test clauses for the individual entries contained in the lexeme lists which were to be formed by native speakers had to fulfil two criteria. Firstly, test clauses were kept as syntactically simple as possible; they contained constituents other than a subject and a non-complex predicate phrase only in cases in which native speakers considered this basic structure incomplete. Secondly, the test clauses were kept as homogeneous as possible with respect to the grammatical categories contained in them.

Only those lexical items were included in the samples which clearly do not import any grammatical 'matter' into the test clauses which could be held responsible for the behavior of a given lexeme with respect to copularization. This restriction is to be taken as another safeguard against the ever-present danger of intermingling copularization triggered by grammatical categories and copularization conditioned by lexical semantics. For instance, in Cantonese and Mandarin, many adjectivals, when used as predicate nuclei, require the presence of an element which is referred to as a nominalizer in the literature (e.g. Li and Thompson 1981: 575ff.). This nominalizer occurs in other syntactic contexts as well, and it triggers copularization. When members of the special class of adjectivals that require the addition of the nominalizer in predicate position figure as predicates, the use of a copula is obligatory, as the following example from Mandarin shows. Neither the nominalizer *de* nor the copula *shì* can be skipped in combination with the predicate nucleus *sōng* 'loose':

3.11. xiédài   shì   sōng   de
       shoestring   COP   loose   NM
       'the shoestring is loose' (author's field data)

3.12. *xiédài   shì   sōng
       shoestring   COP   loose
       'the shoestring is loose' (author's field data)

3.13. *xiédài   sōng   de
       shoestring   loose   NM
       'the shoestring is loose' (author's field data)

3.14. *xiédài   sōng
       shoestring   loose
       'the shoestring is loose' (author's field data)

Thus, it can be assumed that the presence of the nominalizer is responsible for the need to use a copula with such adjectivals. As a consequence, such adjectivals are excluded from the samples. They do not provide any insights as to the interaction of copularization and intrinsic lexical semantics.

Regarding the ascription of feature values to individual lexemes, as a first step the full semantic scope of a given lexeme is determined by considering all of its possible translations. Sometimes a lexical root or stem can be used either with or without a copula, as the Indonesian examples 3.9 and 3.10 show. If this formal distinction co-varies with a semantic distinction, two separate lexemes are posited for statistical purposes. One of these is assigned the feature [+copularizing], the other is classed as [−copularizing]. The alternative would be operating with a single lexical entry that is classified as [+/−copularizing]. A formal class that is ascribed the feature [+/−copularizing], however, is useless in a statistical analysis that is explicitly devised to uncover correlations of the formal contrast of presence *vs.* absence of copulas with semantic features because it does not yield any insights with respect to this contrast.

The semantic feature profiles of individual lexemes were established solely on the basis of native speakers' intuitions. All native speakers interviewed were proficient in at least one Standard Average European language, namely English. In most cases, the interviews were done in English. Given this, one might feel tempted to speculate that feature assignments were influenced by the semantics of the corresponding English lexemes. However, this risk factor was kept at a minimum by explicitly pointing this problem out to the persons interviewed, and asking them to make their judgements exclusively on the basis of their intuitions about the semantic content of individual lexemes in their native language. The fact that in many cases feature values were given that do not coincide with those of the English stimulus lexemes seems to indicate that this method was successful.

3.3. Lexical minimal pairs and semantic features

Lexical minimal pairs are not equally frequent in every language. In some of the languages investigated, only a handful of such minimal pairs could be tracked down by means of the questionnaire reproduced in appendix D. In other languages, dozens of minimal pairs were found. In the majority of cases, the members of the minimal pairs cannot be used interchangeably in all contexts in which they occur—that is, partial synonymies are more widespread than full synonymies.

3.3.1. Dynamicity

The cross-linguistic sample of lexical minimal pairs yields numerous cases in which the respective copularizing and non-copularizing members can be differentiated in terms of the semantic distinction of state *vs.* change of state. An example is the Spanish minimal pair *entristecerse* 'to be sad, grow sad, grieve' vs. *triste* 'sad'. The verb *entristecerse* 'to be sad, grow sad, grieve' denotes a state as well as a process that entails this state, while the adjective *triste* 'sad' *per se* expresses a state only. The adjective *triste* 'sad' copularizes, while the verb *entristecerse* 'to be sad, grow sad, grieve' does not.

3.15. Pedro   se   entristeci-ó
      Pedro   3RFL   be/grow sad-3SG.PST.PRF
      'Pedro was/grew sad' (author's field data)

3.16. Pedro   est-uv-o   triste
      Pedro   COPb-PST.PRF-3SG   sad
      'Pedro was sad' (author's field data)

Additional minimal pairs of this type are given in table 3.2.

TABLE 3.2. *Dynamicity: minimal pairs (part 1)*

	−copula	+copula
Estonian	*vihastama* 'to be/get angry'	*vihane* 'angry'
French	*s'attrister* 'to be/grow sad, grieve'	*triste* 'sad'
Spanish	*alegrarse* 'to be/become happy/glad, to rejoice, to cheer up (itr.)'	*alegre* 'happy, merry, glad'
	igualarse 'to be/become equal'	*igual* 'equal'
	inquietarse 'to worry, get worried'	*inquieto* 'worried, uneasy, anxious'
Swahili	*changamka* 'to be/get to be in a good mood, to cheer up' (itr.), 'to rejoice'	*changamfu* 'to be in a good mood'

From these data, a semantic parameter can be derived which is based on the traditional, and more or less self-evident, distinction between states and processes. This distinction, however, can be more comprehensively phrased in terms of the notion of homogeneity *vs.* inhomogeneity through time, that is, in terms of the presence *vs.* absence of intrinsic change. This semantic parameter covers an additional type of minimal pair that is also frequently encountered in the sample. The semantic relations holding in this case can be illustrated by means of the English minimal pair *to rejoice* vs. *happy*. *Happy* implies an inner emotional state that does not necessarily manifest itself in visible activities. *To rejoice*, on the other hand, indicates that some kind of activity may take place as a consequence of this inner emotional state: '…a person who *rejoices* is probably doing something because of his or her feeling—dancing, singing, laughing and so on' (Wierzbicka 1995: 226).

3.17. John is rejoicing upon his success

3.18. John is happy about his success

Some additional minimal pairs of this type are presented in table 3.3.

In the same vein, Wierzbicka (1995) argues that lexemes expressing emotions in Russian tend to imply a higher degree of agency than their respective English counterparts. In Russian, emotions are usually expressed by verbs, while their English translations, in most cases, happen to be adjectives. According to Wierzbicka, the semantic profiles of Russian emotion verbs correspond to those of English verbs such as *to grieve, to rejoice*, and *to worry*. Wierzbicka concludes:

> …I would venture to propose a universal: if a language has two words for a 'positive emotional attitude', one verb and one adjective, and if one of these words designates a 'stronger', 'more intense', 'more active' feeling than the other, then the stronger feeling will be expressed by the verb, and the 'milder' one by the adjective, never the other way round.

(Wierzbicka 1995: 233)

TABLE 3.3. *Dynamicity: minimal pairs (part 2)*

	−copula	+copula
English	*to grieve*	*sad*
	to rage	*furious*
Estonian	*rõõmustama* 'joyful, to rejoice'	*rõõmus* 'joyful'
French	*[en]rager* 'furious, to rage'	*furibond* 'furious'
		furieux 'furious'
	s'attrister 'to be/grow sad, grieve'	*triste* 'sad'
	se réjouir 'happy, to rejoice'	*joyeux* 'happy'
German	*trauern* 'sad, to grieve'	*traurig* 'sad'
Slovene	*veseliti se* 'happy, to rejoice'	*vesel* 'happy'
Spanish	*alegrarse* 'to be/become happy/glad, to rejoice, to cheer up' (itr.)	*alegre* 'happy, merry, glad'
	entristecerse 'to be/grow sad, grieve'	*triste* 'sad'
	inquietarse 'to worry, get worried'	*inquieto* 'worried, uneasy, anxious'
Swahili	*changamka* 'to be/get to be in a good mood, to cheer up' (itr.), 'to rejoice'	*changamfu* 'to be in a good mood'
	sonona 'sorry, sad, to grieve, be in pain'	*huzunifu* 'sorry, sad'

The insights gained on the basis of the cross-linguistic sample of lexical minimal pairs support Wierzbicka's findings. In all the minimal pairs which show a distinction in terms of state *vs.* change of state, or state *vs.* action/process, the copularizing members—which correspond to Wierzbicka's adjectives—denote a state, while the non-copularizing members—which correspond to Wierzbicka's verbs—express either the meaning combinations of state and change of state, or of state and action/process. Thus, the functional criterion of inherent lexical semantics and the formal criterion of copula use, interact in a non-arbitrary way in these cases.

The semantic parameter which can be distilled from the type of minimal pair represented by Spanish *entristecerse* 'to be sad, grow sad' vs. *triste* 'sad' will henceforth be referred to as DYNAMICITY. A lexeme receives the specification [+dynamic] if it involves at least two disparate component states of affairs, the specification [−dynamic] if it involves homogeneous component states of affairs only, and the specification [+/−dynamic] if it can be interpreted as either involving disparate or homogeneous states of affairs. Thus, concepts such as 'to grow' and 'to jump' are classed as [+dynamic], concepts such as 'round' and 'tall', however, as [−dynamic]. Lexemes such as Spanish *entristecerse* 'to be/get sad' have both dynamic and non-dynamic readings; 'to be sad' is [−dynamic], while 'to get sad' is [+dynamic]. Thus, *entristecerse* 'to be/get sad' is classed as

[+/−dynamic]. The meaning distinction captured by the dynamicity parameter should be quite self-evident in the case of the above examples from Spanish. However, the motivation for interpreting the second type of lexical minimal pair which has been discussed so far, which is exemplified by the English lexemes *happy* and *to rejoice*, as representative of semantic distinction in terms of dynamicity might appear less clear at first glance. As a matter of fact, the connection with dynamicity is mediated by another semantic parameter in this case, namely, by the agency parameter. As indicated above, especially in the quotation from Wierzbicka (1995), the extralinguistic referent of the subject of the verb *to rejoice* is likely to perform some kind of activity that expresses his/her inner emotional state. The adjective *happy*, on the other hand, lacks this semantic connotation.

It should be noted at this point that the concept of agency, or agentivity, as it is sometimes called, is known for the vexing problems of definition it poses. These difficulties are, for the most part, due to the fact that agency is a notion that can be broken down into various semantic subparameters, such as control, volition, and animacy:

> There is a tendency in work on case roles, as elsewhere in linguistics, to assume that notions such as AGENT represent semantically discrete and unitary concepts. This tendency persists in spite of the notorious difficulties in developing a cross-linguistically or even intra-linguistically valid characterization of the concept of agentivity ... The problem with defining agent is that there are a number of semantic categories, notably control, volition, and animacy, which are widely attested as being involved in agentivity but which can be shown to vary independently of each other. This leaves any theory which uses a unitary definition of agent with an insoluble residue of clauses in which an NP has some but not all of the morphosyntactic characteristics of agents.

> (DeLancey 1984: 181)

An additional semantic parameter that might be relevant in the attempt at arriving at a multi-factor definition of agency can be defined in terms of input of physical energy (e.g. Cruse 1973, Lakoff 1977, Talmy 1988). The English verb *to rejoice* can be viewed as an example of a problematic case with respect to the assignment of a clear-cut agency value. At least it can be stated that the agency value of lexemes like *to rejoice* contrasts sharply with the degree of agency observed with lexemes such as *to jump*. While *to jump*, in its prototypical usage, receives positive values on all four of the semantic subparameters of agency, that is, control, volition, animacy, and input of physical energy, *to rejoice* may require an animate protagonist and input of physical energy as well, but is certainly less likely to be controlled and volitional than *to jump*.

In dealing with the relationship between the parameters of dynamicity and agency, the subparameter of physical energy plays a decisive role. Input of physical energy is likely to result in a perceptible change of some sort in the variables that define the physical properties of a given thing or substance in the surrounding universe. For instance, input of energy in the form of heat will make water or other liquids bubble after a while. Presence of perceptible change, however, is tantamount to presence of at least two disparate states of affairs, which, in turn, is the criterion by which a given concept can be classed as [+dynamic]. In contrast to *happy*, *to rejoice* can be characterized as implying input of physical energy which is transformed into perceptible events such as dancing, singing, laughing and so on.

Further, it must be kept in mind that the basic notion of dynamicity or disparateness of states of affairs covers an extremely diverse array of real-world situations. Dynamicity may imply component states of affairs which are radically distinct to the human perceptual apparatus, as with the English verbs *to explode* and *to dissolve* (both of which have an intransitive and a transitive reading). *To explode* and *to dissolve* denote a change from a coherent to a non-coherent, or at least less coherent, state of an entity, or a transition from an original material state to a radically different material state. However, there are also dynamic concepts in which the differences between the component states of affairs that make up a complex state of affairs are more fine-grained, as in the case of the English verb *to shiver*. *To shiver* merely profiles slight oscillations with respect to position in space.

It could be argued that a basic semantic difference between lexemes like *to explode* and *to shiver* is located in the dimension of aspect—more accurately, in the contrast of punctuality *vs.* durativity. The event *to explode* involves an extremely short time span until completion, and can thus be classed as [+punctual]. The event *to shiver*, however, tends to cover a more extended time span than the event *to explode*, and can therefore be characterized as [−punctual]. The difference between *to explode* and *to shiver* with respect to punctuality, however, is notionally independent of the classification of these lexemes with respect to the dynamicity parameter. Both *to explode* and *to shiver* are [+dynamic], although, as is argued above, the difference between the component states of affairs that constitute the respective complex state of affairs is more drastic in the case of *to explode* than in the case of *to shiver*. That dynamicity distinctions cannot be rephrased in terms of the distinction of punctuality *vs.* durativity can be shown, for instance, by comparing *to shiver* with *to dissolve*, rather than with *to explode*. As pointed out above, *to dissolve* involves more radically distinct component states of affairs than *to shiver*, but neither lexeme qualifies for classification as [+punctual], at least if punctual events are defined as covering a time span as short as in the case of *to explode*.

The fact that the diversity of the component states of affairs that make up a given complex state of affairs is more pronounced in some cases than in others is irrelevant for the ascription of the feature values [+dynamic] and [−dynamic] in the system of semantic classification employed in the present study. The feature value [−dynamic] is assigned to lexemes characterized by complete lack of inhomogeneity of their component states of affairs only. This way, the feature dynamicity lends itself to a binary mode of feature representation which includes the feature values [+dynamic], [−dynamic], and [+/−dynamic].

All nominal concepts listed in the questionnaire are [−dynamic]. Only certain types of abstract noun, such as *explosion*, provide counterexamples to the pervasive correlation of (semantic) nounhood and the feature [−dynamic]. Likewise, all adjectival concepts included in the questionnaire are to be classed as [−dynamic]. Verbal concepts are, as a rule, [+dynamic]. Presumably, the most fundamental cognitive archetype the concept of dynamicity is rooted in is motion in space. The majority of verbal concepts contained in the questionnaire display this meaning component. Classification of these verbals with respect to the feature dynamicity is, consequently, not problematic.

Although the majority of concepts contained in the questionnaire do not pose any problems for semantic classification in terms of the dynamicity parameter, the questionnaire contains a residue of verbal concepts which are difficult to classify with respect to dynamicity. The questionnaire comprises 622 lexemes (see appendix D); a total of forty-six verbals are not as straightforwardly classifiable with respect to the feature dynamicity as the remaining lexemes included in the questionnaire are. Most of these belong to a closely circumscribed semantic domain, namely that of mental, perceptive, and emotional states or activities:

3.19. mental, perceptive, and emotional states or activities: *to admire, to believe, to despise, to desire, to doubt, to dream, to fear, to feel, to hate, to hear, to know, to like, to love, to pity, to regret, to remember, to resent, to see, to smell* (tr.), *to suffer, to think, to trust, to wait, to want, to watch, to wish, to worry*

The concepts expressed by these English lexemes cannot be said to involve disparate component states, at least not to the degree to which prototypically dynamic concepts such as 'to jump' do. Instead, they might be regarded as conceptually homogeneous. This is also true for the lexemes listed in 3.20 to 3.26:

3.20. bodily states and sensations: *to ache, to itch, to sleep*

(The lexemes *to feel* and *to suffer*, which are included with the above mental, perceptive, and emotional states or activities could also be classed with bodily states and sensations.)

3.21. existence: *to exist, to live*

3.22. olfactory properties: *to smell* (itr.), *to stink*

3.23. position: *to hang* (itr.), *to lie, to sit* (itr.), *to stand* (itr.)

3.24. possession: *to have, to own*

3.25. resemblance: *to differ, to resemble*

3.26. others: *to glow, to lack, to need, to stay*

All of the forty-six controversial lexemes listed above have, tentatively, been classed as [−dynamic] for the purpose of the statistical analyses described in §3.4. The issue will be addressed again in §3.4.2. Although at least the lexemes contained in the classes position, possession, and resemblance are clearly [−dynamic] in ontological terms, they have been tentatively included in the list of controversial lexemes.

Lexemes denoting sounds might also be felt to be somewhat problematic with respect to the ascription of a dynamicity value. The questionnaire includes 13 sound lexemes:

3.27. sound: *to croak, to cry, to groan, to growl, to hum, to laugh, to purr, to rattle, to ring, to scream, to sneeze, to yawn, to yell*

In these cases, however, the component states involved can be clearly diagnosed as inhomogeneous if oscillations in the quality of sound waves are resorted to as a defining criterion of inhomogeneity. Of the sound lexemes listed in 3.27, *to hum* probably comes closest to exemplifying an entirely homogeneous sound. In the language-specific samples, sound lexemes are uniformly classed as [+dynamic].

The definition of dynamicity employed in the above analysis of lexical minimal pairs is strongly inspired by Langacker's concept of sequential scanning (Langacker 1987). Sequential scanning is a mental operation which co-defines the semantic profiles of certain types of concepts. The interpretation of sequential scanning underlying the definition of dynamicity given above presupposes that real-world events, entities, etc. are 'scanned' at certain intervals in time. If the resulting temporal cross-sections are all identical to each other, that is, if no change occurs from one cross-section to the next, the respective state of affairs is, *per definitionem*, non-dynamic; if the cross-sections are not homogeneous, the state of affairs is dynamic. This is a slightly altered version of Langacker's concept of processuality (Langacker 1987). This modification is necessary because there are some fundamental differences in the approach chosen for the treatment of lexical semantics in this study and Langacker's approach to the issue. For Langacker, it is not the outcome of the sequential scanning process that determines the processuality value of a given lexical item, but rather, the question of whether sequential scanning takes place at all. According to Langacker, any concept for which the mental operation of sequential scanning is constitutive is processual; any concept that undergoes the contrastive process of 'summary scanning' (Langacker 1987: 72ff.) is non-processual—in other words, belongs to the class of 'atemporal relations' (Langacker 1987: 71ff.). The contrast between processual *vs.* atemporal relations, in turn, is parallel to certain traditional parts-of-speech class distinctions:

The set of processual predications is co-extensive with the class of verbs; by contrast, atemporal relations correspond to such traditional categories as prepositions, adjectives, adverbs, infinitives, and participles.

(Langacker 1987: 71f.)

The crucial difference between the approach developed in the present study and Langacker's model lies in the treatment of the idea that the traditional parts of speech might 'impose' meaning. This hypothesis rests on the assumption that clear-cut and unambiguous semantic definitions are in fact available for nominals and verbals, that is, that lexical classes can be characterized exhaustively by means of certain semantic properties:

> ... the noun and verb construe the event with contrasting images, and are therefore semantically distinct.
>
> (Langacker 1987: 57)

A similar view is advocated by Wierzbicka:

> ... formal distinctions in grammar reflect differences in conceptualization, often very subtle differences. Far from being semantically arbitrary they are extraordinarily sensitive—so much that when we come across two quasi-synonyms belonging to two different parts of speech, we can regard the formal difference as a clue suggesting some difference in meaning.
>
> (Wierzbicka 1995: 242)

Such hypotheses are in sharp contrast with the consensus view held in current semantic theory, according to which necessary and sufficient semantic criteria for defining (semantic) nounhood *vs.* verbhood cannot be identified (see §1.3.2). However, such statements are, by and large, based on ontological considerations only. Langacker, on the other hand, derives defining criteria for nounhood *vs.* verbhood from distinctions based on the more abstract mental operation of 'construal' (Langacker 1987: 56ff.), rather than from ontological distinctions.

> Meaning is ... sought in the realm of cognitive processing. It does not reside in objective reality ... Even expressions describing an objective situation may differ in meaning, depending on how the situation is construed.
>
> (Langacker 1987: 56)

Thus, any verbal construes a state of affairs as processual, that is, as undergoing sequential scanning, while any non-verbal profiles states of affairs as undergoing summary scanning (Langacker 1987: 72ff.), the latter being equivalent to construal as an 'atemporal relation' (Langacker 1987: 71ff.).

> [In summary scanning, R.P.] the various facets of a situation are examined in cumulative fashion, so that a more and more complex conceptualization is progressively built up; once the entire scene has been scanned, all facets of it are simultaneously available, and cohere as a single gestalt. With respect to the cognitive events which constitute this experience, we can suppose that, once activated, events that represent a given facet of the scene will remain active throughout. By contrast, sequential scanning involves the successive transformation of one scene into another. The various phases of an evolving situation are examined serially, in non-cumulative fashion; hence the conceptualization is dynamic, in the sense that its contents change from one instant to the next. At the level of cognitive

events, we can suppose that events which represent a given scene will remain active only momentaneously, and will begin to decay as the following scene is initiated.

(Langacker 1987: 72)

The difference between sequential and summary scanning can be illustrated by comparing the semantic profiles of the English verb *to cross* and the corresponding preposition *across*:

The distinction between sequential and summary scanning provides a natural basis for the contrast between processes and atemporal relations. Under this analysis, for instance, the verb *cross* and the preposition *across*...differ in how the component states of this complex relationship are accessed. A verb is thus a 'temporal' predication in the sense of following a situation, state by state, as it evolves through conceived time; its 'dynamic' character reflects the successive transformations which derive each component state from its predecessor. The corresponding atemporal relation employs summary scanning for the same series of states. Though it accesses these states in sequence during the build-up phase (which accounts for its directionality), the cumulative result is a complex conception in which all the component configurations are superimposed and simultaneously active.

(Langacker 1987: 74)

The above quotation illustrates the difference between the notions of sequential and summary scanning very convincingly. Despite its plausibility, however, the present investigation of the putative semantic motivations of copularization will not make use of this conceptual distinction in every detail. The methodological approach chosen in the present project is tracking down semantic parameters governing copula use inductively, that is, on the basis of a careful analysis of large lexical samples from a variety of languages.

Langacker also employs his distinction of sequential *vs.* summary scanning in motivating the semantic difference between the conceptual macro-classes of verbals and adjectivals. According to Langacker, sequential scanning is a fundamental component of the semantic profile of verbals, while adjectivals can be defined as involving summary scanning (Langacker 1987: 55). Thus, for instance, the semantic difference between the English verb *to resemble* and the English adjective *like*, which can be considered synonyms in a more traditional semantic approach than Langacker's, is to be sought in the fact that via cognitive construal, the meaning component of sequential scanning is superimposed on the lexeme *to resemble*, while the meaning component of summary scanning is superimposed on *like*. However, as Langacker himself acknowledges, such construal processes are not open to direct introspection:

The semantic contrasts dealt with here are subtle, and are explicated in terms of cognitive operations to which we have no direct or intuitive access. Thus when I claim that the adjective *like* designates a relation construed atemporally, while the verb *resemble*...scans this same relationship sequentially through conceived time, there is no way to prove this claim directly or autonomously.

(Langacker 1987: 55)

The present project does not operate with theory-dependent semantic distinctions like Langacker's contrast of sequential *vs.* summary scanning which cannot be inductively derived from the lexical minimal pairs under investigation. Although this distinction aptly characterizes the semantic difference between the members of the verbal-prepositional minimal pair *to cross* and *across*, in the case of verbal-adjectival minimal pairs such as *to resemble* and *like*, the distinction is deductively imposed, and will, therefore, not be utilized in the attempt to define semantic parameters that correlate with the formal distinction of copularizing and non-copularizing lexemes. The present approach to dynamicity rests on Langacker's model in so far as it makes use of the basic notion of the conceptual segmentation of states of affairs into component states of affairs, which are compared to each other with respect to whether they are identical to each other or not. If its component states are homogeneous, a given state of affairs is classed as [−dynamic]; if its component states are not homogeneous, the feature value [+dynamic] is assigned. Both *to resemble* and *like* designate states of affairs whose component states of affairs are identical to each other. Consequently, both lexemes are classed as [−dynamic]. On the same grounds, the Spanish adjective *triste* 'sad' and English adjective *happy* are categorized as [−dynamic]. In contrast, the semantic profile of the Spanish verb *entristecerse* 'to be sad, grow sad' comprises at least two distinct component states, at least as far as the second reading 'to grow sad' is concerned: the initial state of affairs of absence of sadness and the subsequent state of presence of sadness. The reading 'to grow sad', therefore, qualifies for assignment of the feature value [+dynamic]. The first reading 'to be sad' is classed as [−dynamic]. Thus, the overall semantic classification of *entristecerse* 'to be sad, grow sad' in terms of the dynamicity parameter is [+/−dynamic]. This is also true for the English verb *to rejoice*. The act of rejoicing is likely to be accompanied by visible activities in which the emotional state in question manifests itself. Visible activities, *per se*, imply some degree of inhomogeneity of their component states of affairs.

To conclude the discussion of the dynamicity parameter, and to justify the general semantic approach outlined above, it may be worthwhile to address some more fundamental issues regarding the status of semantics in linguistic theory at this point.

The stated objective of the present study is evaluating the hypothesis that the presence *vs.* absence of copulas correlates with semantic factors, more specifically, with the intrinsic semantic content of lexemes. Semantics has been banished from the generally approved set of possible factors which shape linguistic surface structure in mainstream linguistics ever since the era of American structuralism. So far, the level of linguistic meaning can be accessed only through ontology, that is, through the association of linguistic items with real-world states of affairs. It is certainly true that semantic categories are immaterial and thus, in some sense, intangible—but how tangible are generative deep structures? There is no obvious reason why semantic categories which map onto ontologically defined, and therefore empirically ascertainable, categories should not be accepted as legitimate tools for describing linguistic structure, and why they should not be credited with the ability of shaping linguistic surface structure at least to some degree.

At such a purely ontology-based level of conceptualization, further, lexemes such as *to be like* and *to resemble* can be considered synonymous. Ontology-based synonymy is also the level of semantic resolution at which lexical minimal pairs of the type *to sleep* vs. *asleep* and *to grieve* vs. *sad*, etc., which are discussed above, can be established. All claims pertaining to the interaction of lexical semantics and copularization made in the present monograph exclusively derive from distinctions observed at this level of semantic description. As has been pointed out above, the sole heuristic in the process of gathering lexical minimal pairs of the type *entristecerse* 'to be sad, grow sad' vs. *triste* 'sad' is mutual substitutability of lexemes according to native speakers' intuitions. Thus, even at the risk of working with inaccurate semantics by Langacker's standards, the goal pursued in this study is determining how far purely ontology-based semantics will lead in trying to uncover the potential semantic motivation of copula usage.

3.3.2. Transience

Many minimal pairs contained in the sample show a meaning differentiation in terms of permanence *vs.* non-permanence. For instance, this semantic parameter may manifest itself in terms of a state *vs.* personality feature contrast, as in the Indonesian minimal pair *berani* 'courageous (in a given situation or inherently/ permanently)' vs. *pemberani* '(inherently/permanently) courageous':

3.28. Tono   berani
       Tono   courageous
       'Tono is being courageous/generally courageous' (author's field data)

3.29. Tono   adalah   pemberani
       Tono   COP   courageous
       'Tono is (generally) courageous/*being courageous' (author's field data)

Other minimal pairs in which the same meaning contrast can be observed are presented in table 3.4.

In Turkish, the contrast between adjectival predicates that contain the copula *-Dlr vs.* the corresponding non-copularizing predicate versions systematically co-varies with a semantic distinction in terms of the feature opposition transitory *vs.* permanent. Thus, the adjectives *öfkeli* 'irritable, furious' and *utangaç* 'shy, ashamed' denote both passing states as well as personality features. However, while the non-copularizing version of the corresponding predicates is ambiguous between a transitory and a permanent reading, the copularizing version can only be interpreted as denoting a permanent quality, that is, a personality feature:

3.30. çocuk   utangaç
       child   shy/ashamed
       'the child is shy/ashamed' (author's field data)

TABLE 3.4. *Transience: minimal pairs (part 1)*

	−copula	+copula
Estonian	*erinema* 'to differ, different' (temporarily/permanently)	*erinev* 'to differ, different' (permanently)
Indonesian	*malas* 'lazy' (temporarily/permanently) *malu* 'shy' (temporarily/permanently)	*pemalas* 'lazy' (permanently) *pemalu* 'shy' (permanently)
Japanese	*noroi* 'slow' (temporarily/permanently)	*noroma* 'slow' (permanently)
Swahili	*kaidi* 'obstinate, headstrong, stubborn, to contradict, resist, behave in a stubborn way' (temporarily/permanently)	*kaidi* 'obstinate, headstrong, stubborn, to contradict, resist, behave in a stubborn way' (permanently)
	kirihi 'to loathe' (temporarily/permanently)	*kirihi* 'to loathe' (permanently)

3.31. çocuk   utangaç-dır
      child   shy-COP
      'the child is shy (inherently/permanently)/*ashamed (author's field data)

3.32. Ömer   öfkeli
      Ömer   irritable/furious
      'Ömer is irritable (inherently/permanently)/furious' (author's field data)

3.33. Ömer   öfkeli-dir
      Ömer   irritable/furious-COP
      'Ömer is irritable (inherently, permanently)/*furious' (author's field data)

As a rule, Turkish adjectives do not copularize. Exceptions are adjectives which can or must be interpreted as conveying the notion of permanence. However, any adjective is compatible with the copula *-DIr* when it is given a generic reading, as in example 3.35; only a few of the adjectives contained in the Turkish sample did not lend themselves to a generic interpretation. When the copula is missing, both a non-generic and a generic interpretation are possible. Thus, example 3.34 can be taken as a simple statement referring to a cup of tea that is being tasted, but it may also be interpreted as a statement about a particular type or blend of tea whose good quality is generally acknowledged. In contrast, the copularizing example 3.35 can only be interpreted as denoting a general quality of Turkish tea.

3.34. bu   çay   iyi
      this   tea   good
      'this tea is good' (author's field data)

3.35. Türk   çay-ı   iyi-dir
      Turkish tea-PSS good-COP
      'Turkish tea is (generally) good' (author's field data)

Presence *vs.* absence of the copula *-DIr* in the context of the adjective *berrak* 'clear' expresses analogous distinctions with respect to the permanence *vs.* non-permanence contrast, as examples 3.36 and 3.37 show.

3.36. bu   su   berrak
     this   water   clear
     'this water is clear (at the moment); this water is (always) clear'
     (author's field data)

3.37. bu   su   berrak-tir
     this   water   clear-COP
     'this water is (always) clear'; *this water is clear (at the moment)'
      (author's field data)

A more pronounced meaning difference is observed in connection with the adjective *uyanık* 'awake, clever'. Both readings are possible when the copula *-DIr* is missing, as in example 3.38, but when the copula is present *uyanık* can only be interpreted as denoting the personality feature 'clever'.

3.38. çocuk   uyanık
     child   awake/clever
     'the child is awake/clever' (author's field data)

3.39. çocuk   uyanık-tır
     child   clever-COP
     'the child is clever/*awake' (author's field data)

In the above examples from Indonesian and Turkish, as well as in table 3.4, the non-copularizing member has both a transitory as well as a permanent reading, while the copularizing member has a permanent reading only. There is, however, an analogous type of minimal pair in which the non-copularizing member can only be interpreted as transitory, while the copularizing member conveys both a transitory as well as a permanent meaning. An example is the Estonian minimal pair *julgema* 'bold (in a given situation, but not always), to dare' vs. *julge* 'bold (in a given situation or inherently/persistently), to dare'. *Julgema* '(temporarily) bold, to dare' is a verb and does not copularize (see 3.40), while *julge* '(temporarily/permanently) bold, to dare' is an adjective and receives a copula in predicate position (see example 3.41).

3.40. mina   julge-n
     1SG   bold-1SG
     'I am (temporarily) bold' (author's field data)

3.41. mina   olen   julge
     1SG   COP.1SG   bold
     'I am (temporarily/permanently) bold' (author's field data)

Other minimal pairs which display this semantic profile are given in table 3.5.

TABLE 3.5. *Transience: minimal pairs (part 2)*

	−copula	+copula
Estonian	*armukadestama* 'jealous' (temporarily)	*armukade* 'jealous' (temporarily/permanently)
	kurvastama 'sad' (temporarily)	*kurb* 'sad' (temporarily/permanently)
	rõõmustama 'joyful, to rejoice' (temporarily)	*rõõmus* 'joyful' (temporarily/permanently)
	tähele panema 'cautious, careful' (temporarily)	*tähelepanelik* 'cautious, careful' (temporarily/permanently)
French	*se réjouir* 'to rejoice' (temporarily)	*joyeux* 'cheerful, joyful' (temporarily/permanently)
	se taire 'silent' (temporarily)	*silencieux* 'silent, taciturn' (temporarily/permanently)
Slovene	*molčati* 'silent' (temporarily)	*molčeč* 'silent, taciturn' (temporarily/permanently)
	veseliti se 'happy, to rejoice' (temporarily)	*vesel* 'happy' (temporarily/permanently)
Spanish	*alegrarse* 'to be/become happy/glad' (temporarily), 'to rejoice, to cheer up' (itr.)	*alegre* 'happy, merry, glad' (temporarily/permanently)
Swahili	*changamka* 'to be/get to be in a good mood, to cheer up (itr.), to rejoice'	*changamfu* 'to be in a good mood, entertaining, entertainer'
	hofu 'afraid' (temporarily)	*oga* 'afraid, cowardly, timid'
	ogopa 'afraid' (temporarily)	(temporarily/permanently)

The semantic parameter that figures in the terminological guise of the permanence *vs.* non-permanence distinction in the above examples is, of course, time-stability. The fact that time-stability plays a role in the distinction between copularizing and non-copularizing lexemes within lexical minimal pairs can be taken as a proof of the validity of the general hypothesis dealt with in Chapter 1. It states that time-stability is a decisive factor in the formation of lexical categories. However, for the purpose of this study, Givón's notion of time-stability is somewhat elaborated on in the following. Although it is beyond dispute that verbals typically express transitory states of affairs, while nominals typically express permanent meanings, it is not entirely obvious what the notion of the 'intermediate' time-stability of adjectivals (Givón 1979: 321) stands for. If it refers to duration in time, the interpretation would be that states of affairs expressed by prototypical adjectivals, in contradistinction to those expressed by prototypical nominals, end after a while, though on the average, they last longer than states of affairs expressed by verbals. This interpretation, however, does not seem to live up to the facts. States of affairs expressed by prototypical adjectivals—that is, by members of semantic classes such as dimension, color, and evaluation—, unlike verbals, do not simply end after a while. States of affairs expressed by verbals, on the other hand, can be expected to end after a more or less brief time-span. But an entity to which an adjectival concept is attributed may, in fact, keep this property throughout its existence. Thus, duration that is intermediate between the duration of states of affairs expressed by nominals and verbals cannot be the correct interpretation of the notion of the 'intermediate' time-stability of adjectivals—although this is intuitively appealing. However, it seems to be the case that LIKELIHOOD of termination is higher with adjectivals than with nominals. For instance, 'redness' can change, 'smallness' can change, and 'goodness' can change. But 'dog-ness', 'stone-ness', or 'house-ness' are non-terminable. Thus, the assumption that the time-stability of adjectivals is 'intermediate' can be rephrased by stating that with adjectivals, termination and non-termination are equally possible.

By splitting the concept of time-stability into two subordinate principles, namely the 'ingressive parameter' and the 'permanency parameter', Stassen (1997: 162) adds another refinement to the time-stability hypothesis. The original version of the time-stability hypothesis operates with the permanency parameter only. According to the permanency parameter, concepts differ with respect to the degree to which they imply an endpoint. The intrinsic time-stability value of individual lexemes, further, is crucial for their assignment to parts-of-speech classes, as has been pointed out above. However, the status of the starting point in the semantic profile of a given concept might also have some bearing on lexical categorization. Taking the ingressive parameter into account would, for instance, explain why a concept such as 'young', which is intrinsically non-permanent, can be realized as an adjective and not as a verb in languages with a structurally-based adjective–verb distinction:

> On the Permanency Parameter . . . the item 'young' must be rated as time unstable: 'young' is a quality which, as sad experience tells us, is very much prone to change, up to the point of cessation.
>
> (Stassen 1997: 176)

If the notion of time-stability is not only defined in terms of whether the duration of a state of affairs extends until a given entity ceases to exist, but also in terms of whether it starts at the beginning of its existence, categorizing 'young' as an adjective in terms of grammatical features makes sense.

The notions of starting point and endpoint can be regarded as facets of the same basic concept, that of boundedness in time. The concept of boundedness employed here derives from Langacker (1987). The opposition of boundedness *vs.* non-boundedness in time, further, is commonly referred to as aspect. Imperfective aspect signals lack of bounding in time. It portrays an event as being in progress; its boundaries, that is beginning and end, are not profiled.

Perfective aspect indicates that one of these boundaries, or both, are included in the semantic scope of a given predication. This commonly held view regarding the relationship of the notions of boundedness and aspect is echoed in the following quotation:

A perfective process is so called because it is bounded; i.e., its endpoints are included within the scope of predication in the temporal domain. No such specification of bounding is made for an imperfective process; it profiles a stable situation that may extend indefinitely far beyond the scope of predication in either direction...

(Langacker 1987: 81)

If aspect is understood as comprising not only the notion of grammatical aspect, but that of lexical aspect or aktionsart as well, the following formula is valid: nominals are, as a rule, intrinsically imperfective, while verbals are intrinsically perfective; nominals tend to cover whole lifespans, verbals only fractions of lifespans. Lexemes expressing prototypical adjectival concepts, on the other hand, are intrinsically unspecified as to bounding in time.

On the basis of what has been said above, two definitions of the semantic parameter which represents bounding in time are possible, depending on whether both the point of incipience and the point of termination of states of affairs is taken as relevant, or only the point of termination. If the concept of boundedness in time is defined as simultaneously embracing both starting point and endpoint, a lexeme receives the specification [+bounded in time] if either the starting point or the endpoint, or both, of the state of affairs it expresses is located within the life span of the entity this state of affairs is predicated on. Neither the starting point nor the endpoint of this state of affairs may coincide with the starting point and endpoint of the existence of the entity this state of affairs is predicated on. According to this definition, the English verb *to run* is [+bounded in time] because it does not cover life spans as a whole. A lexeme receives the specification [−bounded in time] if two conditions apply simultaneously: first, the state of affairs it expresses cannot be expected to end within the life span of the extra-linguistic referent of the entity it is predicated on; second, the starting point of the state of affairs it expresses coincides with the starting point of the existence of the entity it is predicated on. The English noun *bird* is [−bounded in time] because 'bird-ness' is a quality of entities that is neither acquired nor changeable in the physical universe that surrounds human beings. A lexeme receives the specification [+/−bounded in time] if both an interpretation as [+ bounded in time] and as [−bounded in time] is possible.

If the definition of boundedness in time is solely based on the notion of endpoint, thus rendering the potential point of incipience of states of affairs irrelevant, most language-specific lexemes elicited by means of the questionnaire reproduced in appendix D are classified exactly as they are if the alternative definition of boundedness in time is applied. Thus, in both cases, the English verb *to run* is classed as [+bounded in time], while the English noun *bird* is assigned the feature value [−bounded in time]. Both definitions characterize adjectivals such as English *red* as [+/−bounded in time]. Some concepts contained in the questionnaire, however, require reclassification if one possible definition of boundedness in time is replaced with the other. Examples include, in particular, designations of professions and occupations, such as the English noun *cook*, as well as age-related concepts such as the English adjective *old*. According to the definition based on both starting point and endpoint, professions and occupations are to be classed as [+bounded in time] because people are usually not born with the full capacity of performing a certain kind of work for a living; these skills must be acquired. According to the second definition of boundedness in time, for which only the point of termination is relevant, however, professions and occupations must be classed as [+/−bounded in time], because the states of affairs they denote can, but do not have to, extend over whole life spans. The adjective *old* receives the feature value [+bounded in time] when classed on the basis of the first definition of boundedness in time since *old* designates an acquired property which does not cover whole life spans. However, this English adjective must be assigned the feature value [−bounded in time] when the second definition is used because the property 'old' is irreversible.

Initially, within the statistical analyses of complex lexical samples discussed in §3.4, both notional types of boundedness in time have been tested as to their predictive power with respect to the appearance of copulas. The second version of boundedness in time—which is solely based on the notion of endpoint—yields slightly better predictions than the first version and is therefore given preference over the latter. Henceforth, this version of bounding in time will be referred to as TRANSIENCE.

As is pointed out above, the notion of boundedness is crucial for any definition of aspectual categories. An additional concept which is discussed quite extensively in connection with boundedness in current research on aspect is telicity. The following brief discussion of telicity differentiates the latter concept from the specific interpretation of the notion of boundedness which provides the basis for defining the transience parameter.

In the extant literature, the term telicity is given a variety of interpretations. The most widely accepted usage of the term has been coined by Comrie (1976). The concept of telicity implies presence of an endpoint, and it is, according to Comrie's (1976) definition, intimately connected with the notion of resultativity. The difference between the telicity and atelicity can be illustrated by means of the semantic contrast between the atelic predication *John is singing*, and the telic predication *John is making a chair* (Comrie 1976: 44):

...there comes eventually a point at which John completes the action of making a chair, the chair is ready, and at this point the situation described by *make a chair* must of necessity come to an end; moreover, until this point is reached, the situation described by *make a chair* cannot come to an end, but can only be broken off part way through. This is not true of the situation described by *John is singing*: John can stop singing at any point, and it will still be true that he has sung, even if he has not completed the song or songs he set out to sing. Thus the situation described by *make a chair* has built into it a terminal point, namely that point at which the chair is complete, when it automatically terminates; the situation described by *sing* has no such terminal point, and can be protracted indefinitely or broken off at any point.

(Comrie 1976: 44)

Another pair of examples which clarifies the difference between atelicity and telicity is *to eat* vs. *to eat up* (Comrie 1976: 46). *To eat* is atelic, while *to eat up* is telic. Both telicity and transience make use of the concept of bounding in time, but in different ways. The basic difference between telicity and transience lies in the role assigned to interruptions of a given state of affairs. In order to be classifiable as atelic, a given state of affairs can be interrupted and continued at a later point in time. But in order to be classed as [−transient], a given state of affairs must continue without interruption throughout the existence of the referent on whom this state of affairs is predicated. On the transience parameter, both *to sing* and *to make a chair* are assigned the feature value [+transient] because, according to the metaphysics which rules the universe perceived by the human perceptual apparatus, neither activity can be expected to be performed throughout the life span of the performing entity without interruption. This is also true for *to eat* and *to eat up*.

As has been pointed out above, feature ascriptions based on the transience parameter, of necessity, produce the same feature values as the time-stability parameter. Nominals are, as a rule, [−transient], verbals are [+transient], and adjectivals are [+/−transient]. Nominals which must be classed as [+/−transient] include members of the semantic classes profession/occupation and social relation. These concepts are potentially terminable. Some examples from the questionnaire are given in 3.42 and 3.43.

3.42. profession and occupation: *actor*, artist, *beggar*, *cook*, *doctor*, *farmer*, *trader*

3.43. social relation: *enemy*, *friend*, *husband*, *wife*

Certain members of the class age also have to be assigned the feature value [+/−transient]:

3.44. age: *baby*, *boy*, *child*, *girl*

In cases in which a natural life cycle ends before an individual has passed the age implied by the above concepts, the feature value [−transient] has to be assigned. In all other cases, that is if an individual dies after reaching adulthood, the specification [+transient] is appropriate.

Adjectivals denoting certain emotional and bodily states are classed as [+transient].

3.45. emotional and bodily states: *afraid, ashamed, asleep, dizzy, furious, glad, hungry, nervous, pregnant, sore, sorry, thirsty, tired*

Certain adjectivals, in particular, the body features included in 3.46, the age-related concepts given in 3.47, as well as adjectivals denoting material, like *wooden*, express non-terminable states, and are therefore classed as [−transient].

3.46. body features: *color-blind, female, left-handed, male, right-handed*

3.47. age-related: *old, ripe*

Personality features such as the ones given in 3.48, as well as adjectivals expressing nationality, like *French*, are also classed as [−transient].

3.48. personality features: *ambitious, choleric, clever, courageous, intelligent, smart, stingy, stupid, vain*

Certain verbals can be conceived of as denoting either terminable/acquired or non-terminable/non-acquired states of affairs, and are therefore classed as [+/−transient]. Examples can be found in the semantic classes of emotional state/process, olfactory property, position, possession, and resemblance:

3.49. emotional state/process: *to like, to love*

3.50. olfactory property: *to smell, to stink*

3.51. position: *to hang, to lie, to sit, to stand*

3.52. possession: *to have, to own*

3.53. resemblance: *to differ, to resemble*

The above feature assignments are valid for the English vocabulary list given in appendix D. The semantic equivalents or near-equivalents of these lexemes in the languages investigated, of course, do not necessarily comply with the feature profiles of the English test lexemes.

Last but not least, the relationship holding between transience and habitual actions must be addressed. In many languages, such as English, certain verbals can be used to express repeated or habitual actions; no special coding device for habitual action is required:

3.54. he drinks, steals, and lies

In English, only a restricted set of verbals can be used to express habitual action without explicit specification of habituality by means of adverbials or other grammatical elements. In Swahili, on the other hand, a considerable amount of verbals may assume a habitual reading without further grammatical specification of habituality. In Burmese, virtually any verbal may be used to convey a habitual sense without further specification by means of additional grammatical material. The question to be dealt with at this point is whether such verbals should be classed as potentially non-transient or not. For the purpose of this study, the latter option is chosen. Although habitual action may in fact extend over complete life spans, there is a marked difference between non-transience proper and habitual action. The defining criterion for habitual action is regular repetition at certain intervals, that is a constant interplay of inception and cessation, while non-transience proper is characterized by lack of interruption.

3.3.3. Transitivity

The cross-linguistic sample of lexical minimal pairs points to an additional semantic parameter which correlates with the distinction between copularizing and non-copularizing lexemes, namely transitivity. Transitivity distinctions within lexical minimal pairs have also been noted by Wierzbicka (1995: 236). The most obvious structural manifestation of transitivity is grammatical valence. The valence of a prototypical adjectival is 1, while that of a prototypical verbal is either 1 or 2 (see Croft 1991: 63ff.). Lexemes whose valence value is 3 are rare; an example is the English verb *to give*. However, a valence value of 1 is not a reliable diagnostic of adjectivals. If grammatical transitivity is taken as simply referring to the obligatoriness of an argument in addition to the subject, transitive adjectivals exist as well, as examples like *worth* and *devoid of* show. *Worth* requires an object, and *devoid of* is acceptable only in connection with a genitive phrase. The comparison of the lexemes *worth* and *devoid of* further hints at a differentiation which plays an important role in the traditional definition of transitivity, but which is not relevant for the approach to transitivity chosen in the present study. In contrast to the common characterization of transitivity as 'the ability to take an object', the interpretation of transitivity proposed here does not take the coding strategy for the secondary argument into account. With *devoid of*, a genitive phrase is as obligatory as an object phrase is with *worth*. Thus, both *worth* and *devoid of* can be considered transitive.

Oblique coding of obligatory secondary arguments is by no means confined to adjectivals, but occurs with verbals as well. In this context, the English verbs *to hunger for* and *to thirst for* can be cited. Of course, the normal coding device for obligatory arguments are markers for categories such as subject and object, rather than oblique case markers. For this reason, the fact that the valence of a given lexeme is not determined by the marking strategy for its argument(s) is easily overlooked. Object marking of secondary arguments is neither a necessary nor a sufficient condition for bivalence; even objects may be dispensable, as pairings like *to jump a fence* vs. *to jump* demonstrate. Thus, within the framework developed in this study, a lexeme is classed as transitive if its use in discourse obligatorily requires the presence of two arguments, regardless of how these arguments are coded.

Based on these considerations, lexical minimal pairs can be established in which the same semantic type of noun phrase is coded both as a valence-bound argument, and as an argument which is not valence-bound and therefore dispensable. The English verbal-adjectival minimal pair *to fear* vs. *afraid* illustrates this.

3.55. he fears poisonous reptiles

3.56. *he fears

3.57. he is afraid of poisonous reptiles

3.58. he is afraid

The noun phrase *poisonous reptiles* is optional with *afraid*, as examples 3.57 *vs.* 3.58 illustrate, but obligatory with *to fear*, as examples 3.55 *vs.* 3.56 show. Additional examples of lexical minimal pairs exhibiting this syntactic pattern can be found in a variety of languages, as shown in table 3.6.

On the basis of what has been said so far, the transitivity parameter, as compared to the parameters of dynamicity and transience, seems to be special in that it is not defined in purely semantic terms—in fact, it appears to be exclusively based on the syntactic criterion of the structural obligatoriness of a secondary argument. A more detailed evaluation of the facts, however, reveals that just like the parameters of dynamicity and transience, transitivity lends itself to a semantic definition.

It is widely known that syntactic transitivity has semantic underpinnings, as Hopper and Thompson (1980) show. According to Hopper and Thompson, semantic transitivity is a scalar concept that is defined in terms of the interaction of various contributing factors such as kinesis, aspect, volitionality, and agency. Needless to say, the valence of the lexemic representations of a given concept in different languages does not necessarily have to be the same. Thus, the English verb *to fear* is transitive—it requires an object. Its Turkish equivalent, the verb *korkmak* 'to fear', on the other hand, does not require the presence of a secondary argument. Langacker also addresses such cross-linguistic valence fluctuations:

... I am not concerned with trying to predict the valence of a morpheme on the basis of its internal semantic structure. In fact, I do not think it is possible to predict valence in absolute terms ... Instead of absolute predictability, we must settle for predictability of a weaker sort, one more generally appropriate for language: the semantic structure of a morpheme defines its valence potential and determines how readily it lends itself to certain kinds of valence relations exploiting that potential, but whether and how this potential will actually be realized is in some measure a function of linguistic convention.

(Langacker 1988: 99f.)

Since the stated goal of this study is finding out to what degree copula usage correlates with ontology-based semantic parameters, a purely syntactic definition of transitivity is not acceptable in this theoretical context. However, as Langacker argues, semantic and syntactic transitivity are never completely detached from each other. Put differently, a given lexeme will be realized as syntactically transitive in a given language only if its semantic profile shows a sufficient degree

TABLE 3.6. *Transitivity: minimal pairs*

	−copula	+copula
English	*to covet*	*covetous*
	to deserve	*worthy*
	to envy	*envious*
		jealous
	to know	*aware*
	to regret	*sorry*
	to resent	*resentful*
	to thirst	*thirsty*
Estonian	*erinema* 'to differ'	*erinev* 'different'
French	*convoiter* 'to covet'	*avide* 'covetous, greedy'
	envier 'to envy'	*envieux* 'envious'
	jalouser 'jealous'	*jaloux* 'jealous'
	mériter 'to deserve'	*digne* 'worthy'
	se soucier 'to worry'	*inquiet* 'worried'
	s'inquiéter 'to worry'	
German	*beneiden* 'to envy'	*neidisch* 'envious'
	dürsten 'to thirst'	*durstig* 'thirsty'
	geizen 'stingy'	*geizig* 'stingy'
	gieren 'greedy'	*gierig* 'greedy'
	sich sorgen 'to worry'	*besorgt* 'worried'
	verdienen 'to deserve'	*würdig* 'worthy'
Slovene	*obnidati* 'to envy'	*nidečen* 'envious'
	obžalovati 'to regret'	*žal* 'sorry'
	zaslužiti 'to deserve'	*vreden* 'worthy'
	želeti 'to wish, to yearn for'	*poželjiv* 'to wish, to yearn for'
Spanish	*arrepentirse* 'to regret'	*pesaroso* 'sorry'
	sentir 'to regret'	
	codiciar 'to covet'	*codicioso* 'covetous'
	merecerse 'to deserve'	*digno* 'worthy'
Swahili	*chunuka* 'greedy'	*choyo* 'greedy'
	elewa 'to know'	*elevu* 'aware'
	jua 'to know'	
	husudu/husudi 'envious, to admire'	*hasidi* 'envious'
	kaidi 'obstinate, headstrong, stubborn, to contradict, resist, behave in a stubborn way'	*kaidi* 'obstinate, headstrong, stubborn, to contradict, resist, behave in a stubborn way'

of semantic transitivity. Unfortunately, however, valence, or the number of the obligatory arguments of a given lexeme, cannot be regarded as a reliable diagnostic for semantic transitivity or intransitivity. More specifically, although obligatory presence of two arguments can be considered a safe indicator of semantic transitivity, obligatory presence of one argument is not a safe indicator of semantic intransitivity. In other words, a lexeme whose valence frame requires only one obligatory argument is not always semantically intransitive as well—it might still be semantically transitive. Thus, more stringent criteria must be used to determine whether a given lexeme which is structurally intransitive is semantically intransitive or transitive.

According to Fillmore (1986), there are two basic types of secondary argument omission (see also Matthews 1981, Zwicky 1993). The first type is exemplified by the English verbs *to eat* (Fillmore 1986: 96) and *to read* (Matthews 1981: 43). *To eat* and *to read* can be used without a secondary argument, as examples 3.59 and 3.60 illustrate:

3.59. John is eating

3.60. John is reading

In examples 3.59 and 3.60, a semantic object, such as *a sandwich* or *a newspaper*, can, of course, be inferred; the object is, however, pragmatically irrelevant in these cases. As Fillmore (1986: 96) puts it, this argument is either 'a semantic object of considerable generality' which has 'much in common with a syntactically present indefinite noun phrase', or the identity of the referent of this inferred object is 'unknown or a matter of indifference'. In any case, the respective argument is 'obligatorily disjoint in reference with anything saliently present in the pragmatic context'. According to Matthews (1981: 43), the secondary argument in clauses such as 3.59 and 3.60 is simply 'not necessary'.

In contrast, the other basic type of secondary object omission, according to Fillmore (1986) and Matthews (1981: 38ff.), is characterized by the fact that the referent of the secondary argument which is not materially realized in a given clause is, nevertheless, present, either in the general discourse context, or in the extra-linguistic context. Thus, in such 'latent object' (Matthews 1981: 38) constructions, 'the missing element must be retrieved from something *given* in the context' (Fillmore 1986: 96). An example of a lexeme with a latent object is the English verb *to watch* in its intransitive usage (Matthews 1981: 40ff.). With this verb, the missing object is pragmatically salient enough to require retrieval from context. If such retrieval is impossible, the use of *to watch* without an object is ungrammatical. Verbs like *to eat* or *to read*, on the other hand, can be used without an object even if a suitable object phrase cannot be retrieved from context. The type of argument omission which is exemplified by *to watch* will, henceforth, be referred to as CONTEXTUAL ELLIPSIS. The following quotation from Matthews (1981: 43) illustrates the difference between the two types of object omission which becomes evident in the contrast of *to watch* vs. *to eat/to read*:

Suppose I have seen Bloggs sitting opposite you in a railway compartment; I might ask 'Did you talk to Bloggs on the train?' You could not reasonably reply 'No. I'm afraid I was watching all the time.' ... But you could perfectly well reply 'No. I'm afraid I was reading all the time.' What you were reading is immaterial. Likewise if you reply: 'No. I was too busy eating.'

With contextual ellipsis, the object is absent at the structural level only, but not at the semantic level. With *to eat* or *to read*-type lexemes, however, presence of an object is required neither at the structural nor at the semantic level. Since, as is argued above, this study seeks to identify criteria for defining semantic rather than structural intransitivity, lexemes which allow contextual ellipsis of secondary arguments do not qualify as intransitive, whereas *to eat* or *to read*-type lexemes do. Put differently, structural absence of a secondary argument does not suffice as a defining criterion for intransitivity—the missing secondary argument must also be semantically irrelevant. In the present approach to lexical semantics, any structurally intransitive lexeme which does not fulfill the latter criterion is classed as transitive.

It should be noted that *to eat* and *to read* are, actually, special cases of intransitive lexemes because these two verbals are also compatible with object phrases. This fact, however, is the reason why *to eat* and *to read* are particularly suited for the purpose of illustrating the difference between contextual ellipsis and semantic intransitivity proper. The above definition of semantic intransitivity that rests on the criterion of the irrelevance of secondary arguments, of course, also applies to lexemes which are, unlike *to eat* and *to read*, incompatible with object phrases, such as *to doze*. Thus, elaborating on the example by Matthews given above, it can be stated that *to doze* is semantically intransitive because, in response to the question *Did you talk to Bloggs on the train?* the utterance *No. I was dozing all the time* is as acceptable as *No. I was eating/reading all the time*.

As the empirical work with large lexical samples carried out in the present study reveals, there is both intra-linguistic and cross-linguistic variation in the options for second argument omission, particularly with respect to contextual ellipsis. A glance at English suffices to document intra-linguistic variation with respect to contextual ellipsis of secondary arguments. While the English verb *to watch* admits contextual ellipsis of objects, the verbs *to open* or *to shut* do not (Matthews 1981: 41). According to Fillmore (1986), eligibility for contextual ellipsis is lexically determined and more or less unpredictable. Thus, there may be pairs of near-synonyms, such as *to try* and *to attempt*, which behave differently with respect to the applicability of contextual ellipsis. Object omission is possible with *to try*, but ungrammatical with *to attempt*:

3.61. *I tried* (Fillmore 1986: 99)

3.62. **I attempted* (Fillmore 1986: 99)

Examples of cross-linguistic variation with respect to contextual ellipsis are encountered quite frequently, and can even be observed in languages which are related as closely as are English and German. The German counterpart of the English verb *to watch*, the verb *beobachten*, does not allow contextual ellipsis.

With *beobachten* 'to watch', an object has to be present in any case, as the grammaticality contrast between the English example 3.63 and the corresponding German translation 3.64 shows:

3.63. he is watching.

3.64. *er   beobachte-t
      3SG.MSC.NOM watch-3SG.PRS.IND
      'he is watching' (author's field data)

Conversely, the English verb *to lock* does not admit contextual ellipsis (Fillmore 1986: 98). Thus, example 3.65 is ungrammatical. With the German translation of *to lock*, the verb *abschließen*, however, contextual ellipsis is possible, as the grammaticality of example 3.66 demonstrates.

3.65. *did you lock?* (Fillmore 1986: 98)

3.66. ha-st   du   abgeschlosse-n?
      AUX.PST.IND-2SG 2SG.NOM   lock-P
      'did you lock?' (author's field data)

In East Asian languages, the applicability of contextual ellipsis is taken to the extreme. These languages, in contrast to Indo-European languages, do not impose any restrictions on contextual ellipsis. For instance, in Chinese languages, as well as in Burmese, Japanese, Korean, Sgaw Karen, Thai, and others, all types of argument, including subject phrases, tend to fall victim to the process of contextual ellipsis in ongoing discourse. Any argument can be dropped if it can be retrieved from context. The following examples from Burmese illustrate this. In the basic transitive clause 3.67 either the object, as in example 3.68, or the subject, as in example 3.69, or both, as in example 3.70, can be omitted.

3.67. θu   gà   ká   go   tõ̌   ne   ba   ði
      3SG TOP   car   OBJ   push PRG   PLT   POS
      's/he is pushing the car' (author's field data)

3.68. θu   gà   tõ̌   ne   ba   ði
      3SG TOP   push PRG   PLT   POS
      's/he is pushing (it)' (author's field data)

3.69. ká   go   tõ̌   ne   ba   ði
      car OBJ   push PRG   PLT   POS
      '(s/he) is pushing the car' (author's field data)

3.70. tõ̌   ne   ba   ði
      push PRG   PLT   POS
      '(s/he) is pushing (it)' (author's field data)

As in the case of the English verbs *to eat*, *to read*, and *to watch*, which have been dealt with above, only by taking syntactic surface structure into account, the difference between instances of contextual ellipsis of arguments and semantically conditioned absence of arguments cannot be determined in such languages. But in order to show that this distinction is nevertheless relevant to native speakers, the test criteria discussed above can be applied. When a given predicate is to be embedded into a linguistic or extra-linguistic context which does not provide any information regarding the arguments involved, distinctions in terms of semantically conditioned absence of arguments and contextual ellipsis become evident. For instance, in response to a question such as *Why is s/he not having lunch with us?* the statements 3.68 and 3.70, that is, the examples in which the object phrase is missing, could not be uttered, unless the addressee knows that the person the conversation is about is having trouble with his/her car. On these grounds, the missing object can be interpreted as pragmatically relevant. Thus, in connection with the predicate *tŏ* 'push', absence of the object is to be regarded as an instance of contextual ellipsis. Similarly, a question such as 3.71 may evoke a variety of responses:

3.71. question: *Why have you lost your appetite?*

3.72. response A (intransitive): *The carrots are rotten.*

3.73. response B (transitive): *The waitress just poured root beer into John's soup.*

In the East Asian languages named, only the equivalent of the semantically intransitive clause 3.72 may in any case be felicitously uttered without the addition of further arguments, while an analogous syntactic configuration based on statement 3.73, in which all arguments except the subject phrase are omitted, is not acceptable out of context:

3.74. *The waitress just poured.

The translational equivalent of the syntactic configuration exemplified by 3.74 is, in principle, admissible in East Asian languages, but only in cases in which it is clear that the addressee can infer the phrases *root beer* and *John's soup* from context.

As a rule, semantically transitive lexemes are members of the semantic class of verbals. Occasionally, there are transitive adjectivals also, such as English *worth* and *devoid of*. Transitive nominals do not occur in the lexical samples established.

With respect to the process of feature ascription in the language samples investigated, it should be noted that the transitivity parameter diverges from the parameters of dynamicity and transience in that the feature value [+/−] does not occur. The feature value [+/−transitive] does not exist because a given lexeme is either [+transitive]—if it implies a secondary argument on semantic grounds— or [−transitive]—if a secondary argument is not implied.

3.3.4. Dependency

The sample contains many instances of lexical minimal pairs which allow for the identification of a fourth semantic parameter that correlates with the contrast of copularizing *vs.* non-copularizing lexemes. This parameter seems to coincide with the traditional semantic distinction of object concepts *vs.* property concepts, that is, nominals *vs.* adjectivals. Nominal–adjectival minimal pairs in which this semantic parameter manifests itself are discussed in detail particularly in Wierzbicka (1986), but also in Langacker (1988) and Croft (1991). Examples of the concepts involved are 'circle' *vs.* 'round', 'Frenchman' *vs.* 'French', 'fool' *vs.* 'foolish', 'giant' *vs.* 'huge', and 'gold' *vs.* 'golden'. Since both members of such nominal–adjectival pairs copularize in Indo-European languages, the latter do not provide any insights as to the interplay of the semantic parameter which can be assumed to be operative here with copula usage. However, in East Asian languages such as Burmese, Cantonese, and Indonesian, as well as in Lakota, this distinction regularly correlates with presence *vs.* absence of copulas. In the monolexemic minimal pairs found in these languages, presence of copulas indicates that a given lexeme is to be interpreted as an object concept, while absence of copulas imposes a reading as a property concept. For instance, in Lakota, the reduplicated form of *cʰasmú* 'sand', i.e. *cʰasmúsmu* 'sandy', never copularizes and is always interpreted as a property concept. *Cʰasmú* 'sand', on the other hand, is compatible with the copula, and is always interpreted as a mass noun.

3.75. lé   cʰasmú   hécʰa
     this   sand   COP
     'this is sand' (author's field data)

3.76. pahá   ki   líla   cʰasmúsmu
     hill   DEF   very   sandy
     'the hill is very sandy' (author's field data)

An analogous semantic distinction is expressed by presence *vs.* absence of the copula with *cʰáya* 'ice, icy, frozen over':

3.77. lé   cʰáya   hécʰa
     this   ice   COP
     'this is ice/*icy/*frozen over' (author's field data)

3.78. lé   wakpála   ki   cʰháya
     this   creek   the   ice
     'this creek is icy/frozen over/*ice' (author's field data)

In Indonesian, there are numerous nominals which assume an adjectival reading when used without the copula. Such lexemes are mainly met with in the semantic classes gender, personality feature, relationship, shape, and substance.

Thus, in combination with a copula, *raksasa* 'giant/huge' must be translated by 'giant'; if the copula is missing, the semantically adjectival translation 'huge' is appropriate.

3.79. Tono   adalah   raksasa
Tono   COP   giant
'Tono is a giant/*huge' (author's field data)

3.80. Tono   raksasa
Tono   giant
'Tono is huge/*a giant' (author's field data)[1]

Some other lexemes which illustrate this distinction include *kotak* 'box, (a) square, square', *pemarah* 'irritable person, irritable', and *perempuan* 'woman, (a) female, female'.

3.81. Tono   adalah   pemarah
Tono   COP   irritable
'Tono is an irritable person/*irritable' (author's field data)

3.82. Tono   pemarah
Tono   choleric
'Tono is irritable/*an irritable person' (author's field data)[1]

3.83. dia   adalah   perempuan
3SG   COP   woman
'she is a woman/*female' (author's field data)

3.84. dia   perempuan
3SG   woman
'she is female/*a woman' (author's field data)[1]

3.85. ini   adalah   kotak
this   COP   square
'this is a square/a box/*square' (author's field data)

3.86. (meja)   ini   kotak
table   this   square
'this (table) is square/*a box/*a square' (author's field data)[1]

Similarly, many Indonesian mass nouns have an alternative reading as property concepts when used without a copula. An example is *emas* 'gold, made of gold, golden':

3.87. ini   adalah   emas
this   COP   gold
'this is gold/*made of gold/*golden' (author's field data)

---

[1] Since the copula can always be dropped in colloquial Indonesian, the respective non-copularizing predicate versions can be given a nominal reading as well. However, the adjectival readings are incompatible with a copula in any case.

3.88. (cin-cin)   ini   emas
        ring   this   gold
        'this (ring) is made of gold/golden/*gold' (author's field data)[1]

The property concept *emas* may not only indicate material composition, but color
as well, as in example 3.89, which may merely refer to blond hair, rather than to
hair made of gold:

3.89. rambut-nya   emas
        hair-3SG.POR   gold
        'his/her hair is golden' (author's field data)

In addition, some lexemes that designate animals can be used metaphorically
to ascribe certain qualities to human beings. If such a metaphorical reading is
intended, the copula is not admissible, and the predicate is categorized as a
property concept, rather than as an entity concept, by native speakers.

3.90. Tono   adalah   ular
        Tono   COP   snake
        'Tono is a snake/*cunning' (author's field data)

3.91. Tono   ular
        Tono   snake
        'Tono is cunning/*a snake' (author's field data)

The non-copularizing version 3.91 can also be translated by 'Tono is a snake'
because the copula can always be dropped at least in formal Indonesian, but this
kind of interpretation applies in a very restricted set of contexts only, such as
those describing magical transformations.

In Burmese, parallel phenomena can be observed within the semantic classes
personality feature (see examples 3.92 *vs.* 3.93) and shape (see examples 3.94 *vs.*
3.95). Within the respective minimal pairs, presence of the copula $p^hji\mathbf{?}$ regularly
indicates an entity concept, while absence of the copula implies a property
concept.

3.92. θu   gà   ka?síné   p^{h}ji?   pa   ði
        3SG   TOP   miser   COP   PLT   POS
        's/he is a miser/*stingy' (author's field data)

3.93. θu   gà   ka?síné   ba   ði
        3SG   TOP   miser   PLT   POS
        's/he is stingy/*a miser' (author's field data)[2]

---

[2] Since the copula can always be dropped in colloquial Burmese, one might feel tempted to
conclude that a nominal interpretation of a predicate is possible in any case in which a predicate
contains a nominal nucleus. However, there is an additional grammatical criterion that clearly differentiates between cases of copula dropping and adjectival usage of the functionally ambiguous

3.94. i   əja   gà   əpjáwaĩ   pʰjɪʔ   pa   ði
      this   thing TOP   disk   COP   PLT   POS
      'this thing is a disk/*circular' (author's field data)

3.95. i   əja   gà   waĩ   ba   ði
      this   thing TOP   circular PLT   POS
      'this thing is circular/*a disk' (author's field data)[2]

Likewise, the lexeme *əme* 'mother, act like a mother', admits both copularizing and non-copularizing structures when used as a predicate nucleus. This distinction is concomitant with a systematic contrast between a reading as an entity *vs.* activity concept.

3.96. θu   gà   əme   pʰjɪʔ   pa   ði
      3SG   TOP   mother   COP   PLT   POS
      'she is a mother/*acts like a mother' (author's field data)

3.97. θu   gà   əme   ba   ði
      3SG   TOP   act like a mother   PLT   POS
      'she acts like a mother/*is a mother' (author's field data)[2]

Note that example 3.97 can be used to describe women who have no children. Additional minimal pairs of the type discussed above are presented in table 3.7.

The semantic contrast which emerges in the above minimal pairs appears to be coextensive with the traditional distinction between nominal and adjectival concepts. The issue must be dealt with in greater detail at this point, because some innovative insights can be gained from more recent research in this area. These, further, are helpful in the attempt at providing a more rigid definition of the semantic contrast expressed in the above minimal pairs.

Although one might feel tempted to argue that differences in the parts-of-speech class status of the members of nominal–adjectival minimal pairs such as English *circle* vs. *round* are semantically insignificant, that is, arbitrary (Wierzbicka 1986: 355), there are also reasons for advocating the contrary position that nominals differ in meaning from adjectivals in any case, 'in a systematic, largely predictable manner' (Wierzbicka 1986: 356). According to Wierzbicka,

> ... there are at least two crucial and inter-related semantic differences between nouns and adjectives. First, nouns tend to designate 'kinds of things' endowed with certain properties; whereas adjectives designate properties as such. Second, ... a noun tends to suggest a rather large number of properties (even though its meaning cannot be reduced to those properties); an adjective, on the other hand, designates (what is seen as) a single property.
>
> (Wierzbicka 1986: 362)

lexemes in question. Whenever the copula is dropped, the positive statement marker *ði* is also eliminated from the clause. *ði* is compatible with verbals and adjectivals only. If the lexemes in question are to be given an adjectival reading, *ði* is present. If both *ði* and the copula are missing, the respective predicate can be given a nominal reading only.

TABLE 3.7. *Dependency: minimal pairs*

	−copula	+copula
Burmese	*əpʰe* 'to act like a father'	*əpʰe* 'father'
	əpʰódzi' 'old and male'	*əpʰódzi'* 'old man'
	əpʰwádzí 'old and female'	*əpʰwádzí* 'old woman'
	tʃaõ 'weird'	*tʃaõ* 'cat'
Cantonese	*jau* 'greasy'	*jau* 'grease'
	pipi 'baby-like'	*pipi* 'baby'
	sailɔu 'childish'	*sailɔu* 'child'
	sɔːkʷaː 'idiotic'	*sɔːkʷaː* 'idiot'
Indonesian	*anjing* 'vile'	*anjing* 'dog'
	babi 'greedy, lazy'	*babi* 'pig'
	bajingan 'jerkish, villainous'	*bajingan* 'jerk, villain'
	batu 'made of stone'	*batu* 'stone'
	besi 'made of iron'	*besi* 'iron'
	bulatan 'spherical'	*bulatan* 'sphere'
	karet 'made of rubber'	*karet* 'rubber'
	kayu 'wooden'	*kayu* 'wood'
	kubus 'cubical'	*kubus* 'cube'
	kuningan 'made of brass'	*kuningan* 'brass'
	laki-laki 'male' (adj.)	*laki-laki* 'man'
	macan 'cruel, mean, irritable'	*macan* 'tiger'
	perak 'made of silver'	*perak* 'silver'
	perunggu 'made of copper'	*perunggu* 'copper'
	salib 'cross-shaped'	*salib* 'cross'
	segitiga 'triangular'	*segitiga* 'triangle'
	tanah liat 'made of clay'	*tanah liat* 'clay'
	wanita 'female' (adj.)	*wanita* 'woman'
	wol 'woolen'	*wol* 'wool'

These findings rest on the observation that in minimal pairs such as English *fattie* vs. *fat* there is a systematic difference in terms of categorization *vs.* mere description:

An adjective applied to a person, or a thing, doesn't imply that this person or this thing is seen by the speaker in terms of a category, defined by this adjective. For example, if I say: *Max is fat*, I don't wish to imply that Max is the kind of person, or the kind of man who is fat. I merely mention fatness as one of the many things that can be said about Max—not as something which 'defines' Max for me, not even from the point of view of appearance. On the other hand, if I say: *Suzie is a fattie*, I do put a label on Suzie—I do categorize her, at least from the point of view of appearance, in terms of her fatness; I present her as belonging to a certain type, defined by fatness.

(Wierzbicka 1986: 359)

Wierzbicka's definition of semantic nounhood may have been inspired by the following statement by Jespersen:

...there will always...remain an indefinable x, a kernel which may be thought of as 'bearer' of the qualities which we have specified. This again is what underlies the old definition [of nominals, R.P.] by means of 'substance', which is thus seen to contain one element of truth though not the whole truth.

(Jespersen 1924: 80)

Such intuitions are also reflected in Langacker's and Croft's definitions of semantic nounhood. Picking up on the issue of nominal–adjectival minimal pairs of the type *circle* vs. *round*, Langacker writes:

Most broadly, the meanings of linguistic expressions divide themselves into nominal *vs.* relational predications. These two types do not necessarily differ in the nature of their intrinsic content (consider *circle* and *round*, or *explode* and *explosion*), but rather in how this content is construed and profiled. A nominal predication presupposes the inter-connections among a set of conceived entities, and profiles the region thus established. By contrast, a relational predication presupposes a set of entities, and it profiles the inter-connections among these entities.

(Langacker 1987: 68)

Langacker illustrates the distinction of nominal *vs.* relational predications by contrasting the English noun *group* with the preposition *together*:

As a relational predication, *together* presupposes the entities [which are constitutive for the concepts of 'group' or 'together', R.P.]...and profiles the interconnections among them...By definition, these interconnections establish a region...It is precisely this region that the nominal predication *group* puts in profile.

(Langacker 1987: 69)

Furthermore, the notion of 'region' is essential for Langacker's overall definition of semantic nounhood: 'A noun designates a region in some domain' (Langacker 1987: 58).

The English noun *group* specifies a region in the domain of space (Langacker 1987: 69). This domain should also be the one that defines the region profiled by the noun *circle*. However, profiling of regions is not the only conceptual factor that distinguishes nominals from other lexical categories. Another crucial criterion in this respect is the ability of concepts to establish connections with entities. According to Langacker, verbal concepts, such as 'to find', do establish such connections, while nominal concepts, such as 'man' and 'cat', do not:

I speak of [FIND] as being 'conceptually dependent', while [MAN] and [CAT] are 'conceptually autonomous'...[FIND] is conceptually dependent because it presupposes, as an inherent part of its own internal structure, the two things participating in the correspondences; [MAN] and [CAT] are conceptually autonomous because they do not similarly presuppose a salient external relationship. One cannot conceptualize the [FIND] relationship without conceptualizing the two things functioning as trajector [roughly, 'subject', R.P.] and landmark [roughly, 'object', R.P.] of that relation (even if they are conceived only in the vaguest terms, say as blobs), but it is perfectly possible to conceptualize a man or a cat without mentally setting it in a relation with some external object... The dependent structure can be equated with the predicate, in predicate-argument terms, and the autonomous structure with its arguments.

(Langacker 1988: 103)

One of Croft's contributions to a universal definition of semantic nounhood lies in linking Langacker's purely conceptual notion of the contrast of dependency *vs.* autonomy with grammatical valence. By assigning a valence of 0 to prototypical nominals, Croft sets the latter apart from other lexical categories.

It appears that Langacker's definition of 'noun' focuses on the *dependency* of a concept that is expressed by a noun rather than on its classifying conceptual function. His example of *circle* versus *round* illustrates well his distinction, however: a circle is an autonomous object of its own, whereas being round is something associated with an entity. This, however, creates a problem with the abstract noun *roundness*, which does not mean the same thing as *circle*. However, roundness appears to conceptualize a property as an autonomous entity that can be spoken of in abstraction from the entities it presupposes. For that reason, the argument to roundness, in fact the arguments for any nominalized relational entity, can be dropped since they are 'out of focus'. The conceptualization of a nominalized entity as autonomous explains why the core noun lexical semantic classes have zero valence: they can most easily be conceptualized as autonomous entities.

(Croft 1991: 104f.)

According to Croft, the valence value of verbals and adjectivals is 1 or higher than 1. Thus, verbals and adjectivals are 'relational', while nominals are not:

Valence is defined here as inherent relationality. A concept is inherently relational if its existence or presence requires the existence or presence of another entity. I will use the term argument to refer to the additional entity or entities implied by the inherently relational entity. For example, *hit* is inherently relational because its existence requires the existence of two entities, the hitter and the object hit. Likewise, *red* is inherently relational because its existence requires the existence of another entity, namely, the object that possesses the property. On this account, however, *man* is not relational: the existence of a man does not imply the existence of another entity, in the way that the existence of an instance of hitting or of redness does.

(Croft 1991: 62f.)

Croft's definition of semantic nounhood explicitly diverges from the analysis commonly employed in logic, according to which nominals have a valence of 1:

... in terms of inherent relationality, the valence of common nouns is zero. This differs from the way that nouns are usually analyzed in the linguistic and philosophical literature, in which nouns have a valence of one. The standard analysis is based on the predicate nominal construction, translating *John is a man* as *Man(John)*. However, the relation between the predicate and the 'argument' in this analysis is one of class inclusion (the individual John belongs to the class or category 'man'), not to any sort of relationality as defined above.

(Croft 1991: 63)

At this point, it must be emphasized that Langacker's and Croft's approaches to defining the argument structure of nominals *vs.* that of other lexical classes are based on semantic, rather than formal, criteria, and thus correspond to the semantically-based definition of transitivity and intransitivity dealt with in §3.3.3, which also relies heavily on Croft's and Langacker's work. Thus, just like the distinction between transitivity and intransivity, within the domain of semantics, the distinction between autonomy and dependence is gradual rather than absolute: 'I would emphasize that conceptual autonomy and dependence are ultimately matters of degree...'(Langacker 1988: 103).

The criterion of zero valence, or conceptual DEPENDENCY, is suited for describing the semantic distinction which surfaces in the minimal pairs listed above. It captures the intuition that a nominal is conceptually autonomous, that is, it refers to something that can be conceived of as existing in the universe independently, while the corresponding adjectival merely attributes one out of many potentially attributable properties to a given entity. With respect to choice of terminology for the parameter characterized in this section, the extant literature, the most relevant passages of which have been quoted above, offers two options, either 'relationality' or 'dependency'. Henceforth, the term DEPENDENCY will be used to refer to the semantic parameter discussed above.

All adjectivals and verbals contained in the questionnaire reproduced in appendix D are classed as [+dependent], with the sole exception of the verbal concept 'to rain'. Despite the fact that they may require the presence of a dummy pronoun in subject position in some languages, such as English (see example 3.98), in order to be predicable, weather expressions are [−dependent]. They are assigned 0 valence by Croft (1991: 97).

3.98. it is raining

Lexemes to which the feature value [− dependent] must be ascribed are usually nominals. However, in any one of the sampled languages, there are also nominals which must be classed as [+ dependent]. Such nominals are encountered, most notably, in the semantic classes body part (e.g. *toe*) and social relation (e.g. *sister*). These so-called relational nouns imply a possessor phrase and are, consequently, assigned the valence value 1 by Croft (1991: 95).

3.3.5. Generalizations

As the preceding sections show, four semantic parameters can be derived from the cross-linguistic sample of lexical minimal pairs established: dynamicity, transience, transitivity, and dependency. Croft's theoretical approach to lexical categorization anticipates all of them. As is pointed out above, prototypical nominals have a valence of 0, prototypical adjectivals have a valence of 1, and verbals have a valence of 1 (e.g. *to jump*), 2 (e.g. *to hit*), or 3 (e.g. *to give*). Since the feature valence does not distinguish adjectivals from verbals to a sufficient degree, Croft introduces the additional parameters stativity and persistence.

[Stativity is defined as, R.P.] the aspectual distinction between states and processes. This category represents the presence or absence of change over time in the state of affairs described by the concept. One can distinguish prototypical verbs with a valency of one from prototypical adjectives, in that the former are processes while the latter are states. This distinction also identifies prototypical nouns as stative.

(Croft 1991: 63)

Croft's stativity dimension is analogous to the dynamicity parameter introduced in §3.3.1. Croft's notion of persistence is akin to Givón's concept of time-stability, and thus related to the transience parameter discussed in §3.3.2: 'Persistence describes how long the process or state is likely to last over time; processes or states can be persistent or transitory' (Croft 1991: 64).

For the purpose of distinguishing nominals, verbals, and adjectivals in semantic terms, Croft proposes a fourth parameter, that of gradability:

... if the entity denoted by the concept can be manifested in degrees (such as height, coldness, etc.), then the concept is gradable, otherwise not. Prototypical adjectives are gradable, while prototypical nouns and verbs are not.

(Croft 1991: 65)

The sample of lexical minimal pairs investigated does not provide any hints at the relevance of the gradability parameter in distinguishing copularizing from non-copularizing predicates. Since the present approach to copularization is entirely inductive, that is to say, exclusively based on semantic distinctions distilled from lexical mimimal pairs, the gradability parameter is not taken into account in the statistical analysis presented in §3.4.

The most important result of the investigation of lexical minimal pairs carried out in §§3.3.1 to 3.3.4 is that the distribution of semantic feature values among the members of minimal pairs is not random, but rather, rule-governed. This will become evident when the specific pairings of feature values which characterize the members of individual lexical minimal pairs are systematically tabulated for each of the four semantic parameters. As it turns out, in the overall sample of languages investigated with respect to lexical minimal pairs, only a subset of the logically possible pairings do, in fact, occur. In tables 3.8 to 3.11, the respective data are presented separately for each of the four semantic parameters dynamicity, transience, transitivity, and dependency. Those pairings which are documented in the ten-language sample are marked by 'yes', while pairings which are not attested are marked by 'no'.

All four matrices contain cells which are marked by gray shading, and all these cells display the entry 'no', which indicates that the respective pairings of feature

TABLE 3.8. *Dynamicity: combinations of feature values attested in the lexical minimal pairs investigated*

		Non-copularizing member		
		+dynamic	+/−dynamic	−dynamic
Copularizing member	+dynamic	no	no	no
	+/−dynamic	no	no	no
	−dynamic	no	yes	yes

TABLE 3.9. *Transience: combinations of feature values attested in the lexical minimal pairs investigated*

		Non-copularizing member		
		+transient	+/−transient	−transient
Copularizing member	+transient	yes	no	no
	+/−transient	yes	yes	no
	−transient	no	yes	no

TABLE 3.10. *Transitivity: combinations of feature values attested in the lexical minimal pairs investigated*

		Non-copularizing member	
		+transitive	−transitive
Copularizing member	+transitive	yes	no
	−transitive	yes	no

TABLE 3.11. *Dependency: combinations of feature values attested in the lexical minimal pairs investigated*

		Non-copularizing member	
		+dependent	−dependent
Copularizing member	+dependent	yes	no
	−dependent	yes	no

values do not occur in the sample of lexical minimal pairs investigated. The entry 'no' is, of course, found in cells which are not marked by gray shading as well. Unlike the plain cells, the gray cells have a special significance for the model of the semantic motivation of copula usage developed in this study: from the fact that all gray shaded cells in all four of the above matrices show the entry 'no', the four general formulas 3.99 to 3.102 can be derived. In these formulas, the term 'higher than' refers to the feature specifications $+$, $+/-$, and $-$: the value $+$ is higher than the values $+/-$ and $-$, and the value $+/-$ is higher than the value $-$.

3.99. Dynamicity:
    If the members of a given lexical minimal pair show diverging feature values with respect to dynamicity, the dynamicity value of the non-copularizing member is higher than that of the copularizing member, never vice versa.

3.100. Transience:
    If the members of a given lexical minimal pair show diverging feature values with respect to transience, the transience value of the non-copularizing member is higher than that of the copularizing member, never vice versa.

3.101. Transitivity:
    If the members of a given lexical minimal pair show diverging feature values with respect to transitivity, the transitivity value of the non-copularizing member is higher than that of the copularizing member, never vice versa.

3.102. Dependency:
    If the members of a given lexical minimal pair show diverging feature values with respect to dependency, the dependency value of the non-copularizing member is higher than that of the copularizing member, never vice versa.

From the data summarized in tables 3.8 to 3.11, a typologically significant generalization concerning the directionality of the meaning differences within minimal pairs can be derived. Formulas 3.99 to 3.102 can be summarized by a more basic rule which captures the deeper regularities underlying the data. The fundamental observation regarding lexical minimal pairs which is expressed by this rule is that the semantic distinctions involved are always UNIDIRECTIONAL.

3.103. PRINCIPLE OF UNIDIRECTIONALITY of semantic distinctions within lexical minimal pairs:
    Within a given lexical minimal pair, the feature value of the copularizing member with respect to any one of the four semantic dimensions dynamicity, transience, transitivity, and dependency never exceeds the feature value of the non-copularizing member.

This formula rules out the constellations marked by gray shading in tables 3.8 to 3.11, but it allows equal values for copularizing and non-copularizing members of a given minimal pair, and it allows constellations in which the non-copularizing member of a minimal pair, on any one of the four parameters, exhibits a higher value than the copularizing member. As the numerous 'no'-entries in the plain cells of tables 3.8 to 3.11 show, however, not every logically possible instantiation of these two basic patterns of combination of feature values within lexical minimal pairs occurs in the ten-language sample. The general theoretical prediction to be made at this point is that the combinations represented by the plain cells in tables 3.8 to 3.11 which receive a 'no'-entry on the basis of the language data investigated will eventually be proved to exist if additional languages are taken into account. The second prediction to be made on the basis of the lexical minimal pairs investigated is that no language will be found that documents the existence of the combinations represented by the cells marked by gray shading in tables 3.8 to 3.11. After all, the overall size of the ten-language sample of lexical minimal pairs should be comprehensive enough to justify the assumption that the lack of lexical minimal pairs that document the feature combinations represented by the gray-shaded cells is not coincidental. Formula 3.103, therefore, is an aspiring language universal. If this formula withstands further empirical scrutiny, the question of whether the pronounced cross-linguistic variation in copula usage is governed, at least to some extent, by semantic principles must be answered in the affirmative. At this point, it seems safe to conclude that the intrinsic semantic content of lexemes interacts with copularization to a sufficient degree to make the application of the semantic parameters dynamicity, transience, transitivity, and dependency in the statistical analysis of larger language-specific vocabularies appear promising. Even if the unidirectionality principle were valid for the majority of minimal pairs only, rather than in all cases, the four parameters could already be expected to yield positive statistical correlations with copula usage.

In fact, at least at first glance, the cross-linguistic sample of languages discussed in Chapter 2 seems to provide two counterexamples to the principle of the unidirectionality of transience distinctions in monolexemic minimal pairs. In Berbice Dutch Creole and Jacaltec certain lexemes may occur either with or without a copula in predicate position. In these languages, the copularizing predicate conveys a temporary meaning, while the non-copularizing version expresses permanence. This runs counter to the predictions made by the uni-directionality principle, which states that the transience value of the non-copularizing structure is higher than that of the copularizing structure. The Jacaltec case is discussed in detail in §2.3.4; in what follows, the respective data from Berbice Dutch Creole are presented. The uses of the copula *jenda* 'almost suggest a distinction . . . along the lines of attribution of inherent and temporary aspects' (Kouwenberg 1994: 125). For instance, in combination with the copula the lexeme *moi* 'good' indicates a 'temporary' (Kouwenberg 1994: 125) state:

3.104. ɛkɛ   jɛnda   moi
      1SG   COP   good
      'I am all right' (Kouwenberg 1994: 124)

The corresponding predicate version in which the copula is lacking, on the other hand, designates 'inherent qualities of certain beings' (Kouwenberg 1994: 125).

3.105. andə   fan   eni   lombo   bat   enə   ,   mɛrɛ   fan   eni   moi
      some   of   3PL   bad   but   3PL   ,   more   of   3PL   good
      'some of them are bad, but the majority of them are good' (Kouwenberg 1994: 125)

However, there is conclusive evidence that in copularizing structures like example 3.104 the predicate nucleus must be analyzed as an 'adverbial complement' (Kouwenberg 1994: 125). The predicate nucleus *moi* in example 3.104 'must therefore be assumed to be the adverb *moi*, not the adjective' (Kouwenberg 1994: 125). Thus, as in the case of Jacaltec, it can be hypothesized that the copula is not entirely desemanticized here, but rather conveys the explicit meaning of 'being in a state of'. Such elements, however, must be classed as auxiliaries or semi-copulas according to the definition of copula given in §1.2.

   It is also worth noting at this point that the minimal pair method lends additional support to the validity of the scale NOMINALS > ADJECTIVALS > VERBALS, which is posited in Chapter 2. The members of individual lexical minimal pairs investigated usually belong to two different traditional lexical categories. The possible pairings are nominal and adjectival, or verbal and adjectival. No minimal pairs have been found which are composed of a nominal and a verbal, except perhaps for Burmese pairs of the type *əme* 'mother' vs. *əme* 'to act like a mother' (see examples 3.96 and 3.97). In general, if a nominal is substituted for a verbal, and vice versa, severe changes in the overall structural makeup of a clause become necessary. Although semantically corresponding abstract nouns are available for verbals in many languages, the respective lexemes obviously cannot be felicitously substituted for each other in a given clause, at least not as easily as the members of true lexical minimal pairs can be substituted for each other. The English lexeme pair *to explode* vs. *explosion* illustrates this. Attempts at forming a clause on the basis of the noun *explosion* that is semantically equivalent to cxample 3.106, in which the verb *to explode* figures as the predicate nucleus, do not yield convincing results:

3.106. the bomb exploded

3.107. ?? there was an explosion of the bomb

3.108. ?? an explosion of the bomb happened

Likewise, it is difficult to exchange the predicate nucleus *explosion* for the verb *to explode*. Although examples 3.109 and 3.110 are probably semantically equivalent to some degree, they are not structurally equivalent to the extent clauses formed on the basis of true lexical minimal pairs are.

3.109. there was an explosion

3.110. something exploded

Thus, the rules which hold for the macrocosm of lexical categorization via copularization (see §2.3.4) are mirrored in the microcosm of lexical minimal pairs: nominals and adjectivals can be grouped together, as verbals and adjectivals can be grouped together, but nominals and verbals are not grouped together.

3.4. Statistics

In what follows, each of the four semantic parameters—dynamicity, transience, transitivity, and dependency—is tested with respect to its statistical correlation with copula usage in each of the ten languages sampled by means of the questionnaire reproduced in appendix D. The languages for which such data have been compiled are Burmese, Cantonese, German, Hungarian, Indonesian, Japanese, Lakota, Swahili, Thai, and Turkish. Originally, Bambara was also included in this set of languages. However, since Bambara turned out to be a representative of the fully copularizing language type, and thus is not relevant for an investigation of the intra-linguistic contrast between copularizing and non-copularizing lexemes, detailed statistical analyses have not been conducted for Bambara. The ten-language sample is genetically diverse, as the genetic affiliation of the respective languages shows. The classification employed in table 3.12 is based on Ruhlen (1987).

The parameters dependency, transitivity, transience, and dynamicity are, for the most part, logically independent of each other. Each of these parameters can

TABLE 3.12. *Genetic classification of the ten-language sample*

Burmese	Tibeto-Burman
Cantonese	Sinitic
German	Indo-European
Hungarian	Uralic-Yukaghir
Indonesian	Austronesian
Japanese	Japanese-Korean
Lakota	Almosan-Keresiouan
Swahili	Niger-Congo
Thai	Daic
Turkish	Turkic

TABLE **3.13**. *Dynamicity, transience, transitivity, and dependency: logically possible combinations of feature values*

		Dynamicity		Transience	
		+	−	+	−
DYNAMICITY	+				
	−				
TRANSIENCE	+	*to jump*	*glad*		
	−	(complex pred.)	*wooden*		
TRANSITIVITY	+	*to hit*	*to resemble*	*to hit*	*to resemble*
	−	*to fall*	*tall*	*to fall*	*wooden*
DEPENDENCY	+	*to explode*	*tall*	*to explode*	*wooden*
	−	*explosion*	*tallness*	*explosion*	*wood*

be the sole factor that distinguishes the members of a given lexical minimal pair in semantic terms, but, of course, there may be differences between members of minimal pairs on more than one semantic plane as well. Both the positive and the negative values of each parameter are compatible with the positive and the negative values of any of the other parameters, as the existence of lexical items for each logically possible combination proves (see table 3.13). The only exceptions in this respect are the pairings [+dynamic]/[−transient], for which no lexical realization has been found, and any combination of the features transitivity and dependency. The pairing [+dynamic]/[−transient] is ontologically possible, but in construing examples for this combination, it is necessary to resort to complex predications. For instance, electrons and other subatomic particles have the property of being in a spinning motion throughout their existence. Thus, 'being in a spinning motion' constitutes an example of a real-world event which can be characterized as [+dynamic]/[−transient].

The parameters of transitivity and dependency cover the same conceptual domain, that of relationality. As the summary of Croft's approach to relationality in §3.3.4 indicates, valence is a continuum which is defined in terms of the number of required arguments. The segmentation of the valence continuum into the parameters of transitivity and dependency is merely a tentative and artificial one which is prescribed by the empirical findings of the minimal pair method. Transitivity and dependency bisect the overall valence continuum $0 > 1 > 2 > 3$ at different points: transitivity subsumes 0-valence and 1-valence under the feature value [−transitive], and 2-valence and 3-valence under the feature value [+transitive], whereas dependency contrasts 0-valence with all other possible valence values. Thus, the feature value [+dependent] is assigned to 0-valence only, while 1-valence, 2-valence, and 3-valence are subsumed under the feature value [−dependent].

Although the parameters of transitivity and dependency are not logically independent from each other, each of these two features is logically independent from both dynamicity and transience.

In the following section, the predictive power of each of the four semantic parameters with respect to copula usage in each of the ten languages sampled in detail will be determined.

3.4.1. The data

The statistical analyses are based on the materials gathered by means of the questionnaire described in §3.2. Only for Lakota, this questionnaire was not used because an extensive and representative lexical sample compiled during an earlier period of fieldwork was available already. Nevertheless, the concepts contained in the Lakota sample largely coincide with those included in the questionnaire.

After completing the task of filling out the questionnaire and classifying each entry in the sampled languages with respect to the semantic features dynamicity, transience, transitivity, and dependency, the lexeme lists were restructured. Occasionally, two or more English test lexemes were translated by the same lexeme in the sampled languages. Except in cases of clear homonymy, such entries were subsumed in a single entry.

It goes without saying that the feature profiles of the sampled lexemes in the languages investigated do not necessarily mirror those of the corresponding English test lexemes. For instance, when questioned about the entry *beautiful* in the questionnaire, the informant for Bambara stated that the only available lexical equivalent in his native language was the abstract noun *cὲɲa* 'beauty'. The tendency of rendering concepts which figure as adjectives in English by abstract nouns is particularly pronounced in African languages, as Dixon (1977b) already notes.

The statistical data obtained for the sampled languages are summarized in tables 3.14 to 3.23.

3.4.2. Predictive power of semantic features

A superficial glance at the figures in the above tables already reveals that there are significant statistical correlations of all four parameters with presence *vs.* absence of copulas in all sampled languages. The directionality of these correlations is, as expected, the same as in the lexical minimal pairs. The [+] values of all four parameters correspond to absence of copulas, while the [−] values of all four parameters correspond to presence of copulas. The following generalizations can be made:

3.111. The feature value [+dynamic] correlates highly with absence of copulas, while the feature value [−dynamic] correlates highly with presence of copulas.

TABLE 3.14. *Burmese: distribution of copularizing* vs. *non-copularizing lexemes in the sample*

		+copula	−copula
DYNAMICITY	+	0	153
	+/−	0	2
	−	206	165
TRANSIENCE	+	0	186
	+/−	21	123
	−	185	11
TRANSITIVITY	+	0	122
	−	206	198
DEPENDENCY	+	18	319
	−	188	1

Total of sampled lexemes: 526

TABLE 3.15. *Cantonese: distribution of copularizing* vs. *non-copularizing lexemes in the sample*

		+copula	−copula
DYNAMICITY	+	0	155
	+/−	0	0
	−	218	171
TRANSIENCE	+	0	179
	+/−	44	119
	−	174	28
TRANSITIVITY	+	0	119
	−	218	207
DEPENDENCY	+	46	325
	−	172	1

Total of sampled lexemes: 544

TABLE 3.16. *German: distribution of copularizing* vs. *non-copularizing lexemes in the sample*

		+copula	−copula
DYNAMICITY	+	0	174
	+/−	0	2
	−	387	48
TRANSIENCE	+	13	191
	+/−	175	33
	−	199	0
TRANSITIVITY	+	1	118
	−	386	106
DEPENDENCY	+	191	223
	−	196	1

Total of sampled lexemes: 611

TABLE 3.17. *Hungarian: distribution of copularizing vs. non-copularizing lexemes in the sample*

		+ copula	− copula
DYNAMICITY	+	0	201
	+/−	0	1
	−	390	44
TRANSIENCE	+	8	219
	+/−	158	27
	−	224	0
TRANSITIVITY	+	1	123
	−	389	123
DEPENDENCY	+	191	246
	−	199	0

Total of sampled lexemes: 636

TABLE 3.18. *Indonesian: distribution of copularizing vs. non-copularizing lexemes in the sample*

		+copula	−copula
DYNAMICITY	+	0	224
	+/−	0	9
	−	235	284
TRANSIENCE	+	0	257
	+/−	34	205
	−	201	55
TRANSITIVITY	+	0	146
	−	235	371
DEPENDENCY	+	23	516
	−	212	1

Total of sampled lexemes: 752

TABLE 3.19. *Japanese: distribution of copularizing vs. non-copularizing lexemes in the sample*

		+copula	−copula
DYNAMICITY	+	1	223
	+/−	0	8
	−	449	173
TRANSIENCE	+	9	257
	+/−	137	129
	−	304	18
TRANSITIVITY	+	2	179
	−	448	225
DEPENDENCY	+	199	404
	−	251	0

Total of sampled lexemes: 854

TABLE 3.20. *Lakota: distribution of copularizing vs. non-copularizing lexemes in the sample*

		+copula	−copula
DYNAMICITY	+	0	340
	+/−	0	20
	−	223	238
TRANSIENCE	+	0	408
	+/−	20	173
	−	203	17
TRANSITIVITY	+	0	254
	−	223	344
DEPENDENCY	+	10	593
	−	213	5

Total of sampled lexemes: 821

TABLE 3.21. *Swahili: distribution of copularizing vs. non-copularizing lexemes in the sample*

		+copula	−copula
DYNAMICITY	+	0	170
	+/−	0	1
	−	334	45
TRANSIENCE	+	7	183
	+/−	118	32
	−	209	1
TRANSITIVITY	+	1	109
	−	333	107
DEPENDENCY	+	146	215
	−	188	1

Total of sampled lexemes: 550

TABLE 3.22. *Thai: distribution of copularizing vs. non-copularizing lexemes in the sample*

		+copula	−copula
DYNAMICITY	+	0	178
	+/−	0	4
	−	224	201
TRANSIENCE	+	0	201
	+/−	45	149
	−	179	33
TRANSITIVITY	+	0	119
	−	224	264
DEPENDENCY	+	47	382
	−	177	1

Total of sampled lexemes: 607

TABLE 3.23. *Turkish: distribution of copularizing* vs. *non-copularizing lexemes in the sample*

		+/−copula	−copula
DYNAMICITY	+	0	165
	+/−	0	0
	−	366	53
TRANSIENCE	+	0	186
	+/−	136	31
	−	230	1
TRANSITIVITY	+	0	106
	−	366	112
DEPENDENCY	+	194	218
	−	172	0

Total of sampled lexemes: 584

3.112. The feature value [+transient] correlates highly with absence of copulas, while the feature value [−transient] correlates highly with presence of copulas.

3.113. The feature value [+transitive] correlates highly with absence of copulas, while the feature value [−transitive] correlates highly with presence of copulas.

3.114. The feature value [+dependent] correlates highly with absence of copulas, while the feature value [−dependent] correlates highly with presence of copulas.

However, the degree to which the individual parameters correlate with copula usage may differ from language to language. Table 3.24 summarizes the data presented in tables 3.14 to 3.23 by providing both the raw figures as well as the percentages for those lexical items in the overall samples whose behavior with respect to copularization is correctly predicted by the four semantic parameters.

In converting the data in the above tables into the figures in table 3.24 the following procedure is chosen. For instance, on the basis of the data for dependency in Lakota, which are reproduced in table 3.25, the generalizing formulas given in 3.115 and 3.116 can be proposed:

3.115. If a given lexeme has the feature value [+dependent], it does not copularize.

3.116. If a given lexeme has the feature value [−dependent], it copularizes.

These formulas merely describe a hypothetical situation in which the correlation between the dependency parameter and copula usage is perfect. This situation is, however, never encountered in the language samples investigated. Thus,

TABLE **3.24.** *Correct predictions of copula use in the samples*

	DYNAMICITY		TRANSIENCE		TRANSITIVITY		DEPENDENCY	
	Number of items	%	Number of items	%	Number of items	%	Number of items	%
Burmese	361	68.6	494	93.9	327	62.2	507	96.4
Cantonese	373	68.6	472	86.8	337	61.9	497	91.4
German	563	92.1	565	92.5	504	82.5	419	68.6
Hungarian	592	93.1	601	94.5	512	80.5	445	70.0
Indonesian	468	62.2	663	88.2	381	50.7	728	96.8
Japanese	680	79.6	698	81.7	627	73.4	655	76.7
Lakota	583	71.0	784	95.5	477	58.1	806	98.2
Swahili	505	91.8	510	92.7	442	80.4	403	73.3
Thai	406	66.9	529	87.1	343	56.5	559	92.1
Turkish	531	90.9	552	94.5	472	80.8	390	66.8

TABLE **3.25.** *Lakota: distributional data for dependency*

		+copula	−copula
DEPENDENCY	+	10	593
	−	213	5

formulas 3.115 and 3.116 must be understood as capturing strong universal tendencies only.

In the case of Lakota, there are ten exceptions to formula 3.115, and there are five exceptions to formula 3.116. Formula 3.115 predicts the behavior of 593 lexemes correctly, and formula 3.116 predicts the behavior of 213 lexemes correctly. Thus, taken together, the two formulas yield a correct prediction of the behavior of 806 out of the 821 lexemes contained in the Lakota sample. This amounts to an overall rate of 98.2 per cent. The percentages given in table 3.24 determine the overall predictive power of the respective parameters in the languages investigated.

The procedure of calculating percentages is somewhat more complex for features for which [+/−] values can be assigned to individual lexemes, that is for dynamicity and transience. This can be illustrated by means of the data for transience in Swahili, which are reproduced in table 3.26.

In the overall statistical analysis, the lexemes to which [+/−] values have been assigned can, *per se*, either be grouped with those lexemes which display the value [+feature X], or with those which have the value [−feature X]. Lexemes with ambiguous feature values are treated individually in each language in this respect, but always in such a way that the overall predictive power of the parameter in question is maximized. This is accomplished by first determining

TABLE 3.26. *Swahili: distributional data for transience*

		+copula	−copula
TRANSIENCE	+	7	183
	+/−	118	32
	−	209	1

what subclass of lexemes exhibiting the feature value [+/−] for a given parameter, that is either the copularizing or the non-copularizing subclass, comprises the higher amount of members. In the case of transience in Swahili, the copularizing subclass is dominant, since it contains 118 members, while the non-copularizing subclass has only thirty-two members. As a next step, the general correspondences [+transient]/[−copularizing] and [−transient]/[+copularizing] can be established for transience in Swahili. On this basis, the behavior of a total of 209 + 183, which is 392 lexemes, with respect to copula usage can be predicted. The predictive power of the transience parameter can be further improved by adding either the copularizing or the non-copularizing subgroup of lexemes exhibiting the feature value [+/−] to these 392 lexemes. In order to maximize the predictive power of the transience parameter, of course, the lexemes in the numerically dominant subgroup of lexemes exhibiting [+/−] values must be added to the 392 lexemes whose behavior is predictable, rather than the smaller subgroup of lexemes to which [+/−] values have been assigned. This can be justified by linking the dominant subgroup of the semantically ambiguous lexemes—that is those specified as [+/−transient]/[+copularizing]— which comprises 118 lexemes, with the class of 209 lexemes which are specified as [−transient]/[+copularizing] by virtue of the shared feature value [−transient]. Thus, the idealized formulas to be employed in this case are as follows:

3.117. If a given lexeme has the feature value [+transient], it does not copularize.

3.118. If a given lexeme has either the feature value [−transient] or the feature value [+/−transient], it copularizes.

On this basis, copula usage can be predicted by means of the feature transience for a total of 510 lexemes in Swahili.

As table 3.24 shows, the correlations between the four parameters and copula usage are clearly non-random because in the overwhelming majority of cases, the percentages exceed the 50 per cent mark. (Values around 50 per cent must be interpreted as chance distributions—they indicate that there is no interdependence of the factors involved.) Only a single numerical value, that of transitivity in Indonesian, is in the 50 per cent range; transitivity provides correct predictions for copula usage only for 50.7 per cent of the sampled vocabulary in Indonesian. As a rule, however, the percentages are in the 70 to 90 per cent range.

Thus, the hypothesis that the division of language-specific lexical inventories into copularizing and non-copularizing items is not arbitrary, but rather, governed by semantic factors, is borne out by the facts. In order to assess the relative typological relevance of each of the four parameters, the respective features that are most successful in predicting copula usage in each sampled language are listed in table 3.27. As it turns out, top positions are reached only by two of the four parameters, that is, by transience and dependency.

On these grounds, it seems justified to propose a typology of copularization that is based on a differentiation of dependency-dominated *vs.* transience-dominated languages. Such a typology is supported by the finding that this distinction corresponds to the differentiation of AN *vs.* AV languages established in §2.3.4.

TABLE 3.27. *Predictive power of the semantic parameters investigated*

	Parameter with highest predictive power
Burmese	dependency
Cantonese	dependency
German	transience
Hungarian	transience
Indonesian	dependency
Japanese	transience
Lakota	dependency
Swahili	transience
Thai	dependency
Turkish	transience

TABLE 3.28. *Language type and the predictive power of semantic parameters*

	Parameter with highest predictive power	Basic classification in terms of copula usage
Burmese	dependency	AV
Cantonese	dependency	AV
German	transience	AN
Hungarian	transience	AN
Indonesian	dependency	AV
Japanese	transience	split-A
Lakota	dependency	AV
Swahili	transience	AN
Thai	dependency	AV
Turkish	transience	AN

All the AN languages in the ten-language sample are transience-dominated, while all the AV languages are dependency-dominated as shown in table 3.28.

Chapter 4 will deal with the question of whether a language typology based on the dynamicity *vs.* dependency contrast is really the most attractive theoretical model of copularization imaginable, or if alternative approaches are possible. For now, it suffices to know that all four semantic parameters produce remarkably high correlations in any one of the sampled languages, and that it can therefore be assumed that all four parameters contribute to structuring the lexicon with respect to copula usage. However, it is worth noting that the statistical correlations given in table 3.24 are never perfect. This issue will be discussed in greater detail in the next chapter.

In addition to the analysis summarized in table 3.24, chi-square tests of statistical significance can be carried out on the basis of the figures given in tables 3.14 to 3.23. In what follows, chi-square values are calculated for each semantic feature in each of the ten languages investigated. A basic requirement for conducting chi-square tests are figures for the expected occurrences of each sampled category. The number of occurrences of copularizing lexemes to be expected within a given language-specific sample for each of the semantic sub-domains of dynamicity, transience, transitivity, and dependency is calculated on the basis of the percentage of copularizing lexemes in the language-specific sample as a whole. This procedure can be illustrated by means of the following example. The Burmese sample comprises 526 lexemes. Of these, a total of 206 lexical items, that is to say 39.2 per cent, copularize. Consequently, within each of the semantic categories listed in tables 3.14 to 3.23, a total of 39.2 per cent of copularizing lexemes should be expected to occur. For instance, the population of [+dependent] lexemes in Burmese contains a total of 337 lexemes (see table 3.14). Using the percentage of copularizing lexemes obtained for the overall sample as a basis for calculation (39.2 per cent), the group of lexemes which are classed as [+dependent] in Burmese should comprise 132.1 copularizing lexemes.

In order to determine whether the observed deviations from the expected values are statistically significant or not, calculating chi-square values for copularizing lexemes in each sampled category suffices—the non-copularizing lexemes can be ignored because given the nature of chi-square tests, their results would only replicate the results for the copularizing items.

Before the numerical output of the chi-square tests becomes available, the measure of statistical significance to be employed in these tests must be determined. In general, a significance level of $p = 5$ is frequently used in chi-square analyses. For the present study, a significance level of $p = 0.1$ has been chosen, which requires higher values of deviation from the expected number of occurrences than a significance level of $p = 5$. The details of the chi-square analysis are given in tables 3.29 to 3.38.

The individual deviances calculated in tables 3.29 to 3.38 are added up for each semantic parameter in each of the ten sampled languages in table 3.39. In

TABLE 3.29. *Burmese: chi-square analysis*

		+copula expected	+copula observed	Difference expected − observed	χ^2
DYNAMICITY	+	60.8	0	60.8	60.8
	+/−				
	−	145.4	206	60.6	25.3
TRANSIENCE	+	129.4	21	108.4	90.8
	+/−				
	−	76.8	185	108.2	152.4
TRANSITIVITY	+	47.8	0	47.8	47.8
	−	158.4	206	47.6	14.3
DEPENDENCY	+	132.1	18	114.1	98.6
	−	74.1	188	113.9	175.1

TABLE 3.30. *Cantonese: chi-square analysis*

		+copula expected	+copula observed	Difference expected − observed	χ^2
DYNAMICITY	+	62.2	0	62.2	62.2
	+/−				
	−	156.0	218	62.0	24.6
TRANSIENCE	+	137.1	44	93.1	63.2
	+/−				
	−	81.0	174	93.0	106.8
TRANSITIVITY	+	47.7	0	47.7	47.7
	−	170.4	218	47.6	13.3
DEPENDENCY	+	148.8	46	102.8	71.0
	−	69.4	172	102.6	151.7

each case, the values given in table 3.39 exceed the threshold value of statistical significance, which is 10.8 for $p = 0.1$ (1df). In many cases, the deviation is extremely high. Thus, it can be concluded that the deviances from the expected values for each of the four semantic parameters, in each of the ten sampled languages, are statistically significant.

3.4.3. Competing semantic models of copularization

One of the central conclusions arrived at in Chapter 2 is that the behavior of individual lexemes with respect to compatibility with copulas might be determined

TABLE 3.31. *German: chi-square analysis*

		+copula expected	+copula observed	Difference expected − observed	χ^2
DYNAMICITY	+	111.4	0	111.4	111.4
	+/−				
	−	286.8	387	100.2	35.0
TRANSIENCE	+	129.1	13	116.1	104.4
	+/−	257.6	374	116.4	52.6
	−				
TRANSITIVITY	+	75.3	1	74.3	73.3
	−	311.4	386	74.6	17.9
DEPENDENCY	+	262.1	191	71.1	19.3
	−	124.7	196	71.3	40.8

TABLE 3.32. *Hungarian: chi-square analysis*

		+copula expected	+copula observed	Difference expected − observed	χ^2
DYNAMICITY	+	123.8	0	123.8	123.8
	+/−				
	−	266.0	390	124.0	57.8
TRANSIENCE	+	139.2	8	131.2	123.7
	+/−	250.7	382	131.3	68.8
	−				
TRANSITIVITY	+	76.0	1	75.0	74.0
	−	313.9	389	75.1	18.0
DEPENDENCY	+	267.9	191	76.9	22.1
	−	122.0	199	77.0	48.6

TABLE 3.33. *Indonesian: chi-square analysis*

		+copula expected	+copula observed	Difference expected − observed	χ^2
DYNAMICITY	+	72.9	0	72.9	72.9
	+/−				
	−	162.5	235	72.5	32.4
TRANSIENCE	+	155.3	34	121.3	94.7
	+/−				
	−	80.1	201	120.9	182.5
TRANSITIVITY	+	45.7	0	45.7	45.7
	−	189.7	235	45.3	10.8
DEPENDENCY	+	168.7	23	145.7	125.8
	−	66.7	212	145.3	316.5

TABLE 3.34. *Japanese: chi-square analysis*

		+copula expected	+copula observed	Difference expected − observed	χ^2
DYNAMICITY	+	122.3	1	121.3	120.3
	+/−				
	−	327.8	449	121.2	44.8
TRANSIENCE	+	140.2	9	131.2	122.8
	+/−	309.9	441	131.1	55.5
	−				
TRANSITIVITY	+	95.4	2	93.4	91.4
	−	354.7	448	93.3	24.5
DEPENDENCY	+	317.8	199	118.8	44.4
	−	132.3	251	118.7	106.5

TABLE 3.35. *Lakota: chi-square analysis*

		+copula expected	+copula observed	Difference expected − observed	χ^2
DYNAMICITY	+	97.9	0	97.9	97.9
	+/−				
	−	125.4	223	97.6	76.0
TRANSIENCE	+	163.5	20	143.5	126.0
	+/−				
	−	59.8	203	143.2	342.9
TRANSITIVITY	+	69.1	0	69.1	69.1
	−	154.2	223	68.8	30.7
DEPENDENCY	+	164.0	10	154.0	144.6
	−	59.3	213	153.7	398.4

TABLE 3.36. *Swahili: chi-square analysis*

		+copula expected	+copula observed	Difference expected − observed	χ^2
DYNAMICITY	+	103.8	0	103.8	103.8
	+/−				
	−	230.1	334	103.9	46.9
TRANSIENCE	+	115.3	7	108.3	101.7
	+/−	218.5	327	108.5	53.9
	−				
TRANSITIVITY	+	66.8	1	65.8	64.8
	−	267.1	333	65.9	16.3
DEPENDENCY	+	219.1	146	73.1	24.4
	−	114.7	188	73.3	46.8

TABLE 3.37. *Thai: chi-square analysis*

		+copula expected	+copula observed	Difference expected − observed	χ^2
DYNAMICITY	+	67.2	0	67.2	67.2
	+/−				
	−	156.8	224	67.2	28.8
TRANSIENCE	+	145.8	45	100.8	69.7
	+/−				
	−	78.2	179	100.8	129.9
TRANSITIVITY	+	43.9	0	43.9	43.9
	−	180.1	224	43.9	10.7
DEPENDENCY	+	158.3	47	111.3	78.3
	−	65.7	177	111.3	188.6

TABLE 3.38. *Turkish: chi-square analysis*

		+/−copula expected	+/−copula observed	Difference expected − observed	χ^2
DYNAMICITY	+	103.5	0	103.5	103.5
	+/−				
	−	262.7	366	103.3	40.6
TRANSIENCE	+	116.6	0	116.6	116.6
	+/−	250.0	366	116.0	53.8
	−				
TRANSITIVITY	+	66.5	0	66.5	66.5
	−	299.7	366	66.3	14.7
DEPENDENCY	+	258.3	194	64.3	16.0
	−	107.8	172	64.2	38.2

TABLE 3.39. *Chi-square values in the 10-language sample*

	DYNAMICITY: χ^2	TRANSIENCE: χ^2	TRANSITIVITY: χ^2	DEPENDENCY: χ^2
Burmese	86.1	243.2	62.1	273.7
Cantonese	86.8	170.0	61.0	222.7
German	146.4	157.0	91.2	60.1
Hungarian	181.6	192.5	92.0	70.7
Indonesian	105.3	277.2	56.5	442.3
Japanese	165.1	178.3	115.9	150.9
Lakota	173.9	468.9	99.8	543.0
Swahili	150.7	155.6	81.1	71.2
Thai	96.0	199.6	54.6	266.9
Turkish	144.1	170.4	81.2	54.2

p = 0.1, 1 df: 10.8

by its inherent semantic properties. As is argued in §§1.3.4.3 and 2.5, Givón's time-stability scale could, at least theoretically, be taken as the semantic principle which conditions the markedness phenomena described in Croft (1991). The intrinsic time-stability/transience value of a given lexeme determines its predicate worthiness, that is its statistical frequency in predicate position. The less frequently a lexeme appears as a predicate nucleus, the more likely it will be found in combination with a copula, that is, in a predicate construction which is more marked with respect to the amount of morphosyntactic input. Thus, markedness and time-stability/transience can be interpreted as forming two parallel, and interacting, scales. Such a joint approach to copularization is intuitively appealing because it seems to provide a unified account for the behavior of copulas in cross-linguistic perspective. On this basis, it can be argued that AN languages, such as German or English, partition the lexicon in terms of the feature value [−transient]. Nominals are usually ascribed the feature value [−transient], while verbals are generally be characterized as [+transient]; prototypical adjectivals are ambiguous with respect to transience and therefore receive the specification [+/−transient]. As a consequence, nominals and adjectivals can be said to share the feature value [−transient]. Thus, in AN languages, the following rule might be operative:

3.119. Lexemes whose intrinsic semantic profile contains the feature value [−transient] copularize; lexemes whose intrinsic semantic profile does not contain the feature value [−transient] do not copularize.

AV languages such as Burmese or Mandarin, on the other hand, partition the lexicon on the basis of rule 3.120:

3.120. Lexemes whose intrinsic semantic profile contains the feature value [+transient] do not copularize; lexemes whose intrinsic semantic profile does not contain the feature value [+transient] copularize.

However, the semantic analyses discussed in §3.4.2 indicate that the transience parameter, in five of the ten sampled languages, loses out to the dependency parameter in terms of predictive accuracy. Thus, one is left wondering how seriously the joint approach based on transience and markedness should be taken as a possible universal model for motivating copularization. Besides, the distributional types AN and AV can be motivated by means of the other semantic parameters derived from the minimal pair method as well. For instance, the AN type might be thought of as based on the dynamicity parameter, if the following rule holds:

3.121. Lexemes whose intrinsic semantic profile contains the feature value [+dynamic] do not copularize; lexemes whose intrinsic semantic profile does not contain the feature value [+dynamic] copularize.

Or, alternatively:

3.122. Lexemes whose intrinsic semantic profile contains the feature value [−dynamic] copularize; lexemes whose intrinsic semantic profile does not contain the feature value [−dynamic] do not copularize.

Both of these rules separate verbals from both nominals and adjectivals, since prototypical verbals are [+dynamic], while nominals and adjectivals are generally [−dynamic].

The AV type, on the other hand, might be sensitive to rules such as 3.123 or 3.124:

3.123. Lexemes whose intrinsic semantic profile contains the feature value [+dependent] do not copularize; lexemes whose intrinsic semantic profile does not contain the feature value [+dependent] copularize.

3.124. Lexemes whose intrinsic semantic profile contains the feature value [−dependent] copularize; lexemes whose intrinsic semantic profile does not contain the feature value [−dependent] do not copularize.

These two rules single out nominals and contrast them with both verbals and adjectivals. Prototypical nominals are [−dependent], while verbals and adjectivals are usually [+dependent].

Thus, in order to account for the implicational hierarchy NOMINALS > ADJECTIVALS > VERBALS, theoretical models of copularization do not have to rely on the transience parameter alone. Moreover, the semantic parameters of dynamicity and dependency can be linked with the markedness principle as convincingly as transience. The gradual cline between the respective frequency of nominals, adjectivals, and verbals in predicate position observed by Croft (1991: 87ff.) may also be conditioned by dynamicity or dependency. The predicate worthiness of nominals may be low because nominals are intrinsically [−dynamic] (with the exception of certain types of abstract noun such as English *explosion*), or because nominals are intrinsically [−dependent]. The pragmatic function of predicate may be seen as accommodating the need to establish a setting in time as well as in space for a given state of affairs. Furthermore, 'setting in time' can be associated with the expression of time-oriented categories such as aspect and tense. 'Setting in space' can be interpreted as the conceptual archetype for relationality, that is for categories expressing interconnections among entities.

Given the above, it is plausible that lexemes which are *per se* [−dynamic] and [−dependent], that is to say nominals, do not lend themselves to usage as predicate nuclei as easily as do lexemes which are intrinsically [+dynamic] and [+dependent], that is to say, verbals. Lexemes which are classed as [−dynamic] *per se* neutralize potential oppositions holding in the dimension of time; they are, in some sense, atemporal. The feature value [+dynamic], on the other hand, implies variety in time, that is change and processuality, and therefore fosters the expression of aspectual oppositions such as perfective *vs.* imperfective, and perhaps of tense oppositions as well. For instance, a process can be profiled as ongoing or as completed, that is as imperfective or as perfective. This distinction, however, does not make much sense for a non-process such as 'to be a dog'; 'dogness' is intrinsically non-transient. Likewise, the feature value [−dependent] is conceptually opposed to the notion of relationality, while the feature value [+dependent] implies the presence of valence structure. Valence structure, however, is intimately linked with the expression of focal predicate categories such as person and voice.

In sum, lexemes which are [+dynamic] and [+dependent], that is verbals, yield 'better' predicates than lexemes which are [−dynamic] and [−dependent], that is, nominals. The majority of adjectivals are appropriately characterized in terms of the combination [−dynamic]/[+dependent]. Thus, they are conceptually intermediate between nominals and adjectivals, and, as a consequence, intermediate between the latter in terms of predicate worthiness as well.

However, in the context of the search for the driving forces behind the phenomenon of copularization in general, and the existence of the specific distributional patterns of copularizing *vs.* non-copularizing lexemes in the lexicon of individual languages, in particular, the more marginal distributional patterns split-A, split-V, and—if this type exists—split-N also deserve a more thorough discussion. Within these types, the correlations between the four semantic parameters and copula usage do not hold to the same degree as within the types AN and AV, as the Japanese data suggest. The figures for lexemes whose behavior with respect to copularization is predictable on the basis of each of the four semantic parameters dynamicity, transience, transitivity, and dependency range between 70 and 80 per cent in Japanese. In AN and AV languages, however, predictability regularly exceeds the 90 per cent mark for at least one parameter. It could be hypothesized that split-N, split-A, and split-V languages are extremely rare because they operate with a cognitively unnatural division of the lexicon, that is, a division that is not mirrored by some distinction at the semantic level. This points to another factor which may have to be taken into account in the search for functional principles which govern copularization: cognitive economy.

In any language in which copulas occur, their use is controlled by strict rules which prescribe, for instance, whether a given lexeme must be combined with a copula in predicate position or not; copula usage is lexically fixed. Thus, compatibility *vs.* non-compatibility with a copula is part of the morphosyntactic information that must be stored in the brain separately for any given lexeme. The storage and memorizing processes involved here require considerable cognitive effort. It is a truism that patterns of categorization which minimize cognitive effort are superior to others. As a consequence, theoretical models of categorization are evaluated, among other things, in terms of the degree of cognitive parsimony or economy they involve (Barsalou and Hale 1993: 105ff.). Rules for copula usage which more or less cling to the divisions imposed by any of the four semantic dimensions dynamicity, transience, transitivity, and dependency reduce the cognitive effort which has to be spent on memorizing, processing, and learning for a variety of reasons. Most importantly, such rules have the advantage that pre-existing patterns of the segmentation of the lexicon, which are anchored in the intrinsic semantic content of lexical items, can be utilized. For instance, the feature dynamicity correlates highly with copula usage in German. If cognitive processes associated with copula use are backed up by a general rule such as 3.121 or 3.122, the cognitive effort required presumably decreases. Conversely, if such support from the semantic level is missing, as in the case of split-N, split-A, and split-V languages, cognitive economy is not maximized. Of course, the possibility that such languages operate with semantic parameters other than dynamicity, transience, transitivity, and dependency, which correlate with the respective distinction between copularizing and non-copularizing lexemes, cannot be ruled out—but it is entirely unclear at that point what these parameters should be.

In conclusion, it can be stated that in the ten sampled languages, semantic parameters other than transience, alias time-stability, most notably dynamicity and dependency, not only exhibit statistical correlations with copula usage that equal, and in many cases even exceed the predictive power of the transience parameter. What is more, the latter parameters can be integrated into a joint approach to copularization that rests crucially on Croft's markedness theory as elegantly as the transience parameter. These findings entail the hypothesis that copula distribution in a given language is best motivated in terms of the dominant semantic parameter, that is, in terms of the parameter that yields the highest number of correct predictions of copula use for the language in question. Whether this is really the most convincing theoretical model of copularization, however, remains an open question. As stated above, the Achilles heel of the dominant parameter model is the observation that in none of the ten sampled languages did any of the four semantic parameters discussed in this chapter yield predictions of copula use that reach the 100 per cent mark. There always remains a small residue of counterexamples. In the next chapter, an alternative semantic model will be proposed which combines all four parameters which, according to the investigations conducted above, can be claimed to correlate with the structural criterion of presence *vs.* absence of copulas. A decisive advantage of this multi-factor model of copularization lies in the fact that it is capable of explaining away such inconvenient counterexamples as well.

4 The Multi-factor Model of Copularization

4.1. The limited predictive power of semantics

As Chapter 2 has shown, there are often striking similarities in the organization of the lexicon of genetically unrelated languages with respect to the distribution of copularizing *vs.* non-copularizing items. Obviously, certain distributional patterns are favored across languages. Although the cut-off point between copularizing and non-copularizing lexemes may be located anywhere in the scale NOMINALS > ADJECTIVALS > VERBALS, as the discussion in §2.3.4 suggests, even within these semantic macro-classes, cut-off points that more or less coincide with the segmentation of the lexicon imposed by these semantic macro-classes are preferred, as revealed in table 4.1, which is a simplified version of table 2.5.

The majority of the languages contained in the global sample belong to either one of the types AN or AV, in which the semantic macro-classes of nominals, verbals, and adjectivals each contain either copularizing or non-copularizing lexemes only, rather than a mixture of both lexeme types, as is the case in split-A and split-V languages. The percentage of AN-languages and AV-languages in the overall sample, when calculated under exclusion of languages that do not employ copulas at all, that is under exclusion of the non-copularizing language type, is extremely high: together, AN- and AV-languages constitute 90.1 per cent of the sampled languages which have copulas. This crucial issue, which should be accounted for in a general theory of copularization, will be dealt with in greater detail in §4.5. At this point, it can only be hypothesized that the prevalence of the types AN and AV in the cross-linguistic sample hints at the possibility that there

TABLE **4.1.** *Typology of copularization patterns: quantitative distribution in the sample*

	Number of occurrences	%
non-copularizing	41	31.5
split-N	0	0.0
AV	27	20.8
split-A	6	4.6
AN	54	41.2
split-V	1	0.8
fully copularizing	2	1.5

is some fundamental cognitive salience to the traditional division of the lexicon into the semantic macro-classes of nominals, verbals, and adjectivals.

The semantic approach to copularization developed in Chapter 3 reveals that the parameters dynamicity, transience, transitivity, and dependency each produce highly accurate predictions of copula usage. However, these predictions never reach the 100 per cent mark. This, of course, does not mean that the hypothesis of the semantic motivation of copularization must be rejected, since any non-random statistical correlation between two variables indicates that there is an inter-dependence between these variables—and the statistical correlations between each of the semantic parameters and copula usage given in table 3.24 are clearly non-random. Moreover, the observation that the correlations display the same directionality in all languages investigated adds some additional force to the assumption that copularization is sensitive to semantic factors. The [+] values of the four features always correspond to absence of copulas, while the [−] values correspond to presence of copulas. The most important argument in favor of the hypothesis of the semantic motivation of copularization, however, is that all four parameters correlate positively, and in a statistically significant way, with copula usage in all sampled languages, despite their genetic diversity.

Thus, there is good reason for considering dynamicity, transience, transitivity, and dependency the universal semantic primitives underlying copularization. One of the major objectives of this chapter is providing an explanation for the existence of counterexamples to the overall statistical correlations which decrease the predictive power of the four semantic parameters dynamicity, transience, transitivity, and dependency. Before this issue will be dealt with in detail in §4.5, however, a closer look will be taken at diachronic developments which may change the distributional scope of copulas in the lexicon, and which might, at least to some extent, be held responsible for the fact that the four semantic parameters fail to produce entirely accurate predictions of copula use.

4.2. Migration of copulas in the lexicon

At least as rewarding as the question about the historical origin of copulas, which has been addressed in §2.3.3, is the question about the subsequent development of linguistic items, once they have acquired the status of copulas. The behavior of a specific set of copulas in several Romance languages, which can be traced back to the Latin verb *stare* 'to stand', is a case in point. According to Hengeveld (1992: 245), *stare* first evolved into a localizing predicator of a very general meaning, and then spread across the domain of adjectival predication. This developmental stage is documented by today's representation of *stare* in Spanish, the copula *estar*. *Estar* can be used as a localizing predicator, or as a copula, but only with adjectivals, not with nominals. This situation also holds in Modern Catalan and Galician. In Judeo-Spanish, this stage of expansion into the adjectival domain has

TABLE 4.2. *Distribution of copular verbs derived from Latin* stare *'to stand' in the lexicon of five languages (adapted from Hengeveld 1992: 245)*

	ADJECTIVALS	NOMINALS
Judeo-Spanish	−	−
Catalan	+	−
Spanish	+	−
Galician	+	−
Portuguese	+	+

never been reached. In Portuguese, however, today's representation of *stare* combines with both nominal and adjectival predicates. Table 4.2 summarizes these findings. Thus, copulas seem capable of migrating in the lexicon, that is to say of taking over different parts of speech in the course of time.

An analogous process of copulas entering a new lexical domain has taken place in Basque. In Basque, all nominals and adjectivals, and all verbals with the exception of about three dozen, employ the same periphrastic construction that is built on the copular verbs *izan* 'to be' and *ukan* 'to have' in all categories of predicate inflection. Intransitive predicates are formed with *izan* 'to be'; with transitive predicates, the verb *ukan* 'to have' is used.[1] Copularizing predicate types with nominal, adjectival, and verbal nuclei are presented in examples 2.179 to 2.181, which are repeated below for convenience.

4.1. hura   gizon-a   d-a
      3SG.ABS   man-SG.ABS   3ABS-PRS.COP
      'he is a man' (Saltarelli 1988: 150)

4.2. mutil-a   haundi-a   d-a
      boy-SG.ABS   big-SG.ABS   3ABS-COP.PRS
      'the boy is big' (Saltarelli 1988: 150)

4.3. bi   ordu   barru   itzuli-ko   n-a-iz
      two   hour   inside   return-FUT   1SG.ABS-PRS-COP
      'I will return in two hours' (Saltarelli 1988: 191)

However, there are some relics left of an older, so-called synthetic inflection, which attaches person, number and tense/aspect/mood affixes directly to the predicate nucleus. Synthetic inflection is limited to a few dozen verbals only, including the copulas *izan* and *ukan*, and does not occur with nominals and adjectivals. The majority of the thirty-nine synthetically inflecting verbals listed

---

[1] Some scholars analyze *izan* and *ukan* as forming a single paradigm. With certain lexemes, the localizing verb *egon* 'to be at' assumes copular function (M. Bauer, p.c.).

by Bouda (1933) are transitive. However, synthetically inflecting verbals are not incompatible with periphrastic paradigms. For one, like periphrastically inflecting verbals, synthetically inflecting verbals regularly employ auxiliaries in the formation of certain tense/aspect/mood categories. Further, according to Campión (1884: 323), there is no synthetically inflecting lexeme in Basque that does not possess an alternate periphrastic form for each synthetically formed tense/aspect/mood category, except *izan* and *ukan* themselves, of course. However, the meaning of synthetically formed tense/aspect/mood categories differs somewhat from that of their periphrastic counterparts. The synthetic present expresses the semantically unmarked present (see example 2.182, which is reproduced below), whereas the periphrastic present, whose base is formed by adding the imperfective suffix *-t(z)en* to the root (see example 4.5), has a habitual connotation (Umandi 1976: 38).

4.4. laku-ra   n-oa
      lake-ALL   1SG.ABS-PRS.go
      'I am going to the lake' (Saltarelli 1988: 22)

4.5. laku-ra   joa-ten   n-a-iz
      lake-ALL   go-IPF   1SG.ABS-PRS-COP
      'I usually go to the lake' (author's field data)

The distinction of synthetically *vs.* periphrastically inflecting verbals is subject to some dialectal variation in that verbals which are inflected synthetically in one dialect may be inflected periphrastically in another (M. Bauer, p.c.).

In the past, the number of synthetically inflecting lexemes was higher. The decline of the synthetic inflection has been observed since the earliest documentation of Basque, which dates back to the sixteenth century. It is due to the extreme categorial complexity of predicate inflection in Basque:

El verbo ... es la gloria y el orgullo de la lengua bascongada ... se ... representa como un edificio de colosales dimensiones, levantando sobre anchos y resistentes cimientos. Si atendemos a la abundancia y a la solidez de los materiales, calificámoslo de labor de cíclopes; pero en dirigiendo los ojos a las esbeltas torrecillas y afiligranadas agujas, lo debemos calificar de labor de hadas.

(Campión 1884: 307)

[The verb ... is the glory and pride of the Basque language ... it presents itself as a building of colossal dimensions, rising above broad and solid foundations. If we look at the abundance and firmness of the materials we declare it the work of cyclops; but in directing our eyes at the slender turrets and filigree spires, we have to declare it the work of fairies.]

This inflectional system had apparently grown too glorious and proud to be an economical means of communication. Consequently, it was replaced with the periphrastic inflection (Tovar 1957: 94), for which only two synthetic paradigms, namely those of *izan* and *ukan*, had to be mastered. Thus, it can be hypothesized that copularization might have been in use for nominal and adjectival predicates only at an earlier stage, but finally invaded the domain of verbal predication as the result of the pressure of cognitive economy.

Further evidence in favor of the assumption that a given etymological root may acquire the ability to copularize in the course of time comes from the behavior of certain etymological cognates in Indo-European languages. For instance, the English adjective *tacit* and the French verb *se taire* 'to be silent' both derive from the Latin verb *tacēre* 'to be silent'. The verb *tacēre* 'to be silent' coexisted with the adjective *tacitus* 'silent' in Latin; *tacitus* 'silent' is a participial form of *tacēre* 'to be silent', which had grammaticalized into an adjective. The verbal form *tacēre* survives in the French verb *se taire*. In contrast, the English adjective *tacit* is based on the adjectival form *tacitus*. French does not have an adjectival equivalent of the Latin adjective *tacitus*, while English does not have a verbal equivalent of Latin verb *tacēre*. Thus, different members of the Latin verbal-adjectival minimal pair *tacēre* 'to be silent' vs. *tacitus* 'silent' have been adopted by the modern languages English and French. As a consequence, the realizations of the common etymological root differ with respect to copula usage: *tacit* copularizes, while *se taire* does not. Thus, lexical minimal pairs carry with them the potential for lexical recategorization through loss of one of its members in diachronic change. It is not being claimed here that French *se taire* and English *tacit* are semantically equivalent—the semantic overlap between Latin *tacēre* and *tacitus* is, if the available lexical glosses can be trusted, much more pronounced. However, the diachronic mechanisms which are documented by the above examples may well result in lexical recategorization proper, that is in constellations in which the semantic content of the lexemes involved remains constant through time, but in which parts-of-speech class status changes.

A slightly different situation holds with respect to the development of the lexical root represented by the Latin verb *ardēre* 'to burn, glow, sparkle' in the daughter languages French and Spanish. In Modern Spanish, both the verb *arder* 'to burn, glow, blaze, shine, flash', and the adjective *ardiente* 'burning, glowing, shining, blazing', which derives from a participial form, are in use. In French, on the other hand, the verbal form is missing; only the adjectival form *ardent* 'burning, glowing, blazing, fiery', which is based on an Old French participle, has survived. Thus, one could argue that the Latin verb *ardēre* 'to burn, glow, sparkle' has been recategorized into an adjective in French. Spanish, which has retained both the verbal as well as the adjectival form, can be interpreted as representing the diachronic link between the synchronic states encountered in Latin and French.

In English, a different mechanism of lexical innovation has created various verbal-adjectival minimal pairs. Adjectives of the type represented by *aglow* or *asleep* derive from locative constructions formed by means of the preposition *at*. Such adjectives now exist side by side with etymologically corresponding verbs, such as *to glow* and *to sleep*. If a language in which such lexical innovation has taken place eliminates the older forms—in this case, the verbal forms *to glow* and *to sleep*—from its vocabulary, the recategorization cycle is complete.

At least in Indo-European languages, participles constitute a rich diachronic source for copularizing lexemes which can be classed as adjectivals in semantic terms. Homonymies between auxiliaries which accompany participles in predicate position and copulas presumably facilitate the rise of such neologisms. As participles grammaticalize into morphosyntactic adjectives, the auxiliary is gradually reanalyzed as a copula. The English forms *astonished*, *scared*, and *worried*, among many others, are currently undergoing the transition from participle to adjective. These three forms have already acquired some adjectival characteristics, such as compatibility with the modifier *very* (B. Comrie, p.c.). True participles, on the other hand, cannot be combined with *very*. For instance, the syntactic configuration **very seen* is not acceptable. Moreover, copula acquisition via participles may produce discrepancies in the parts-of-speech class membership of semantically equivalent lexemes in genetically related languages. The English adjective *ashamed* and its semantic and etymological equivalent in German, the verb *sich schämen*, provide an example of such a lexeme pair.

On the basis of the comparative data from Indo-European it can be hypothesized that individual lexemes may be recategorized with respect to copula usage as languages drift apart in their evolution, and that copulas, as a consequence, may 'migrate' in the lexicon. Such shifts, which are safely attested for Romance languages and Basque, may well have some bearing on the fact that the statistical correlations between the semantic parameters dynamicity, transience, transitivity, and dependency on the one hand, and copula usage on the other, are always high but never perfect. It must be kept in mind that any diachronic change which turns a copularizing lexeme into a non-copularizing lexeme, or vice versa, has an impact on the statistical correlations holding between the four semantic features and copula usage. If a correlation between a given feature and copula usage is perfect at the outset, that is if it reaches the 100 per cent mark, any diachronic change that interferes with this correlation will decrease its statistical value. Thus, if perfect statistical correspondences between semantic features and copula usage should ever exist, they are inevitably destroyed by the migration of copulas in the lexicon. On assuming further that copula migration takes place in any one language, it comes as no surprise that the statistical correlations summarized in table 4.1 (p. 153) are never perfect. This observation potentially explains the existence of counterexamples to the otherwise quite pronounced correlations of copula use with any of the four semantic parameters. However, the language data compiled in this study also invite an alternative, more comprehensive analysis, which circumvents the problems created by the existence of counterexamples.

4.3. Combining the parameters

The division of the lexicon of individual languages into a copularizing and a non-copularizing part can be considered an instance of CATEGORIZATION by means of the grammatical feature of compatibility *vs.* non-compatibility with copulas. This structure-based categorial dichotomy can, unfortunately, not be linked to a corresponding distinction at the semantic level, as the results of the statistical analyses carried out in §3.4 reveal. Although the semantic parameters dynamicity, transience, transitivity, and dependency predict the occurrence of copulas to a considerable extent, none of the parameters ever reaches the point of a perfect statistical convergence with copula use.

But difficulties in defining linguistic categories in semantic terms have become all too familiar from the more practically oriented linguistic enterprises such as lexicography. It is, in many cases, impossible to provide a fixed set of necessary and sufficient defining criteria for a given lexeme that applies to all real-world denotata for which the lexeme can be used. There are, of course, categories for which clear-cut definitions do exist, such as the categories 'odd number' and 'even number' (Armstrong, Gleitman, and Gleitman 1983). However, over the past few decades, research into human categorization has identified a great number of natural categories which defy such simple feature list definitions.

The main result of the global survey discussed in §2.3 is that in all languages which make use of copulas, copula distribution can be described in terms of the implicational scale NOMINALS > ADJECTIVALS > VERBALS: in any one language, adjectivals may behave either like nominals or like verbals with respect to copularization, but nominals and verbals never display uniform behavior which contrasts with the behavior of adjectivals. Further, it is argued in §3.4.3, that each of the four semantic parameters—dynamicity, transience, transitivity, and dependency—partitions the lexicon in a way that matches the 'cuts' imposed by the scale NOMINALS > ADJECTIVALS > VERBALS. Thus, the scale NOMINALS > ADJECTIVALS > VERBALS and the semantic parameter model are, in principle, compatible with each other. As a consequence, the question of how these two explanatory models relate to each other in detail must be raised. It can be hypothesized at this point that the semantic parameters uncovered by means of the minimal pair method, rather than the scale NOMINALS > ADJECTIVALS > VERBALS, are the actual regulators of copula distribution. But if the semantic parameter model is taken as the underlying motivation for copula usage, and the scale NOMINALS > ADJECTIVALS > VERBALS is replaced with the latter, there is a price to pay: an apparently universal, unifying formula that is valid for any one language must be given up in favor of four competing explanatory models. The typology introduced in §3.4.3 classifies languages according to the semantic feature that shows the highest statistical correlation with copula distribution. Within such a model, only one feature, that is the statistically dominant feature, determines copula usage in a given language. Thus, the scale NOMINALS > ADJECTIVALS > VERBALS could be dismissed as a mere theoretical construct that has no explanatory value of its own. In this view, the explanatory efficiency of this scale is due to the fact that incidentally, it partitions the lexicon the same way as the four semantic parameters, the true regulators of copula distribution, do. However, the question remains whether this convergence is really coincidental, or rather, conditioned by the fact that dynamicity, transience, transitivity, and dependency are not only the deeper principles governing the phenomenon of copularization, but constitute the defining criteria for the basic semantic macro-categories of nominals, verbals, and adjectivals as well. This issue will be addressed in greater detail towards the end of this chapter. For now, it suffices to state that since all four semantic features, in any one of the sampled languages, correlate strongly with copula use, an analytical option should be tested that has not been considered so far: integrating all four parameters in a combined semantic model.

The multi-factor model requires full specification of each lexical entry contained in the individual language samples described in §3.4 in terms of the four features dynamicity, transience, transitivity, and dependency. For instance, for the Indonesian adjectival *kecil* 'small' the following feature profile can be established:

4.6. *kecil* 'small'   [−dynamic]   [+/−transient]   [−transitive]   [+dependent]

However, conflating the four parameters in a unified model makes a modified treatment of the parameters of transitivity and dependency necessary. As Croft (1991: 62f.) points out, these two semantic dimensions represent a single semantic parameter, that of valence. In Croft's model, transitive lexemes receive the feature value 2, which symbolizes two obligatory arguments; intransitive lexemes are, analogously, ascribed the feature value 1. Lexemes which are classed as [−dependent] receive the feature value 0. Thus, the erstwhile separate parameters dependency and transitivity are united to form a single descriptive dimension, which will hitherto be referred to as VALENCE. The feature profile of the Indonesian adjectival *kecil* 'small' must therefore be revised:

4.7. *kecil* 'small'   [−dynamic]   [+/−transient]   [1 valence]

The triple-parameter model yields twenty-seven logically possible combinations of feature values, which are summarized in table 4.3.

It is interesting to note that not all of the logically possible combinations of feature values, or feature profiles, occur in the ten language samples investigated with approximately equal statistical frequency. On the contrary, the sizes of the lexical classes defined by each feature profile differ drastically. Some classes may comprise over 100 or even over 200 members within a given language sample, others just about a dozen or even fewer members, and some classes are completely absent in the samples. The classes which are attested in the ten-language sample are listed in table 4.4, together with examples of the concepts

TABLE 4.3. *Valence, transience, and dynamicity: logically possible combinations of feature values*

VALENCE	TRANSIENCE	DYNAMICITY
0	−	−
0	−	+/−
0	+/−	+/−
0	+/−	−
0	−	+
0	+	+
0	+	−
0	+	+/−
0	+/−	+
1	−	−
1	−	+/−
1	+/−	+/−
1	+/−	−
1	−	+
1	+	+
1	+	−
1	+	+/−
1	+/−	+
2	−	−
2	−	+/−
2	+/−	+/−
2	+/−	−
2	−	+
2	+	+
2	+	−
2	+	+/−
2	+/−	+

they represent. For further analytical purposes which will be made explicit in what follows, each class is specified by a letter in the leftmost column.

It has to be pointed out that in many, but not all, cases, the above classification produces lexical classes that conform to conceptually natural, intuition-based, semantic classes. In classes B (body features; adjectivals denoting nationality ('French'), personality features ('smart'), body features ('color-blind'), relational nouns including body parts and terms of relationship, age adjectivals denoting permanent membership in age group ('old')) and D (prototypical adjectivals ('big', 'good', 'red'), positionals ('to sit', 'to stand') and other statives ('to stink')), concepts are grouped together that may not be felt to be sufficiently similar semantically to warrant such treatment. In class B, for instance, adjectivals like

TABLE 4.4. *Semantic classes attested in the 10-language sample*

Class	VALENCE	TRANSIENCE	DYNAMICITY	Examples
A	0	−	−	prototypical nominals ('house', 'dog'); nominals designating sex ('woman'); age nominals denoting permanent membership in age group ('old man'); nominals referring to bodily or mental disposition ('glutton', 'genius')
B	1	−	−	body features; adjectivals denoting nationality ('French'); personality features ('smart'); body features ('color-blind'); relational nouns including body parts and terms of relationship; age adjectivals denoting permanent membership in age group ('old')
C	0	+/−	−	occupations/professions ('teacher'); nominals for shape ('triangle')
D	1	+/−	−	prototypical adjectivals ('big', 'good', 'red'); positionals ('to sit', 'to stand') and other statives ('to stink')
E	1	+/−	+/−	'to get up/to stand' (represented by a single lexeme)
F	1	+/−	+	'to flow'; 'to glitter'
G	2	+/−	−	emotional/mental acts or states ('to love', 'to know'); concepts denoting possession ('to have'); concepts denoting resemblance ('to resemble')
H	2	+/−	+/−	'to cover' (temporarily or permanently)
I	2	+/−	+	'to understand'
J	0	+	−	'to be chilly' (weather)
K	0	+	+	meteorological events ('to rain')
L	1	+	−	bodily/mental states ('tired', 'angry')
M	1	+	+/−	'to recover/to be well' (represented by a single lexeme)
N	1	+	+	prototypical intransitive verbals ('to go')
O	2	+	−	transitive transient non-dynamic events ('to hold')
P	2	+	+/−	'to carry/to wear' (represented by a single lexeme)
Q	2	+	+	prototypical transitive verbals ('to buy')

personality features and body features appear together with relational nouns. In class D, prototypical adjectivals are grouped with positionals. However, it should be kept in mind that the primary goal of the research presented here is testing the suitability of the semantic parameters which have been uncovered inductively via the minimal pair method as building blocks of a general theory of copularization, rather than developing a classification of the lexicon that is in line with 'natural' semantic classifications in any case. The intuition that the adjectivals contained in classes B and D are conceptually distinct from the relational nouns and positionals which share their lexical class membership may stem from the fact that typical adjectivals on the one hand, and relational nouns and positionals on the other, differ with regard to a specific semantic parameter which has not been included in the set of classificatory parameters. The semantic parameter in question is gradability (Croft 1991: 65). In principle, the multi-factor model potentially accommodates any semantic parameter that produces significant statistical correlations with copula use; any such parameter can be added to the list of semantic dimensions upon which the overall classification of the lexicon is based. The sole reason for not including gradability in the set of semantic parameters which participate in the definition of semantic classes is that the minimal pair method, at least in the sampled languages, has failed to identify gradability as a parameter which is operative in distinguishing copularizing from non-copularizing lexemes. It should also be remembered that if a semantic parameter functions to distinguish 'natural' semantic classes, this does not automatically imply that it plays a decisive role in the categorization processes that bring about a division of the lexicon into two structural classes on the basis of compatibility *vs.* non-compatibility with copulas.

In appendix E, the relevant distributional figures for the languages investigated are presented. Only those lexical classes for which actual class members are found in the language samples are listed. A comparison of these frequency tables shows that the sizes of the individual classes remain relatively constant across the sampled languages. Across the sampled languages, the statistically dominant feature profiles are A (prototypical nominals ('house', 'dog'), nominals designating sex ('woman'), age nominals denoting permanent membership in age group ('old man'), nominals referring to bodily or mental disposition ('glutton', 'genius')); D (prototypical adjectivals ('big', 'good', 'red'), positionals ('to sit', 'to stand') and other statives ('to stink')); N (prototypical intransitive verbals ('to go')); and Q (prototypical transitive verbals ('to buy')). In some of the language-specific samples, class B (body features, adjectivals denoting nationality ('French'), personality features ('smart'), body features ('color-blind'), relational nouns including body parts and terms of relationship, age adjectivals denoting permanent membership in age group ('old')) is, approximately, in the same frequency range as classes N and Q. Moreover, the four focal feature profiles A, D, N, and Q happen to coincide with the semantic profiles of the lexical macro-classes of nominals, adjectivals, and verbals. These three macro-classes, further, define the prototypical semantic profiles of the traditional parts of speech noun, adjective, and verb. Nominals, or entity concepts, can be characterized by the feature profile [0 valence]/[−transient]/[−dynamic]. Verbals, or event concepts, on the other hand, can either be classed as [1 valence]/[+transient]/[+dynamic], or as [2 valence]/[+transient]/[+dynamic], depending on whether they are transitive or intransitive. Many adjectivals, or property concepts, can be characterized by the formula [1 valence]/[+/−transient]/[−dynamic].

Skeptical readers might feel tempted to object that the clustering of lexemes in particular areas in semantic space might be an artifact of the specific lexical samples compiled on the basis of the English questionnaire reproduced in appendix D. This possibility, however, can be ruled out for a variety of reasons. First, it is not the case that the semantic feature profile of a given lexeme A in language X is always identical to the feature profile of a semantically equivalent lexeme B in language Y. Still, it might be argued that in cases in which the semantic profiles of translational equivalents are, in fact, identical, the native speakers consulted, in preparing the lexical samples, chose only those lexemes for inclusion in the respective samples which exhibit the greatest semantic similarity to the English test lexemes. But these lexemes can, of course, also be expected to be extremely similar to the English test lexemes with respect to their semantic feature profiles. Being able to make such choices in the compilation of the lexical sample, however, would require the existence of a wide range of near-synonyms in the vocabulary of a given language. More importantly, an effort was made to control for such unwanted bias in the structure of the samples by encouraging native speakers to provide several possible translations of each English test lexeme (see §3.2). And, in fact, on the basis of such instructions, especially for languages with large vocabularies such as Indonesian and Japanese, various alternative translations were obtained for a multitude of English test lexemes.

4.4. The cognitive basis: prototypes

In response to the well-known fact that in too many cases, attempts at establishing features that are singly necessary and jointly sufficient for defining a category are unsuccessful, a theoretical approach to categorization has been devised which rejects the Platonic view that categories can be defined by means of fixed sets of necessary and sufficient features. Instead, categories are conceived of as organized around prototypes. This idea originates with Wittgenstein and was fully developed by Rosch and associates (e.g. Rosch 1973a, Rosch 1973b, Rosch 1975a, Rosch 1975b, Rosch 1978, Rosch and Mervis 1975, Rosch *et al.* 1976). Although prototype theory has never been without its critics, its impact on scientific thinking in general has been tremendous. Prototype theory crystallizes around several types of psychological experiments which indicate that certain category members are treated differently than others. Those category members that coincide with categorial prototypes tend to be learned and processed faster, rated as better examples of the category, named more often as examples of the category, and so on. Such prototype effects can be traced back to the fact that in the absence of necessary and sufficient features, category boundaries cannot be clearly defined; they are fuzzy. Thus, membership in a category can be graded: some items included in a category are more focal representatives of the category than others. Evidence for the presence of graded category structure is not only to be found at the psychological level, but at various levels of linguistic description as well. For instance, metaphor and hedges (Lakoff 1973, Lakoff 1987, Lakoff and Johnson 1980, Lakoff and Johnson 1999) are quite thoroughly studied phenomena that support prototype theory. Bybee and Moder (1983) track down prototype structures at the phonology/morphology interface. In addition, particularly in typologically oriented work, numerous applications of prototype theory can be found. Examples include the prototype approach to transitivity proposed by Keenan's (1976) investigation of the universal properties of subjects, Hopper and Thompson in 1980 and Shibatani's (1985) prototype analysis of the category of passive.

Although within prototype models, individual features are not treated as singly necessary and jointly sufficient for defining a category, this does not imply that feature-based descriptions can be dismissed as unnecessary. On the contrary: it is widely assumed in contemporary cognitive science that human categorization essentially operates in the basis of feature ascription. Thus, the mental representations of categories are generally thought to be atomistic, that is, decomposable into features. Unfortunately, decades of research into categorization in the field of cognitive science culminate in the insight that 'it is not notably easier to find the prototypic features of a concept than to find the necessary and sufficient ones' (Armstrong, Gleitman, and Gleitman 1983: 272).

Identifying semantic features that can be used as building blocks of a theoretical approach to the phenomenon of the categorization of the lexicon via copula use is not an issue here; by means of the minimal pair method, semantic parameters which undeniably correlate with copula use have already been inductively extracted from an extensive data corpus.

Investigating language-specific lexical samples with respect to the size of the lexical classes which can be established on the basis of the parameters valence, transience, and dynamicity (see table 4.3) yields statistical figures that bear out one of the most important aspects of Rosch's prototype theory. Rosch predicts the occurrence of the very same discrepancies in class size which characterize the composition of the lexical samples discussed in §4.3. Such CLUSTERING EFFECTS are an essential component of the original versions of prototype theory, whose proponents assume that there is an imbalance between the statistical frequencies of certain combinations of features within natural scts of items and other combinations in that some feature combinations are significantly more widespread than others, sometimes to the point at which some logically possible feature combinations are not documented in the universe perceived by human beings (Mervis and Rosch 1981, Rosch *et al.* 1976). The most frequently occurring feature clusters can be equated with categorial prototypes. Mervis and Rosch (1981: 91f.) use the following example to illustrate this hypothesis:

...consider some of the qualities ordinarily treated as attributes in classifying animals: 'coat' (fur, feathers), 'oral opening' (mouth, beak), and 'primary mode of locokinesis' (flying, on foot). If animals were created according to the total set model, then there would be eight different types:

(a) those with fur and mouths, which move about primarily on foot;
(b) those with fur and mouths, which move about primarily by flying;
(c) those with fur and beaks, which move about primarily on foot;
(d) those with fur and beaks, which move about primarily by flying;
(e) those with feathers and mouths, which move about primarily on foot;
(f) those with feathers and mouths, which move about primarily by flying;
(g) those with feathers and beaks, which move about primarily on foot;
(h) those with feathers and beaks, which move about primarily by flying.

...any of the several schemes... would be equally plausible... Thus, given the total set type of categorization, it makes sense that the category assignments should be originally arbitrary. However, it hardly requires research to demonstrate that the perceived world of objects is *not* structured in this manner. Just two of the eight theoretically possible combinations of attribute values, types *a* and *h* (mammals and birds, respectively), comprise the great majority of existent species in the world that are possible based on this total set.

Types other than *a* and *h* also occur, but they are much less frequent. For instance, type *b* is represented by bats, type *g* by ostriches and other birds that are not capable of flying. In Rosch's terminology, the special composition of natural sets of items which results from the occurrence of clustering effects is referred to as CORRELATIONAL STRUCTURE (e.g. Rosch *et al.* 1976: 428; Rosch 1978: 37). Basically, Rosch's claim is that the universe of objects *per se* displays a prototype structure based on statistical frequency. If human categorization reflects this hypothetical innate structure of the perceived world, human categorization is, of necessity, organized around prototypes:

Rosch's original account of the theory was that the world is structured in such a way that the similarity space in which we define our categories falls directly out of the stimulus structure. Now the kind of qualities that end up as concept attributes involve a number of dimensions: physical appearance obviously, but also origin, constitution, common location, function or use, and behavior. The Roschian hypothesis... is that we start off with a particular set of sensory processors, and a particular set of needs and goals. We therefore categorize the world along a number of basic, 'elemental' dimensions... Starting with these attributes, the mind then performs some kind of quasi-statistical cluster analysis— grouping things together to maximize similarity within groups and minimize similarity between groups. The result is a basic level of categorization, and seems to characterize the understanding of preschoolers with some success.

(Hampton 1993: 86)

Systems of categorization should exhibit a high degree of cognitive economy in order to be effective (e.g. Barsalou and Hale 1993). The fact that categorization by means of prototypes meets this requirement lends additional support to the assumption that human categorization does in fact make use of prototypes. In particular, a maximally effective system of categorization should be capable of processing as many real-world items as possible by means of a minimal set of categories. A system of categorization based on feature clustering, or the statistical convergence of specific features, significantly reduces the cognitive effort that goes into categorization processes:

...prototype models need only track the frequency of specific features and possibly the frequency of categories. Prototype models perform classification quickly, because they need not examine large numbers of exemplars but instead process compact prototypes. Learning is simple in prototype models. Instead of having to compute absolute rules, prototype models simply update frequency information and revise prototype composition using a simple threshold rule.

(Barsalou and Hale 1993: 118)

4.5. A scalar model of the lexicon

The multi-factor approach to copularization outlined in the preceding sections implies additional analytical possibilities. Cognitive approaches to categorization operating with feature analyses often use statistical methods which allow calculating the overall degree of similarity of the entities investigated, for instance, the similarity relations holding between members of a category (e.g. Tversky 1977, Hampton 1998). Some of these analytical methods rely on the representation of similarity relations in two- or three-dimensional space. A problem that multi-factor models using larger sets of features are confronted with when data representations in two-dimensional or three-dimensional space are desired is subsuming a multitude of quality dimensions in fewer dimensions. The statistical method of multidimensional scaling (Young 1987), which is widely used in anthropology, biology, cognitive psychology, commerce, physics, the social sciences, etc. makes such mathematical reductions of descriptive dimensions possible. Since the semantic model of the lexicon proposed in §4.3 comprises three quality dimensions only, i.e. the parameters valence, transience, and dynamicity, it is not necessary to resort to mathematical transformations by means of multidimensional scaling in order to depict the similarity relations holding between lexical classes in a three-dimensional space diagram.

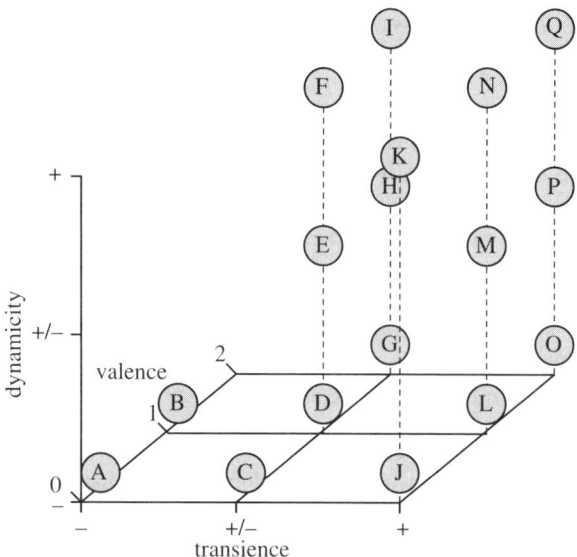

FIG. 4.1. *Semantic space as defined by the parameters of valence, transience, and dynamicity*

The arrangement of the lexical classes established by using the semantic parameters valence, transience, and dynamicity as defining criteria (see figure 4.1) in three-dimensional space is as follows. The horizontal axis and the vertical axis in figure 4.1 represent the parameters transience and dynamicity, respectively. Both of these axes comprise three positions: a position '−', a position '+/−', and a position '+'. The feature values for valence are entered in the axis pointing to the back in figure 4.1. For valence, there are the positions 0, 1, and 2, representing the number of arguments required by the lexeme type to which a location in semantic space is to be assigned.

The location of a given lexical class in semantic space is defined by its coordinates in the three axes, which converge in a specific point in three-dimensional space. Figure 4.1 depicts the position of all the semantic classes attested in the sampled languages, which are listed in table 4.4 (p. 162).

Graphic representation of similarity relations holding between individual lexical classes yields surprising results. Once again, it has to be emphasized that only those lexical classes which are represented by at least one lexical item in at least one of the language samples have been included in figure 4.1. The most startling property of the spatial structure which emerges in figure 4.1 is the fact that the focal classes A, D, N, and Q, which correspond to the semantic macro-classes of nominals, adjectivals, and intransitive and transitive verbals, respectively, are arranged in a sequence that parallels the scale NOMINALS > ADJECTIVALS > VERBALS, which describes the global distribution of copulas.

Class A comprises prototypical nominals ('house', 'dog'), nominals designating sex ('woman'), age nominals denoting permanent membership in age group ('old man'), nominals referring to bodily or mental disposition ('glutton', 'genius'); class D includes prototypical adjectivals ('big', 'good', 'red'), positionals ('to sit', 'to stand') and other statives ('to stink'); class N comprises prototypical intransitive verbals ('to go'), and class Q includes prototypical transitive verbals ('to buy'). The feature profiles [0 valence]/[−transient]/[−dynamic] and [2 valence]/[+transient]/[+dynamic], which mark the opposite ends of an im- aginary, somewhat twisted line connecting the focal classes A, D, N, and Q in figure 4.1, are those of prototypical nominals and transitive verbals, respectively. The feature profile [1 valence]/[+/−transient]/[−dynamic], which is, roughly, located in the middle of the line, characterizes prototypical adjectivals. Proto- typical intransitive verbals, which can be characterized by means of the feature profile [1 valence]/[+transient]/[+dynamic] are located at a point between transitive verbals and adjectivals in three-dimensional similarity space which is closer to transitive verbals than to adjectivals. Figure 4.2, which exclusively depicts the position of the focal classes A, D, N, and Q—alias nominals, adjectivals, and intransitive and transitive verbals—, illustrates this.

   In §2.3 it has been argued that regarding the structural feature of copula use, members of the semantic classes of nominals, adjectivals, and verbals, alias object, property, and event concepts, which represent the semantic cores

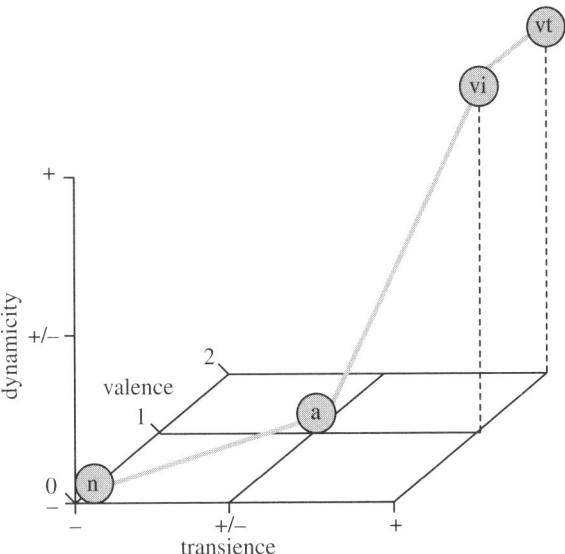

n = nominals; a = adjectivals; vi = intransitive verbals; vt = transitive verbals

Fig. 4.2. *Nominals, adjectivals, and intransitive and transitive verbals in semantic space as defined by the parameters of valence, transience, and dynamicity*

of the traditional parts of speech noun, adjective, and verb, and which can be equated with the semantic classes A, D, and N/Q respectively, are treated uniformly in the overwhelming majority of the languages contained in the global sample. Thus, languages seem to avoid structural constellations which break these focal semantic classes up into distinct formal classes. As the discussion of putative cognitive principles underlying human categorization in §4.4 implies, treating especially focal, that is to say statistically large, lexical classes uniformly with respect to copula use (or any other structural feature) is cognitively advantageous because such categorization patterns are more economical with regard to information storage in the brain. Thus, the principle of cognitive economy, which has been used to motivate the general avoidance of the language types split-N, split-A, and split-V within the hypothetical mono-factor models of copularization introduced in §3.4.3, can be successfully applied within the multi-factor approach as well. Certain cut-off points in semantic space, which mark the borderline between the copularizing and the non-copularizing section in the lexicon of individual languages, are encountered more frequently than others. By and large, the more popular cut-off points are those that cut around, rather than across, those lexical classes which can, by virtue of the amount of class members they comprise, be considered focal and which are equivalent to the semantic macro-classes of nominals, verbals, and adjectivals.

In particular, in any of the ten sampled languages, all members of the classes A on the one hand, and N and Q on the other, show uniform behavior with respect to copularization: class A (prototypical nominals ('house', 'dog'), nominals designating sex ('woman'), age nominals denoting permanent membership in age group ('old man'), nominals referring to bodily or mental disposition ('glutton', 'genius')), always copularizes, while the two verbal classes N (prototypical intransitive verbals ('to go')), and Q (prototypical transitive verbals ('to buy')) never do. Figures 4.3 to 4.12, which represent the behavior of lexical classes in the individual languages, demonstrate this. A black rimmed box marks those lexical classes which copularize; a gray rimmed box subsumes the non-copularizing classes. The boxes overlap in areas in which those lexical classes are located which contain both copularizing and non-copularizing lexemes. In each diagram, the focal classes A (prototypical nominals ('house', 'dog'), nominals designating sex ('woman'), age nominals denoting permanent membership in age group ('old man'), nominals referring to bodily or mental disposition ('glutton', 'genius')); D (prototypical adjectivals ('big', 'good', 'red'), positionals ('to sit', 'to stand') and other statives ('to stink')), N (prototypical intransitive verbals ('to go')), and Q (prototypical transitive verbals ('to buy')) are set off by dark gray shading.

Class D (prototypical adjectivals ('big', 'good', 'red'); positionals ('to sit', 'to stand') and other statives ('to stink')) is mixed with respect to copularization in all sampled languages except Lakota and thus, at least at first glance, seems to refute the claim that focal classes always show uniform behavior. However, a

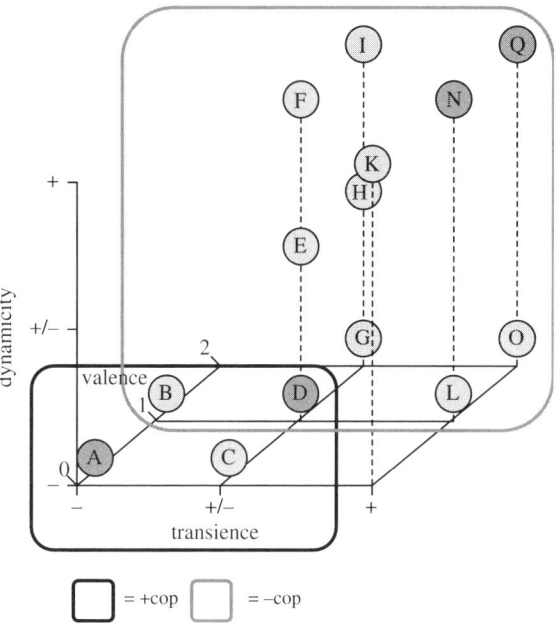

FIG. 4.3. *Burmese: lexical classes in semantic space*

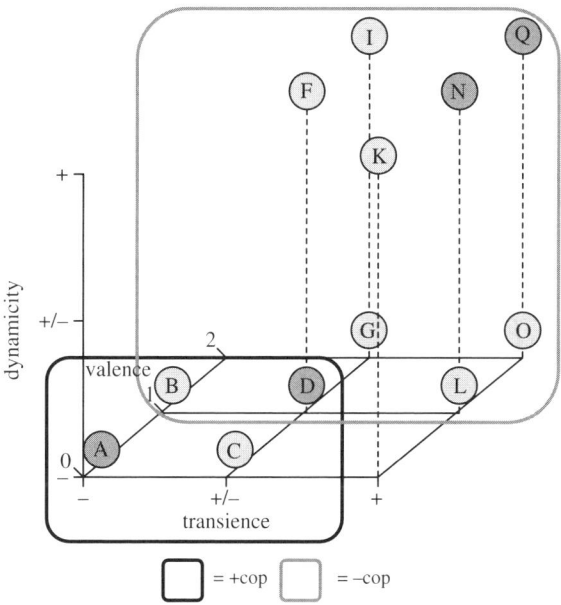

FIG. 4.4. *Cantonese: lexical classes in semantic space*

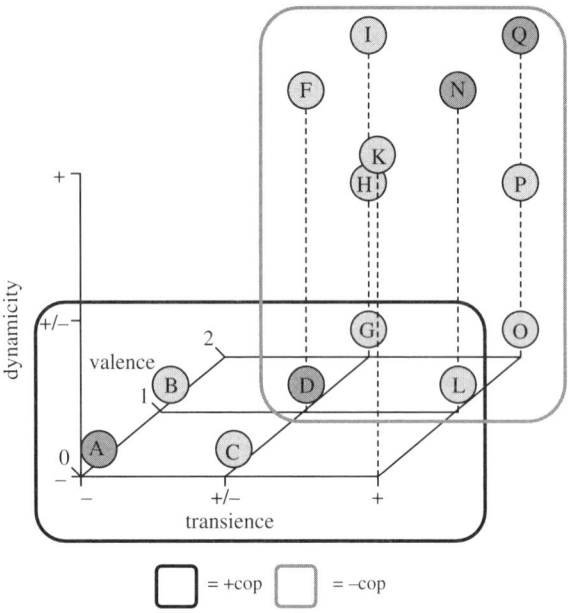

FIG. 4.5. *German: lexical classes in semantic space*

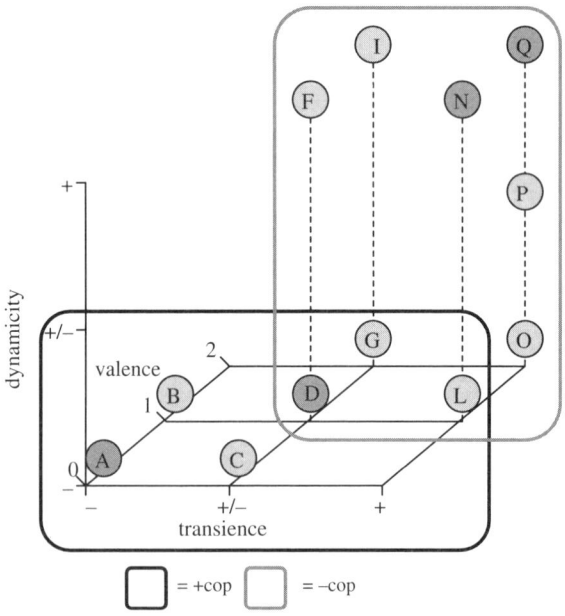

FIG. 4.6. *Hungarian: lexical classes in semantic space*

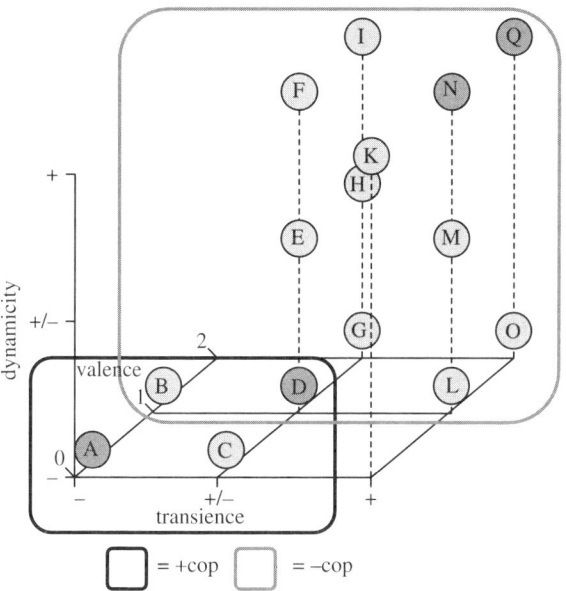

Fɪɢ. 4.7. *Indonesian: lexical classes in semantic space*

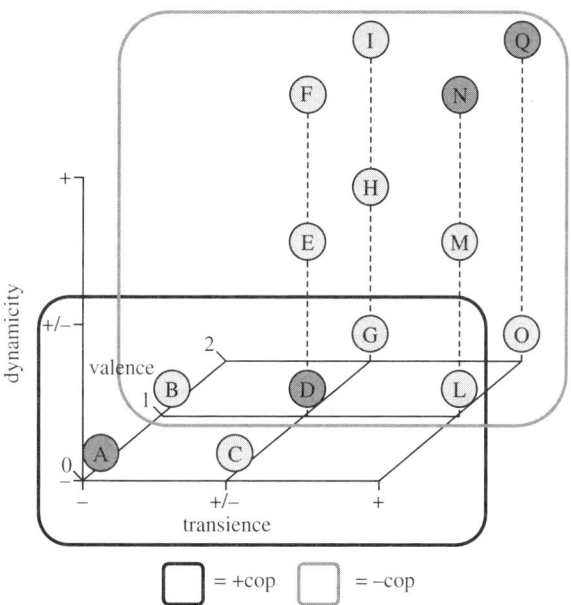

Fɪɢ. 4.8. *Japanese: lexical classes in semantic space*

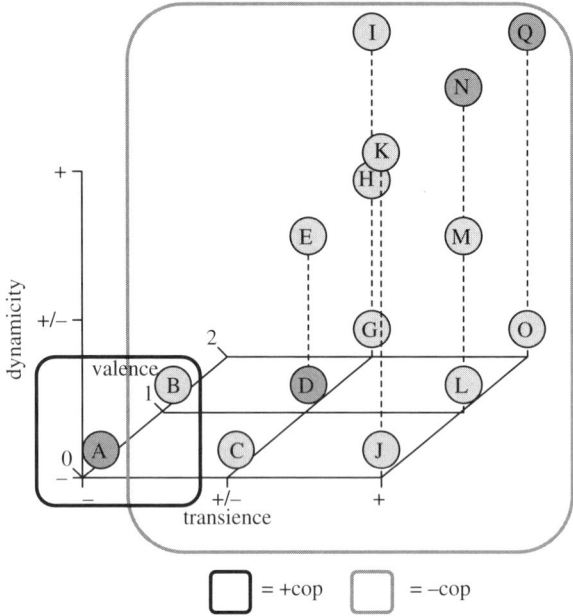

Fig. 4.9. *Lakota: lexical classes in semantic space*

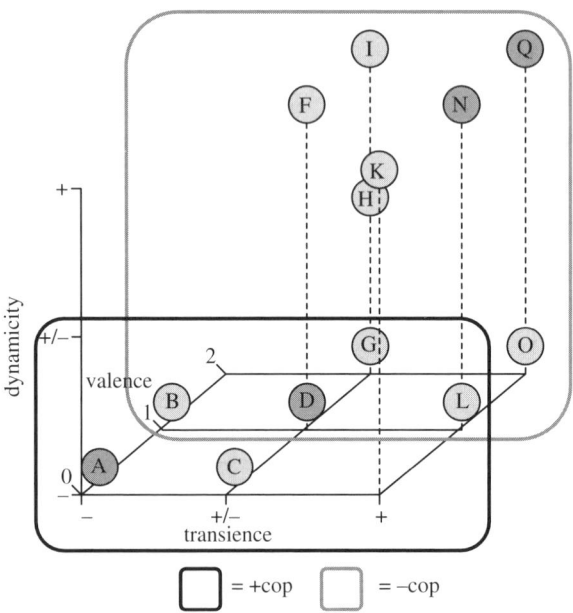

Fig. 4.10. *Swahili: lexical classes in semantic space*

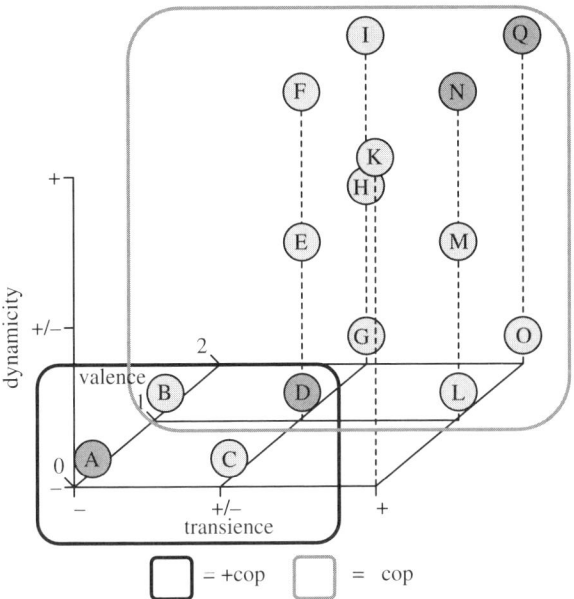

Fig. 4.11. *Thai: lexical classes in semantic space*

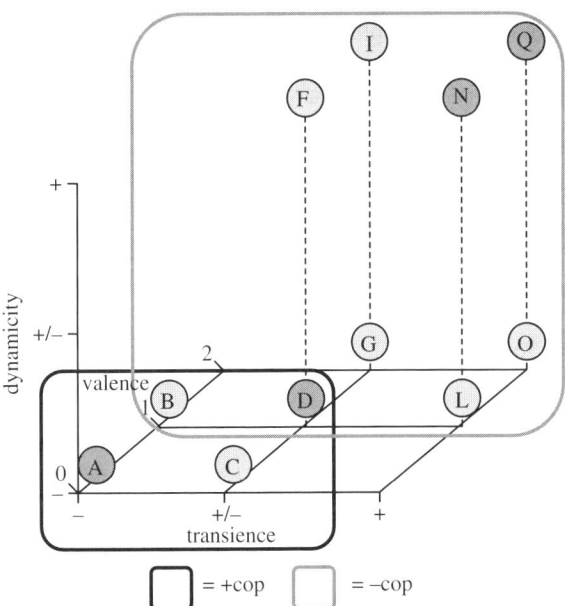

Fig. 4.12. *Turkish: lexical classes in semantic space*

TABLE 4.5. *Class D: copularizing* vs. *non-copularizing lexemes*

	Class D: +copula	Class D: −copula
Burmese	2	104
Cantonese	19	96
German	145	13
Hungarian	132	10
Indonesian	3	174
Japanese	95	97
Lakota	0	143
Swahili	94	14
Thai	21	125
Turkish	118	15

closer look at the exact distributional figures given in appendix E shows that in all languages except Japanese, the composition of the mixed adjectival class D is extremely unbalanced as to the contrast between copularizing and non-copularizing lexemes. Table 4.5 summarizes the statistical figures on class D.

In all cases, with the exception of Japanese, one structural type clearly prevails. If the majority of class members behave uniformly with respect to copularization, a general rule is applicable which states that the lexemes contained in class D either copularize, or do not copularize, depending on the behavior of the dominant structural type in a given language. Only for the small residue of class members that do not comply with this rule an additional rule that characterizes their behavior as idiosyncratic must be learned. In Japanese, however, class D cannot be treated this way. In Japanese, the amount of exceptions is approximately as large as the amount of lexemes which conform to a hypothetical copularization rule, since the ratio of copularizing vs. non-copularizing members is 95 : 97 in class D. Thus, even if a general copularization rule that accounts for the behavior of about 50 per cent of the members of class D is operative in the Japanese case, the large amount of exceptions which have to be dealt with renders the Japanese pattern of categorization extremely uneconomical. Given the fact that languages, by and large, avoid categorizing class D lexemes in the way Japanese does, it can be concluded that the principle of cognitive economy is also effective in the organization of the adjectival class D.

In sum, it can be stated that the inductive research into the semantic motivation of copula distribution carried out in the present project, which discloses prototype structures in the lexicon of ten languages, corroborates traditional intuitions about the fundamental segmentation of the lexicon into the three semantic macro-classes of entity, property, and event concepts, which are referred to by the labels of nominals, adjectivals, and verbals in this study. The results obtained so far converge with Croft's (1991) model of the lexicon, which is based on multi-factor definitions of the semantic prototypes of entity, property, and event concepts (see §1.3.4.2).

The multi-factor model of the lexicon not only accounts for the questions concerning copula use which have been raised in the preceding chapters, it also offers a semantic classification of language-specific vocabularies which is more fine-grained than the traditional division of the lexicon into nominals, verbals, and adjectivals. According to the data given in table 4.4 (p. 162), language-specific vocabularies include numerous lexical classes whose semantic profiles do not coincide with those of prototypical nominals, verbals, and adjectivals, and which usually are relatively small in size. These minor classes, just like the focal classes, comply with the rules that turn the scalar structure schematized in figure 4.2 into an implicational hierarchy. These rules prescribe (a) that in any one language in which both copularizing and non-copularizing lexemes exist, there is a bipartite segmentation of the lexicon into a copularizing *vs.* a non-copularizing part which is defined by a single cut-off point in semantic space, and (b) that any lexical item located to the left of this cut-off point copularizes, while any lexical item located to the right of the cut-off point is incompatible with copulas. Thus, if a given lexical class X is positioned between two other classes in semantic space, both of which behave the same way with respect to copula use, class X will behave the same way as the adjacent classes do with respect to copula use. Areas in semantic space which deserve special attention are those located between classes which display internally uniform but distinct behavior with respect to copularization. Only lexical classes positioned in such areas exhibit a mixed composition, that is, they contain both copularizing and non-copularizing lexemes. Further, as a generalization that is valid in any one of the sampled languages, it can be stated that exclusively copularizing and exclusively non-copularizing sections of the lexicon are never directly adjacent to each other. They are always separated by mixed classes. For instance, in Cantonese, all members of class C (occupations/ professions ('teacher'), nominals for shape ('triangle')) copularize; the members of class G (emotional/mental acts or states ('to love', 'to know'), concepts denoting possession ('to have'), concepts denoting resemblance ('to resemble')), never admit copularization. At the halfway point between classes C and G, the mixed class D (prototypical adjectivals ('big', 'good', 'red'), positionals ('to sit', 'to stand'), and other statives ('to stink')) is located. Mixed classes constitute points of transition, or gray zones, between areas in the lexicon which diverge with respect to copula use. Thus, the presence and specific location of mixed classes in the space diagrams underscores the hypothesis that the distribution of copulas mirrors, and might even be controlled by, the coherent architecture of semantic similarity space. Again, the occurrence of configurations involving gray zones in category formation is predicted by Rosch's prototype theory, which claims that categories arc fuzzy. That is, they have unclear boundaries. This entails the possibility that there may be areas of overlap between categories (e.g. Givón

TABLE 4.6. *Areas of categorial overlap in the lexicon*

	A	B	C	D	E	F	G	H	I	J	K	L	M	N	O	P	Q
Burmese		*		*													
Cantonese		*		*													
German				*			*					*					
Hungarian				*			*					*					
Indonesian		*		*													
Japanese		*		*			*					*					
Lakota		*															
Swahili		*		*			*					*					
Thai		*		*													
Turkish		*		*													

1995: 13f., Taylor 1989: 51). Such overlap scenarios originate in the fact that there exist real-world items whose properties potentially justify ascribing them to more than one category. Thus, mixed classes can be interpreted as areas of categorial instability and vagueness, which define the borderline or cut-off point between areas in the lexicon that diverge with respect to copula use.

Interestingly, the areas in the lexicon in which categorial overlap occurs tend to be constant across languages. The classes in question are marked by an asterisk (*) in table 4.6, which summarizes the respective data on the sampled languages. Only a handful of the seventeen lexical classes encountered in the samples participate in gray zone formation at all, namely the classes B (body features: adjectivals denoting nationality ('French'), personality features ('smart'), body features ('color-blind'), relational nouns including body parts and terms of relationship, age adjectivals denoting permanent membership in age group ('old')); D (prototypical adjectivals ('big', 'good', 'red'), positionals ('to sit', 'to stand'), and other statives ('to stink')); G (emotional/mental acts or states ('to love', 'to know'), concepts denoting possession ('to have'), concepts denoting resemblance ('to resemble')), and L (bodily/mental states ('tired', 'angry')). There are three attested combinations of mixed classes: B/D (in five languages), D/G/L (in two languages), and B/D/G/L (in two languages). Thus, the size of categorial gray zones may vary from language to language. Minimally, a categorial gray zone involves two classes in the sampled languages; maximally, it extends over four classes. The central question arising from these data is why mixed classes are found only in special restricted locations in the space diagrams. Although mixed classes can be expected to occur anywhere in semantic similarity space, only four of the seventeen semantic classes which are present in the samples—classes B, D, G, and L—do in fact exhibit mixing.

In this context, another noteworthy observation that is in need of an explanation must be addressed. In all the language samples investigated, some semantic domains are more likely to produce lexical minimal pairs, or instances of double categorization, than others. These semantic domains include in particular those representing emotional, mental, or bodily acts or states ('to love', 'to know', 'to itch'); or those representing personality features, body features, and material composition ('stingy', 'cross-eyed', 'golden'). It comes as no surprise that these semantic domains are characterized by semantic feature profiles which define lexical classes participating in gray zone formation. Emotional, mental, or bodily acts or states often show either the feature profile [2 valence]/ [+/−transient]/[−dynamic] or the feature profile [1 valence]/[+transient]/ [−dynamic]. These feature profiles define classes G (emotional/mental acts or states ('to love', 'to know'), concepts denoting possession ('to have'), concepts denoting resemblance ('to resemble')), and L (bodily/mental states ('tired', 'angry')). Lexemes indicating personality features, body features, and material composition are characterized by the feature profile [1 valence]/[−transient]/ [−dynamic], which defines class B (body features, adjectivals denoting nationality ('French'), personality features ('smart'), body features ('color-blind'), relational nouns including body parts and terms of relationship, age adjectivals denoting permanent membership in age group ('old')). This connection between lexical minimal pairs and semantic classes participating in gray zone formation is, of course, not a coincidence. Categorial overlap, which creates categorial gray zones in which assignment of lexical items to one of two possible categories is arbitrary, fosters the emergence of lexical minimal pairs. The theoretical model introduced above offers an explanation for the increased frequency of categorial gray zones, and thus, implicitly, of lexical minimal pairs, in certain lexical domains, and their conspicuous absence in others. According to the principle of cognitive economy, which has been addressed in §4.4, areas of categorial overlap are more tolerable in specific areas of the lexicon than in others. The smaller the group of lexical items affected by category merging, the more economical the overall system of categorization will be. As a consequence, focal—that is, large—classes strongly resist category merging. Thus, in general, the members of focal classes display uniform behavior with respect to compatibility with copulas, or the amount of class members which show idiosyncratic behavior is greatly reduced. Thus, if category mixing occurs in minor classes, rather than in focal classes, the decrease in cognitive economy that category mixing always entails is kept within limits.

As is argued in the preceding section, the existence of categorial gray zones, which literally 'build a bridge' between copularizing and non-copularizing parts of the lexicon, can be taken as evidence for the assumption that cross-linguistically, copula usage follows patterns which are imposed by a coherent semantic superstructure that organizes the lexicon of any one language. This hypothesis is underscored by the findings gained from a more detailed analysis of the composition of mixed lexical classes. At this point, it should be noted that proximity and distance in three-dimensional space translate directly into semantic similarity and dissimilarity. For instance, in figure 4.1 (p. 168) the classes B (body features, adjectivals denoting nationality ('French'), personality features ('smart'), body features ('color-blind'), relational nouns including body parts and terms of relationship, age adjectivals denoting permanent membership in age group ('old')), and C (occupations/professions ('teacher'), nominals for shape ('triangle')) are both equidistant from class A (prototypical nominals ('house', 'dog'), nominals designating sex ('woman'), age nominals denoting permanent membership in age group ('old man'), nominals referring to bodily or mental disposition ('glutton', 'genius')). The distance between class A and class D (prototypical adjectivals ('big', 'good', 'red'), positionals ('to sit', 'to stand') and other statives ('to stink')) is greater than the distance between class A and classes B and C. Class B is characterized by the semantic profile [1 valence]/ [−transient]/[−dynamic] and thus diverges from class A, which is defined by the semantic profile [0 valence]/[−transient]/[−dynamic], solely with respect to the feature value for valence. Class C, which is defined by the feature values [0 valence]/[+/−transient]/[−dynamic], also diverges from class A with respect to a single semantic dimension only, namely transience. Class D, on the other hand, which is characterized by the semantic profile [1 valence]/[+/−transient]/ [−dynamic], diverges from class A with respect to two parameters, namely valence and transience. This example illustrates how spatial distance corresponds to, and therefore is symbolic of, semantic distance in the space diagrams used.

Obviously, the semantic distance of a given mixed class from a given lexical prototype has a direct impact on the composition of the class. At least, within the sampled languages, for any mixed class X which is part of a gray zone, the following generalization holds: as the distance of class X from any of the two categorial prototypes—either the nominal prototype, which coincides with class A (prototypical nominals ('house', 'dog'), nominals designating sex ('woman'), age nominals denoting permanent membership in age group ('old man'), nominals referring to bodily or mental disposition ('glutton', 'genius')), or the verbal prototype, which is coextensive with the classes N (prototypical intransitive verbals ('to go')) and Q (prototypical transitive verbals ('to buy'))—increases, the percentage of lexemes contained in class X which behave like one of the two prototypes with respect to copularization decreases. As a consequence, in cases in which there are chains of mixed classes in three-dimensional similarity space, the figures for lexemes behaving like the prototype in question drop continuously from class to class, the more the respective distance of these classes from the prototype increases. Thus, gray zones display an algorithmic structure. The relevant figures which define the internal structure of gray zones in the sampled languages, which are presented in appendix E, can be transformed into diagrams (see appendix F).

The claim that the categorization of the lexicon by means of copulas involves categorial gray zones, or points of transition in which categorizarion is arbitrary, is substantiated by independent evidence from a different area of research. Lexical minimal pairs whose members are fully synonymous so that mutual substitution in all contexts investigated is possible are frequent in the sampled languages. An example is the English verbal-adjectival minimal pair *to sleep* vs. *asleep*. The existence of full synonyms which diverge with respect to the structural criterion of compatibility with copulas *per se* implies the existence of areas of categorial overlap in the lexicon.

Last but not least, the assumption that the multi-factor model of the lexicon is more suited for explaining the empirical facts regarding copula distribution than the mono-factor models introduced as an analytical option in §3.4.3 is supported by the following considerations. Since none of the semantic parameters used in analyzing the language-specific lexical samples produces entirely accurate predictions of presence or absence of copulas, the predictive power of the mono-factor models is restricted. In any case, there remains a residue of exceptions that have to be dealt with. In the multi-factor model of the lexicon, on the other hand, such exceptions do not actually exist. Theoretically, within the multi-factor model, residual lexemes in mixed classes which do not conform to the majority of lexemes with respect to compatibility or non-compatibility with copulas would have to be treated as exceptions as well. However, in all sampled languages, the mixed classes happen to be located between exclusively copularizing and exclusively non-copularizing sections of the lexicon—they always form part of a categorial gray zone. By virtue of this specific property of mixed classes, their occurrence can, on the grounds of what has been said above, be interpreted as a manifestation of category overlap, and can thus be regarded as a natural, rather than a disturbing phenomenon.

4.6. Discourse frequency

As is argued in Chapter 1, Croft's (1991) discourse-based markedness theory can be used to motivate the special rules governing copula distribution at the cross-linguistic level, which have been described in §2.3. Among other things, Croft's analyses reveal a correlation between the discourse frequency of predicate types, and markedness patterns as defined by the criterion of structural complexity. Nominal predicates are less frequent in discourse than adjectival and verbal predicates are, and they are also structurally more complex than adjectival and verbal predicates, if predicate types in a given language differ as to the degree of their structural complexity. Further, adjectival predicates are less frequent in discourse than verbal predicates, and they are structurally more complex than the latter. One of the factors which contribute to the structural complexity of predicates is the presence of copulas. Thus, nominal predicates are more likely to contain a copula than adjectival predicates are, and adjectival predicates are more likely to contain a copula than verbal predicates are.

In what follows, discourse data from Burmese, Cantonese, German, Hungarian, Indonesian, Japanese, Lakota, Swahili, Thai, and Turkish will be presented, and the question of whether the statistical data support the hypothesis proposed in the preceding sections of this chapter will be discussed. For all languages except German and Lakota, stories told by the native speakers consulted have been used as databases. The German data are derived from samples from novels, and the Lakota data are taken from Pustet (forthcoming).

In §3.4.3 it is hypothesized that the intrinsic semantic profile of lexical items might directly determine their predicate worthiness. If this is correct, the traditional parts of speech become dispensable as building blocks of a general theory of copularization, not only at the level of semantic description, as is argued in §4.5, but also with regard to the motivation of the varying discourse frequencies of predicate types. The respective discourse data are represented in table 4.7, which is based on the semantic classification of the lexicon established in table 4.4.

The data reproduced in the above table are quite complex. Graphic representation of the data entails technical problems because a combination of the three-dimensional space diagrams used in the preceding section with statistical modes of representation, such as bar charts, would be required. However, the representation of the data given above can be simplified, so that the relevant correlations between semantic class membership and discourse frequency become visible. On the basis of figures 4.3 to 4.12, for each language investigated, three lexical macro-categories can be posited: the first category subsumes those of the lexical classes A to Q whose members never copularize; the second category subsumes all mixed lexical classes, which contain both copularizing and non-copularizing lexemes; the third category subsumes those lexical classes which contain copularizing lexemes only. This cruder segmentation of the lexicon yields a substantial analysis of the discourse data if the language-specific figures given for the lexical classes A to Q in table 4.7 are added up within each macro-category. The resulting figures are given in table 4.8.

TABLE 4.7. *Discourse frequency of semantic classes*

	A	B	C	D	E	F	G	H	I	J	K	L	M	N	O	P	Q
Burmese	4	3	2	22			31					19		72	2		156
Cantonese				11			34	2						26			49
German		2	1	23			23					4		56	1		81
Hungarian	1			7			3							6			21
Indonesian	11	4	6	33	4	2	23					8	4	59	6		84
Japanese	6	6	1	26	1		8	1		2		15		31			53
Lakota	5	3	1	27	4		23					21		93			203
Swahili	1			2			10	1				7		51	2	1	74
Thai	1	1		15			11					5		48	2		46
Turkish	4	10		17			4					4		10			34

TABLE 4.8. *Discourse frequencies of lexical classes as defined by copula use*

	+copula	Gray zone	−copula
Burmese	6	25	280
Cantonese	0	11	122
German	3	50	138
Hungarian	1	10	27
Indonesian	17	37	190
Japanese	7	55	103
Lakota	5	3	372
Swahili	1	19	129
Thai	1	16	112
Turkish	4	27	56

The numerical values are as expected. Discourse frequency in predicate position is lowest for the copularizing macro-category; it increases drastically within the mixed lexical macro-category, and reaches its climax within the non-copularizing macro-category. The only exception to this general pattern is found in Lakota. There are five members in the copularizing category, but the mixed category contains only three members. This minor deviation from the expected distributional pattern is conditioned by the extremely small size of the mixed macro-category in Lakota, which comprises a single lexical class only, namely B (body features, adjectivals denoting nationality ('French'), personality features ('smart'), body features ('color-blind'), relational nouns including body parts and terms of relationship, age adjectivals denoting permanent membership in age group ('old')). Basically, the problem is not caused by the language-specific data in this case, but rather, by the simplified mode of analysis which had to be chosen for the reasons addressed above. As a matter of fact, the Lakota data do bear out the prediction that discourse frequency in predicate position decreases as proximity to the lexical prototype represented by the semantically nominal class A in semantic space increases. A glance at the focal classes A, D, N, and Q in table 4.7 is particularly revealing: class A (prototypical nominals ('house', 'dog'), nominals designating sex ('woman'), age nominals denoting permanent membership in age group ('old man'), nominals referring to bodily or mental disposition ('glutton', 'genius')) has five members; class D (prototypical adjectivals ('big', 'good', 'red'), positionals ('to sit', 'to stand'), and other statives ('to stink')), has twenty-seven members; class N (prototypical intransitive verbals ('to go')) has ninety-three members; class Q (prototypical transitive verbals ('to buy')) has 203 members. The minor classes B, C, E, G, and L also conform to the general rule that discourse frequency decreases as proximity to class A in semantic space increases. Classes B (body features, adjectivals denoting nationality ('French'), personality features ('smart'), body features ('color-blind'), relational nouns including body parts and terms of relationship, age adjectivals denoting permanent membership in age group ('old')) and C (occupations/professions ('teacher'), nominals for shape ('triangle')) are equidistant to class A but closer to class A than classes E ('to get up/to stand'), G (emotional/mental acts or states ('to love', 'to know'), concepts denoting possession ('to have'), concepts denoting resemblance ('to resemble')), and L (bodily/mental states ('tired', 'angry')). The distributional values for classes B and C are lower than the values for classes E, G, and L. Class E, further, is closer to class A than classes G and L are, which are equidistant to class A. The value for class E is lower than the values for classes G and L. It is advisable to treat focal and minor classes separately in this case because with respect to relative size, the minor classes, *per definitionem*, will never be on a par with the focal classes. Thus, in quantitative terms, the two class types are not directly comparable.

Judging by the data on discourse frequency of lexical items in predicate function given above, the position of a lexical item in semantic similarity space does in fact determine its frequency of occurrence as nucleus of a predicate phrase in discourse, and, as a consequence, its compatibility with copulas. Thus, as the overall result of the present study, it can be stated that the universal distributional patterns governing copula use described in § 2.3 are, basically, motivated by the interaction of structure-imposing forces at different levels of language description. Semantics can be considered the most fundamental of these structuring factors. Semantics, more specifically, the parameters valence, transience, and dynamicity, which, in conjunction, define the semantic space diagram of the lexicon shown in figure 4.1, determines the shape of the gradually sloping scale of discourse frequencies established in table 4.8. Discourse frequency, finally, correlates systematically with the dimension of physical complexity of linguistic units, or structural markedness, one possible manifestation of structural markedness being copularization.

5 Synopsis

The point of departure for the present study of copularization had been the discovery of a prospective language universal, that is the scale NOMINALS > ADJECTIVALS > VERBALS, which translates the existing distributional patterns of copularizing *vs.* non-copularizing lexemes into a compact formula. In the extant literature on the parts-of-speech issue, particularly in Pustet (1989) and Stassen (1997), this scale has been proposed repeatedly as it can be used to describe certain aspects of the morphosyntactic properties of lexical items at the universal level. The analysis of the global language sample established in Chapter 2 for the purpose of investigating patterns of copula distribution is based on the division of the lexicon into the semantic macro-classes of nominals, alias entity concepts, adjectivals, alias property concepts, and verbals, alias event concepts. The scale NOMINALS > ADJECTIVALS > VERBALS, in addition, lends itself to a general characterization in terms of the semantic parameter of time-stability as proposed by Givón (1979, 1984). Consequently, in the conclusion to Chapter 2, the possibility of explaining the behavior of copulas by means of a model that redefines the semantic macro-classes of nominals, verbals, and adjectivals in terms of the more profound semantic dimension of time-stability is taken into consideration. Elaborating on this semantic approach in Chapter 3, in the attempt to uncover potentially relevant semantic factors that correlate systematically with presence *vs.* absence of copulas, lexical minimal pairs are investigated, which prove to be a rich source of information. The minimal pair method discloses four semantic parameters which correlate systematically with presence *vs.* absence of copulas: dynamicity, transience, transitivity, and dependency. The parameters transitivity and dependency can be subsumed under the label of valence. These findings bear out the model of lexical categorization proposed by Croft (1991), in which the three semantic parameters of dynamicity, transience, and valence are used to define the semantic distinctions between the semantic prototypes referred to by the labels of nominals, verbals, and adjectivals. Combining the semantic parameters established via the minimal pair method in a final analytical step in Chapter 4 creates a theoretical model that provides plausible answers for many questions surrounding the phenomenon of copularization. The most important result of the multi-factor approach to copularization is that in quantitative terms, presumably, the lexicon of any language is structured around the semantic prototypes of entity, event, and property concepts, alias nominals, verbals, and adjectivals. The implicational hierarchy NOMINALS > ADJECTIVALS > VERBALS, which has been derived from the cross-linguistic sample investigated in §2.3.4

and which captures the universal rules governing the distribution of copularizing and non-copularizing lexemes in the lexicon of individual languages, can be redefined in terms of the semantic parameters valence, dynamicity, and transience.

The empirical results that emerge from the inductive research carried out in Chapters 2, 3, and 4, can be integrated into a more general theoretical context. In Chapter 1, on the basis of previous research into the parts-of-speech issue, some potential building blocks of such a comprehensive functional model of copularization have been identified. In the attempt to answer the initial question about the motivation of the existence and the specific distributional properties of copulas the concept of markedness, as formulated by Croft (1991, 2001), plays a crucial role. Markedness theory provides a theoretical framework that links the various empirical findings obtained in the present study of copularization. What is more, markedness theory is capable of offering an answer to the fundamental questions about the nature of copulas and the reason for their existence. These questions are particularly challenging in the case of copulas because, as has been pointed out in §1.2, copulas are, essentially, devoid of meaning. This is what constitutes what is referred to in §1.1 as one of the various aspects of the copula paradox. Since the purpose of language is the coding of meaning, the very fact that copulas exist seems to lead this most basic assumption about language *ad absurdum*.

5.1. Copularization and markedness

The copula paradox can be resolved by the following line of reasoning, in which markedness theory figures as the key factor. A marked linguistic structure is physically more complex than an unmarked structure. Presence of a copula renders a predicate construction physically more complex than a predicate construction that does not contain a copula. The frequency of occurrence of linguistic structures, which include predicate constructions, in discourse corresponds to their markedness status: marked structures are employed less frequently than unmarked structures. Thus, in the discourse of any language, copularizing predicates will be encountered less frequently than non-copularizing predicates. Furthermore, as is argued in detail in §3.4.3, in the pragmatic function of predicate—the only position in which copulas are found—the occurrence of certain lexeme types is favored. The semantic motivation for such processes of selection is to be sought in the interaction of the three basic semantic parameters of valence, dynamicity, and transience at the level of lexical semantics. Various semantic profiles are created which, in turn, exhibit different degrees of compatibility with the inherent semantic function of the predicate slot. In short, lexemes which designate events are more likely to function as nuclei of predicate phrases than lexemes expressing property concepts; property concepts, in turn, are more likely to function as predicates than entity concepts are. As a consequence of this cline of predicate worthiness of lexeme types, a lexeme with a high frequency of occurrence in predicate position is less likely to be accompanied by a copula than a lexeme which displays a low frequency of occurrence in predicate position. The basic idea underlying the theoretical model proposed in this study is that the semantic scale NOMINALS > ADJECTIVALS > VERBALS, which can be defined in terms of the three semantic parameters valence, dynamicity, and transience, translates into a scale of 'predicate worthiness' which determines the discourse frequency of individual lexemes in predicate position. Frequency of occurrence in discourse, however, is one facet of the markedness principle, which goes hand in hand with the physical manifestation of markedness, namely, presence of a greater or smaller amount of coding material. Low discourse frequency of a given lexical item in predicate position tends to increase the structural complexity of the respective predicate construction as a whole. The appearance of a copula within a given predicate construction, further, does a lot to increase the structural complexity of the latter.

The hypothesis that copularization is, basically, one of the numerous manifestations of the markedness principle, which has been proposed in Chapter 1 on the basis of Croft's theoretical approach to lexical categorization, is supported by some additional observations.

First, as is stated in §2.2, copula usage is sensitive to grammatical categories in many languages. Particularly in the present tense, copulas tend to be dropped. Present tense can be considered the least marked form of predicates in terms of cognitive complexity. In addition, some languages admit or demand copula dropping with pronominal subjects. This syntactic context is unmarked with respect to discourse frequency, if compared to the alternative syntactic configuration in which the subject is realized as a full noun (Givón 1995: 377f.). Thus, the markedness principle seems to control copula usage not only in conjunction with intrinsic lexical semantics, but in conjunction with grammatical categories as well.

Secondly, in some languages, copula usage is determined by stylistic factors. If there is a distinction between formal and/or literary *vs.* colloquial style, copulas always occur in formal and/or literary style, never in colloquial style. Since formal/literary style is, on the whole, employed less frequently than colloquial style, such facts can be regarded as another instance of the interaction of discourse frequency with copula usage. For instance, the Burmese copula $p^h j\imath\textit{?}$ is sensitive to the distinction between literary and colloquial style. $P^h j\imath\textit{?}$ is encountered in literary style, but not in conversations. Similarly, the Indonesian copula *adalah* occurs only in formal style (see example 5.1), never in colloquial style (see example 5.2).

5.1. ini   adalah   rumah
    this   COP   house
    'this is a house (formal)' (author's field data)

5.2. ini   rumah
     this   house
     'this is a house (colloquial)' (author's field data)

Likewise, the Thai copulas *khɨ:* and *pen* mark formal style. They are not used in everyday conversation.

5.3. nî: khɨ: rɨ:
     this   COPa   boat
     'this is a boat (formal)' (author's field data)

5.4. nî: pen   rɨ:
     this   COPb   boat
     'this is a boat (formal)' (author's field data)

5.5. nî: rɨ:
     this   boat
     'this is a boat (colloquial)' (author's field data)

A third possible argument in favor of the assumption that the frequency principle interacts with copula usage can be derived from the cross-linguistic generalization that the fully copularizing language type is very scarce, while the non-copularizing type is relatively frequent. Thus, there seems to be a global markedness principle of copularization as well.

On this basis, it can be concluded that markedness, together with the semantic parameters obtained through the minimal pair approach, constitutes an indispensable building block of a functional model of copularization.

In this connection, the Basque case must be taken into consideration once more. The correlation of high discourse frequency with low structural complexity of predicate types, which has been taken for granted so far as one of the major ingredients of a general functional model of copularization, holds in all the languages investigated except Basque. In fact, Basque reverses the normal markedness relation: because copularizing predicates in Basque are much more frequent than non-copularizing predicates, high discourse frequency correlates with presence of copulas, that is high structural complexity, in this language, while low discourse frequency correlates with absence of copulas, that is low structural complexity. Still, the Basque case does not invalidate the approach to copularization outlined above. But in order to assign Basque its rightful place in the overall puzzle, some more fundamental issues of functional language theory must be addressed.

As is stated in §4.2, the system of verbal inflection in Basque is extremely complex. Speakers have difficulty mastering it since too many, often suppletive, forms have to be memorized. The history of the language shows that, as a consequence, speakers started to avoid these forms, and replaced them with periphrastic verb forms, that is, verb forms that contain a copula. This periphrastic predication strategy is more economical than the synthetic alternative in cognitive terms because only two verbal paradigms, those of the copulas *izan* and *ukan*, have to be memorized and reproduced. Thus, the special situation given in Basque led to an 'overextension' of copularization—cognitive economy now overrides the markedness principle.

But the decisive point to be made here is that, at a basic level, the conflict between markedness and cognitive economy observed in Basque is not a conflict at all because markedness itself is nothing more than one of the manifestations of the principle of cognitive economy. It has been widely known ever since Zipf's studies of the statistical interaction between the structural complexity and discourse frequency of linguistic items that more frequent forms are less complex, that is, they are structurally more marked than less frequent forms. As a consequence, more frequent forms are shortened in the course of time.

... all speech-elements or language-patterns are impelled and directed in their behavior by a fundamental law of economy in which is the desire to maintain an equilibrium between form and behavior.

(Zipf 1935: 19)

The law of abbreviation seems to reflect on the one hand an impulse in language toward the maintenance of an equilibrium between length and frequency, and on the other hand an underlying law of economy as the *causa causans* of this impulse toward equilibrium ... That economy, or the saving of time and effort, is probably the underlying cause of the maintenance of equilibrium is apparent from the fact that the purpose of all truncations ... is almost admittedly the saving of time and effort.

(Zipf 1935: 38)

While economic motivation of copula usage in all sampled languages, except Basque, operates indirectly—that is, via lexical semantics, which controls the frequency of lexeme types in predicate position—cognitive economy in Basque operates more directly, by blocking the use of synthetic paradigms almost thoroughly, and replacing them with copularizing structures. The result is a deviant markedness pattern. But both the Basque system of copula usage and all other copularization systems investigated are, ultimately, shaped by a single underlying principle: that of cognitive economy.

Despite the promising insights offered in the preceding Chapters, the copula paradox, as formulated in §1.1, may not yet have been resolved to universal satisfaction. One might still wonder why a language 'needs' a copula, given that there are so many languages that fulfill their communicative purposes effectively without employing copulas. In response, it can be stated that languages might in fact produce structures they do not 'need'. Copulas can be interpreted as mere morphosyntactic ballast, as nothing more than the material outgrowth of the markedness principle. The potential problems connected with the attempt to characterize copulas in terms of function should also be viewed in the context of the widespread compulsion of practicing descriptionists to associate any linguistic item encountered in a given language with some kind of function (Givón

1995:62). Givón argues that this inclination originates in the following tacit but erroneous assumption:

> Because most structures reveal a considerable measure of isomorphism with paired functions, no structure could possibly hang around without some obvious function paired to it.

(Givón 1995: 62)

Givón's view implies that there may be linguistic elements which do not fulfill a specific function. Copulas, which have so often been claimed to be semantically empty, are first-rate candidates for this hypothetical class of afunctional elements, although the hypothesis that copulas might indeed be entirely afunctional in every respect runs counter to the traditional intuitions about copulas. Usually, copulas are portrayed as fulfilling at least some pragmatic or syntactic functions, such as making certain lexemes admissible in predicate position, or linking the predicate to its arguments, or serving as a 'hitching post' for categories of predicate inflection. However, as the line of argumentation pursued in Chapter 1 already suggests, there is no cogent need for integrating such pragmatic and syntactic functions into clause structure at all. What is more, the hypothesis of the afunctional nature of copulas is indirectly supported by analogies from biology:

> Some components of biological structure cannot be paired isomorphically in an obvious way to any specific function. In many cases, such excess structures perform more abstract global functions that are harder to pin down. In other cases, excess structures are the bio-design consequence of the way more concrete—obvious—functions are represented isomorphically. An example of this can be seen in the design of DNA as a code for protein production. The most concrete elements in this code are sequences of nucleotide triplets. Each triplet on the DNA chain codes for a particular amino acid on the protein chain. This correspondence is 100% isomorphic. However, interspersed between such concrete segments of the DNA code are occasional nucleotide sequences that do not correspond to any amino acid in the protein chain. Some of these seemingly redundant nucleotides function as higher-level governors, they block or release entire sequences of the more concrete—isomorphic—code. Their function is thus more global and abstract. But other sequences in the linear DNA chain are apparently fillers, they seem to be there in order to ensure a particular spacing of the more concrete elements in the code. And others yet may be there as mere by-products of the way other elements of the complex structure, elements with more obvious functions, are organized.

(Givón 1995: 62)

By way of deductive reasoning, it can be hypothesized that afunctional elements may indeed occur in human language. Whether copulas should be analyzed as such, or perhaps as abstract 'fillers' or 'governors' in syntax, is not clear at this point. Like any more abstract linguistic function which is detached from ontology proper, the function of copulas, if there is any, defies direct introspection. For this reason, the present study does not subscribe to any of the current theories which seek to ascribe a specific function to copulas—the answer to the question about the functional content of copulas will be left to future research, which will, hopefully, come up with more subtle means of defining linguistic elements with respect to their functional range.

5.2. Towards a new approach to the parts-of-speech issue

The analysis of the language data presented in the preceding Chapter yields a theoretical model of copularization that is not derived from a particular theoretical framework. It is based, first of all, on the conviction that linguistics, being a young science, is well advised to proceed strictly inductively, and that it is advantageous to investigate a large amount of genetically and geographically diverse languages before general theoretical conclusions are proposed. That the multi-factor model of copularization, further, can be linked with theories advanced in the neighboring discipline of cognitive science, in particular, with prototype theory, is a highly welcome but not necessarily expected corollary of this study. Prototype theory has been readily—maybe too readily—accepted in linguistics. Wierzbicka (1990: 365) cautions against giving in to the temptation of relying on prototypes as convenient, superficial labels that legitimize or even invite analytical carelessness:

In too many cases, these new ideas have been treated as an excuse for intellectual laziness and sloppiness. In my view, the notion of prototype has to prove its usefulness through semantic description, not through semantic theorizing . . . But if it is treated as a magical key to open all doors without effort, the chances are that it will cause more harm than good.

Within the multi-factor model of copularization, the concept of prototype does not have the status of a descriptive label that is deductively superimposed on the data to facilitate dealing with categories which defy simple definitions. Rather, the emergence of prototype structures is the result of a purely inductive line of reasoning in this case. In Chapter 3, semantic parameters which correlate with copula use are derived from large language-specific samples by means of the minimal pair approach. As it turns out, the bulk of the lexical items contained in the language samples investigated can be characterized in terms of a small number of specific combinations of the feature values provided by the semantic parameters of valence, transience, and dynamicity. The feature bundles in question, therefore, define lexical prototypes. It so happens that these specific combinations of semantic features coincide with the popular semantic definitions of the traditional parts of speech noun, verb, and adjective in terms of the concepts of entity, event, and property, which have always figured as lexical prototypes in semantic theory (e.g. Croft 2001: 103). The simple equations 'noun = entity', 'verb = event', and 'adjective = property' are apparently sufficient for compartmentalizing the majority of lexical items of—presumably—any one language in semantic terms. This accounts for the fact that the traditional parts of speech have been successfully used as descriptive primitives of grammar writing for so long. According to the theoretical model developed in Chapter 4, the special status of the lexical prototypes entity, event, and property derives from their quantitative dominance in language-specific vocabularies. Thus, at least indirectly, this model confirms the age-old intuition that nominals, verbals, and adjectivals, alias entity concepts, event concepts, and property concepts, are, in some way, fundamental components of human language. Another noteworthy aspect of the multi-factor model of the lexicon introduced in Chapter 4 is that by portraying the lexicon as a coherent system at the semantic level, a connection can be established between the semantic prototypes of nominals, verbals, and adjectivals, which are usually regarded as more or less monolithic units in current linguistic theory.

However, the present study also touches upon a deeper issue in contemporary linguistic theory—the question of whether, and if so, to what degree, linguistic form or surface structure is determined by linguistic function, that is, by semantic or pragmatic content. Copularization is one of the many aspects of linguistic surface structure. Current generative dogma denies that there exist any interdependencies between linguistic form and function. The theoretical model introduced above, on the other hand, claims that the basic factor determining copula distribution is the intrinsic semantic content of individual lexemes, and thus supports the hypothesis that interdependencies between surface form and meaning do in fact exist. First, the semantic differences between copularizing and non-copularizing members of the lexical minimal pairs investigated in §3.3 are, obviously, of a systematic nature. If members of lexical minimal pairs diverge with respect to any of the four basic parameters dynamicity, transience, transitivity, and dependency, the copularizing member of the pair is always less dynamic, less transient, less transitive, and less dependent than the non-copularizing member. This is a strong generalization to which, at least in the language samples established, no counterexamples have been found. Thus, in the microcosm of lexical minimal pairs, a systematic correlation between formal and semantic properties of lexical items holds. Secondly, the semantic parameters dynamicity, transience, transitivity, and dependency show high statistical correlations with presence *vs.* absence of copulas in the macrocosm of comprehensive language-specific vocabularies as well. The respective statistical figures do not reach the point of a perfect convergence of the formal feature of presence or absence of copulas with any of the semantic parameters tested, but they usually range around the 80 or 90 per cent mark and thus clearly exceed random values. Such significant statistical correlations between linguistic form and meaning must be taken seriously as empirical facts, regardless of whether they can be reconciled with scientific dogma or not. American structuralism marks the beginning of an era in linguistic theory in which semantics is explicitly banned from the set of potential factors that shape language structure. The role of the elusive parts of speech noun, verb, and adjective, which have long been known to defy exact semantic definitions (see §1.3), in this development should not be underestimated. The following emphatic statement by Bloomfield (1933: 266) is quite illustrative in this respect:

...every lexical form is assigned always to the customary form-classes. To describe the grammar of a language, we have to state the form-classes of each lexical form, and to determine what characteristics make the speakers assign it to these form-classes.

The traditional answer to this question appears in our school grammars, which try to define the form-classes by the class-meaning—by the feature of meaning that is common to all the lexical forms in the form-class. The school grammar tells us, for instance, that a noun is 'the name of a person, place, or thing.' This definition presupposes more philosophical and scientific knowledge than the human race can command, and implies, further, that the form-classes of a language agree with the classifications that would be made by a philosopher or scientist . . . Class-meanings, like all other meanings, elude the linguist's power of definition . . . To accept definitions of meaning, which at best are makeshifts, in place of an identification in formal terms, is to abandon scientific discourse.

One aspect of the theoretical approach to copularization introduced in the preceding Chapters is that it provides a methodology which may turn out helpful in developing a general approach to the parts-of-speech issue. Since the phenomenon of copularization is, apparently, inextricably linked with the parts-of-speech issue, a fact which has already been addressed in Chapter 1, one of the implicit goals of the present study of copularization is contributing to a better understanding of lexical categorization in general. If lexical categories are to be defined, at least in part, by means of formal criteria, as is done in traditional approaches to the parts-of-speech issue (see §1.3.2), copula usage will have to be included in the complex catalog of formal criteria which differentiate the morphosyntactic profiles of individual lexical items within a given language. But if copula usage is taken as one of the defining criteria for lexical categories, the theoretical model developed in the present study can be expected to shed some more light on the nature of the controversial parts of speech noun, verb, and adjective, which have so far resisted universal definitions at all levels of language description, as the discussion in Chapter 1 shows. Thus, a comprehensive theoretical model of copula usage can also be regarded as a partial theory of lexical categorization, and it should be of some interest to current typological research, which increasingly advocates the position that the traditional division of the lexicon into nouns, verbs, and adjectives is in need of re-evaluation (e.g. Anward, Moravcsik, and Stassen 1997, Croft 1991, Dixon 1977b, Schachter 1985, Stassen 1997).

The theoretical framework presented in Chapter 4 offers the opportunity of defining lexical classes as semantic feature bundles, which can be arranged in coherent semantic similarity space. In the quotation given above, Bloomfield recommends replacing semantic definitions with 'formal' ones, that is with definitions using compatibility of individual lexical items with grammatical units, such as copulas, as criteria for establishing lexical classes. Such formal definitions of lexical classes are, in principle, viable. But formal and semantic definitions of parts of speech are certainly not mutually exclusive. On the contrary, following the functionalist tenet of the non-autonomy of linguistic form or surface structure, they can be fruitfully combined. The present study provides ample evidence in support of the hypothesis that the meaning of lexical items determines their formal properties, and that linguistic form and meaning are, therefore, intimately connected. Additional factors such as markedness, discourse frequency, and cognitive economy, whose vital role in sculpting the surface shape of language is generally acknowledged, supplement the semantics-based theoretical approach developed in this study.

The theoretical approach outlined in this monograph has been designed to account for a single formal feature only, that of copula use. But the formal make-up of lexical items comprises a variety of grammatical features, such as compatibility with tense/aspect/mood/person categories, or with case/number/ definiteness categories, and a general theory of lexical categorization will have to deal with any of these formal criteria. Theoretically, all these grammatical categories, as well as their subcategories, can be investigated by means of the methodology developed in this study. Future research might reveal that the specific regularities observed within the domain of copularization hold in other areas of grammar as well. More specifically, it can be hypothesized that ultimately, the interplay of the three basic semantic parameters of valence, transience, and dynamicity acts to assign grammatical features other than compatibility with copulas to individual lexical items in exactly the same way as with copulas. Thus, other formal criteria might produce compatibility patterns with respect to the lexicon that mirror the ones obtained for copulas. If they do, these patterns lend themselves to description by means of the implicational hierarchy NOMINALS > ADJECTIVALS > VERBALS as well. The extant typological literature on the subject does in fact provide some evidence supporting the hypothesis that the lexicon of any one language is organized around the basic semantic scale NOMINALS > ADJECTIVALS > VERBALS. In languages in which adjectivals do not display any structural features that distinguish them from either nominals or verbals, the inventory of adjectival lexemes is absorbed either by the nominal or the verbal class, or by both classes; but nominal and verbal lexemes are apparently never grouped together in a single lexical class that contrasts with the adjectival class (e.g. Croft 2001: 97, Hengeveld 1992: 69, Pustet 1989, Stassen 1997). This places adjectivals in an intermediate position between nominals and verbals in structural terms, so that the attested patterns of partial indistinction between nominals, verbals, and adjectivals can be summarized by means of the implicational hierarchy NOMINALS > ADJECTIVALS > VERBALS: only categories which are adjacent to each other in the hierarchy can be classed together at the structural level.

Prospective theories of lexical categorization, further, can be evaluated within various domains of empirical research. For instance, the lexical categories established by means of an adequate model of lexical categorization can be expected to have some cognitive relevance which might manifest itself, among other things, in the process of first and second language acquisition, or in the way in which grammatical properties are assigned to new words entering a language through mechanisms such as derivation, composition, or borrowing.

In sum, whatever the final answer to the question about the true nature of the elusive parts of speech noun, verb, and adjective will be, the theoretical approach presented in this monograph offers an analytical tool that might take linguistic research one step closer to the solution of one of the most challenging problems in language theory, that of lexical categorization.

Appendix A
Genetic affiliation of the languages quoted

The genetic classification used is based on Ruhlen (1987).

Abkhaz	Caucasian
Acehnese	Austronesian
Acooli	Nilo-Saharan
Af Tunni	Cushitic
Ainu	Japanese-Korean
Alacatlatzala Mixtec	Oto-Manguean
Alamblak	Indo-Pacific
Alyawarra	Pama-Nyungan
Arabana-Wangkangurru	Pama-Nyungan
Arabic	Semitic
Arbore	Cushitic
Ateso	Nilo-Saharan
Athpare	Tibeto-Burman
Awtuw	Indo-Pacific
Ayacucho Quechua	Andean
Bambara	Niger-Congo
Barasano	Equatorial-Tucanoan
Bari	Nilo-Saharan
Basque	isolate
Belizean Creole	(pidgins & creoles)
Berbice Dutch Creole	(pidgins & creoles)
Blackfoot	Almosan-Keresiouan
Boumaa Fijian	Austronesian
Buriat	Mongolian-Tungus
Burmese	Tibeto-Burman
Burushaski	isolate
Canela-Krahó	Ge-Pano-Carib
Cantonese	Sinitic
Chalcatongo Mixtec	Oto-Manguean
Chamorro	Austronesian
Classical Nahuatl	Uto-Aztecan
Copala Trique	Oto-Manguean
Cubeo	Equatorial-Tucanoan

Desano	Equatorial-Tucanoan
Diyari	Pama-Nyungan
Djapu	Pama-Nyungan
Dumi	Tibeto-Burman
Dyirbal	Pama-Nyungan
English	Indo-European
Epena Pedee	Chibchan-Paezan
Estonian	Uralic-Yukaghir
Finnish	Uralic-Yukaghir
French	Indo-European
Fulfulde	Niger-Congo
Gbeya	Niger-Congo
German	Indo-European
Gooniyandi	isolate
Guugu Yimidhirr	Pama-Nyungan
Halkomelem Salish	Almosan-Keresiouan
Hausa	Chadic
Hebrew	Semitic
Hindi	Indo-European
Hixkaryana	Ge-Pano-Carib
Hua	Indo-Pacific
Hungarian	Uralic-Yukaghir
Ila	Niger-Congo
Imonda	Indo-Pacific
Indonesian	Austronesian
Iraqw	Cushitic
Japanese	Japanese-Korean
Kabardian	Caucasian
Kambera	Austronesian
Kannada	Dravidian
Karo Batak	Austronesian
Kawaiisu	Uto-Aztecan
Kayardild	Pama-Nyungan
Kenya Luo	Nilo-Saharan
Kilivila	Austronesian
Kisi	Niger-Congo
Koasati	Penutian
Kobon	Indo-Pacific
Korean	Japanese-Korean
Koromfe	Niger-Congo

Koyra Chiini	isolate
Kriyol	(pidgins & creoles)
Kwaio	Austronesian
Ladakhi	Tibeto-Burman
Lakota	Almosan-Keresiouan
Lango	Nilo-Saharan
Lezgian	Caucasian
Limbu	Tibeto-Burman
Logbara	Nilo-Saharan
Loniu	Austronesian
Maasai	Nilo-Saharan
Malayalam	Dravidian
Maltese	Semitic
Mam	Penutian
Manam	Austronesian
Mandarin	Sinitic
Manipuri	Tibeto-Burman
Maori	Austronesian
Margi	Chadic
Martuthunira	Pama-Nyungan
Michoacán Nahuatl	Uto-Aztecan
Misantla Totonac	Penutian
Mojave	Hokan
Mokilese	Austronesian
Mundari	Munda
Nandi	Nilo-Saharan
Navaho	Athabaskan-Eyak
Ndyuka	(pidgins & creoles)
Ngankikurungkurr	Non-Pama-Nyungan
Ngiti	Nilo-Saharan
Nigerian Pidgin	(pidgins & creoles)
Nootka	Almosan-Keresiouan
Northern Paiute	Uto-Aztecan
Nuer	Nilo-Saharan
Nung	Daic
Palauan	Austronesian
Panyjima	Pama-Nyungan
Papago	Uto-Aztecan
Pero	Chadic
Persian	Indo-European
Polish	Indo-European

Ponapean	Austronesian
Punjabi	Indo-European
Rapanui	Austronesian
Retuarã	Equatorial-Tucanoan
Rotuman	Austronesian
Russian	Indo-European
Samoan	Austronesian
Sgaw Karen	Tibeto-Burman
Shilluk	Nilo-Saharan
Shona	Niger-Congo
Slovene	Indo-European
So	Nilo-Saharan
Somali	Cushitic
Spanish	Indo-European
Squamish	Almosan-Keresiouan
Sranan	(pidgins & creoles)
Swahili	Niger-Congo
Tagalog	Austronesian
Tamil	Dravidian
Tarma Quechua	Andean
Telugu	Dravidian
Thai	Daic
Tok Pisin	(pidgins & creoles)
Tswana	Niger-Congo
Turkish	Turkic
Tzotzil	Penutian
Tzutujil	Penutian
Uzbek	Turkic
Vietnamese	Mon-Khmer
Wambaya	Non-Pama-Nyungan
Warí	Equatorial-Tucanoan
West Futuna-Aniwa	Austronesian
Woleaian	Austronesian
Written Mongolian	Mongolian-Tungus
Yagaria	Indo-Pacific
Yapese	Austronesian
Yidiɲ	Pama-Nyungan
Yimas	Indo-Pacific
Yoruba	Niger-Congo
Yucatec Maya	Penutian

Appendix B
Pilot study/semantic classification

action (verbal)
Intransitive lexemes which are agentive, controlled, and not included in 'mental process', 'motion', 'social behavior', 'sound' and 'speech'. Examples: *to fight, to play, to work.*

age (nominal/adjectival)
Concepts such as *new, old, young*; also concepts such as *adult, baby, boy, child, girl, man, woman*, which are in part also members of the class 'sex'.

animate entity (nominal)
Entities which perform cell division, that is, mainly human beings, animals and plants.

animate part (nominal)
Component parts of entities which perform cell division, especially body parts; also plant parts such as *branch, leaf.*

artifact (nominal)
Examples: *car, house, knife, sweater.* Notionally, 'artifact' is a subclass of 'inanimate entity'. Nevertheless, 'artifact' is treated as a separate class here.

bodily state/experience (adjectival/verbal)
Transitory bodily states, sensations and emission processes, i.e. bodily 'events' which are low in agency and more or less uncontrolled. Examples: *awake, to blush, dizzy, drunk, to faint, healthy, hungry, to itch, to perspire, pregnant, sick, to sleep, tired*; also body sounds which have a tendency to be uncontrolled, as *to breathe, to cough, to hiccup, to pant, to sneeze, to snore, to yawn.*

body feature (nominal/adjectival)
Permanent physical properties of animates. Examples: *bow-legged, color-blind, cripple(d), glutton, left-handed, midget, near-sighted.*

carries substance (adjectival)
Examples: *dirty, dusty, juicy, moldy, muddy, oily, rusty, smoky, sticky, wet*; also concepts referring to the absence of a substance: *clean, clear, dry, pure.*

change of state (verbal)
Lexemes denoting dynamic intransitive events: *to break* (itr.), *to burst, to congeal, to decay, to explode, to freeze* (itr.), *to grow* (itr.), *to harden* (itr.), *to melt* (itr.), *to rot, to rust, to shrink* (itr.), *to swell, to wither, to widen* (itr.).

consistency (adjectival)

Examples: *brittle, coarse, crisp, crude, elastic, firm, fluffy, fragile, hard, liquid, porous, rough, smooth, soft, solid, tender, tough, viscous.*

dimension (adjectival)

Examples: *big, broad, deep, high, huge, large, long, low, narrow, shallow, short, small, tall, thick, thin, wide.*

emotion (adjectival/verbal)

Examples: *afraid, angry, ashamed, bold, courageous, to despair, desperate, enthusiastic, envious, to exult, furious, glad, happy, melancholic, nervous, optimistic, to panic, pessimistic, sad, serious, sullen, to worry.*

emotional response (adjectival)

Examples: *awful, boring, despicable, disgusting, funny, horrible, impressive, miserable, pitiable, poor, ridiculous, scandalous, shocking, terrible.*

evaluation (adjectival)

Examples: *attractive, bad, beautiful, difficult, easy, excellent, good, gorgeous, noble, perfect, precious, pretty, shabby, ugly.*

inanimate entity/substance (nominal)

Entity concepts such as *moon, star, stone*; substance concepts such as *clay, earth, iron, oil, rain, sand, snow, water, wood.*

intensity (adjectival)

Examples: *extreme, fierce, intensive, slight, strong, vehement, weak.*

location/position (adjectival/verbal)

Examples: *central, distant, to hang* (itr.), *horizontal, to kneel, to lie, near, parallel, prone, to protrude, to sit, to squat, to stand, upright, vertical.*

material (adjectival)

Examples: *golden, wooden, woolen.*

mental process (verbal)

Examples: *to ponder, to think, to dream.*

mental property (adjectival)

Examples: *alert, attentive, careful, cautious, clever, crazy, curious, cynical, diligent, forgetful, ingenious, insane, intelligent, naive, negligent, obstinate, sagacious, skeptical, sensible, stupid, untidy, wasteful, wise.*

mental value (adjectival)

Examples: *certain, cheap, concrete, dangerous, detrimental, direct, dubious, evident, exact, exceptional, expensive, extreme, false, general, guilty, important, innocent, legal, likely, logical, mysterious, necessary, normal, paradox, possible, real, right, safe, secret, simple, special, strange, sufficient, sure, trivial, true, useless, wrong.*

motion (verbal)
Examples: *to dance, to dangle, to drive* (itr.), *to fall, to float, to fly* (itr.), *to go, to move* (itr.), *to rise, to run* (itr.), *to sink, to swim, to walk* (itr.).

nationality/race (nominal/adjectival)
Examples: *American, French, Frenchman, Italian.*

natural phenomenon (nominal)
Lexemes denoting non-material entity concepts such as *fire, ghost, lightning, shadow*; also lexemes denoting time concepts like *day, evening, morning, night, noon, summer.*

personality feature (nominal/adjectival)
Examples: *coward, crank, dreamer, genius, gossip, loser, macho, maverick, timid.*

profession/occupation (nominal)
Examples: *actor, artist, politician, scientist, teacher, thief.*

proper name (nominal)
Although the class 'proper name' is, strictly speaking, not on a par with the other semantic classes contained in this classification, because it usually produces identificational rather than ascriptive predicates, it is included in this classification.

quantity (adjectival)
Examples: *all, few, many, much, numerous, several.*

resemblance (adjectival/verbal)
Examples: *alike, to differ, different, (to) equal, heterogeneous, homogeneous, similar.*

section of entity (nominal)
Sections of, or formations on, entities belonging mainly to the classes 'artifact' and 'toponym'. Examples: *bump, center, edge, end, hole, point.*

sex (nominal/adjectival)
Examples: *female, hermaphrodite, male.* This class may overlap with 'age', as in the case of *boy, girl, man, woman.*

shape (nominal/adjectival)
Examples: *angular, arch, bent, blunt, circle, circular, cone, concave, conical, cross, cube, cubic, flat, hollow, oval, pointed, round, sharp, straight, triangle, triangular.*

smell/taste (adjectival/verbal)
Examples: *acidic, bitter, fetid, fragrant, pungent, rancid, salty, to smell* (itr.), *sour, stale, to stink, sweet, tangy.*

social behavior (adjectival/verbal)
Examples: *aggressive, arrogant, to brag, brusque, cordial, cruel, faithful, frank, friendly, generous, harsh, honest, humble, jealous, kind, to lie, nasty, obedient, obstinate, opportunistic, polemic, polite, to pout, rebellious, selfish, shy, sincere.*

social relation (nominal)
Focal examples: terms of relationship; also: *ally, boss, enemy, foreigner, friend, orphan, widow.*

sound (adjectival/verbal)
Examples: *to call, to croak, to crunch, to cry, to growl, to hiss, to holler, to howl, to hum, to laugh, loud, to moan, to purr, to rattle, to ring, to rustle, to scream, to shout, silent, to sing, to tinkle, to whisper, to whistle.*

speech (verbal)
Examples: *to babble, to speak, to stammer, to talk.*

speed (adjectival/verbal)
Examples: *fast, to hurry* (itr.), *slow.*

temperature (adjectival/verbal)
Examples: *to boil* (itr.), *to burn* (itr.), *cold, cool, hot, tepid, warm.*

time (adjectival)
Examples: *early, late, permanent, recent, simultaneous.*

toponym (nominal)
Examples: *canyon, cliff, hill, mountain, river, sea.* Notionally, 'toponym' is a subclass of 'inanimate entity/substance'. Nevertheless, 'toponym' is treated as a separate class here.

transitive (verbal)
Lexemes which obligatorily require more than one argument when used as predicate nuclei. This is the only class in this classification which is defined in purely structural, rather than semantic, terms. On this basis, lexemes which require a possessor phrase, such as terms of relationship, are members of the class 'transitive'. However, such lexemes are, herewith, systematically excluded from the class 'transitive'; possessor phrases are not taken into account. This class has a special status in this investigation because its members hardly ever combine with a copula. An exception is the English adjective *worth*, which requires an object.

visual property/state (adjectival/verbal)
Color terms; also visual impressions like *to blink, to glimmer, to glitter, to glow, iridescent, to radiate, to shine, to sparkle, speckled, striped, transparent.*

wealth (nominal/adjectival)
Examples: *millionaire, poor, rich.*

weather (adjectival/verbal)
Examples: *cloudy, foggy, to hail, to rain, rainy, to snow, sultry, sunny, stormy.*

Appendix C
Pilot study/statistics

German

	+COP	–COP
age	100%	
animate entity	100%	
animate part	100%	
artifact	100%	
body feature	100%	
consistency	100%	
dimension	100%	
evaluation	100%	
emotional response	100%	
toponym	100%	
inanimate entity	100%	
intensity	100%	
material	100%	
mental property	100%	
mental value	100%	
nationality/race	100%	
natural phenomenon	100%	
personality feature	100%	
proper name	100%	

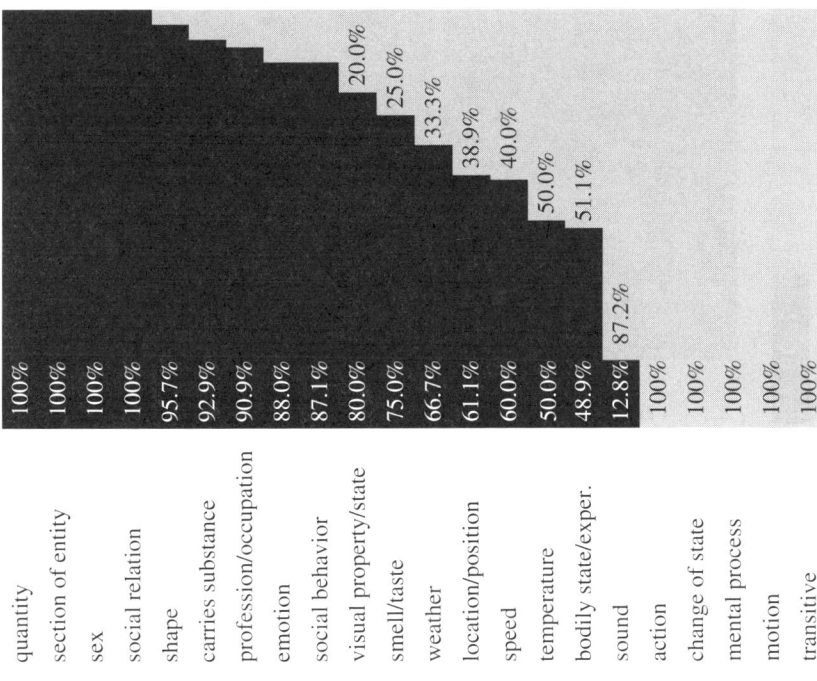

quantity	100%
section of entity	100%
sex	100%
social relation	100%
shape	95.7%
carries substance	92.9%
profession/occupation	90.9%
emotion	88.0%
social behavior	87.1%
visual property/state	80.0% / 20.0%
smell/taste	75.0% / 25.0%
weather	66.7% / 33.3%
location/position	61.1% / 38.9%
speed	60.0% / 40.0%
temperature	50.0% / 50.0%
bodily state/exper.	48.9% / 51.1%
sound	12.8% / 87.2%
action	100%
change of state	100%
mental process	100%
motion	100%
transitive	100%

Japanese

	+COP	−COP
animate entity	100%	
animate part	100%	
artifact	100%	
toponym	100%	
inanimate entity/subs.	100%	
material	100%	
nationality/race	100%	
natural phenomenon	100%	
profession/occupation	100%	
proper name	100%	
section of entity	100%	
sex	100%	
social relation	100%	
wealth	100%	
personality feature	95.6%	
time	93.0%	
location/position	90.7%	
quantity	90.5%	
age	89.2%	
resemblance	87.2%	
mental value	87.1%	

Category		
body feature	84.4%	15.6%
shape	82.5%	17.5%
evaluation	81.6%	18.4%
mental property	77.7%	22.3%
consistency	76.7%	23.3%
social behavior	73.6%	26.4%
visual property/state	72.6%	27.4%
carries substance	71.7%	28.3%
speed	61.5%	38.5%
emotional response	57.5%	42.5%
dimension	56.8%	43.2%
emotion	52.3%	47.7%
bodily state/exper.	45.6%	54.4%
intensity	42.1%	57.9%
smell/taste	41.2%	58.8%
temperature	33.3%	66.7%
weather	28.6%	71.4%
sound	26.9%	73.1%
motion	21.1%	78.9%
action	100%	
change of state	100%	
mental process	100%	
speech	100%	
transitive	100%	

Lakota

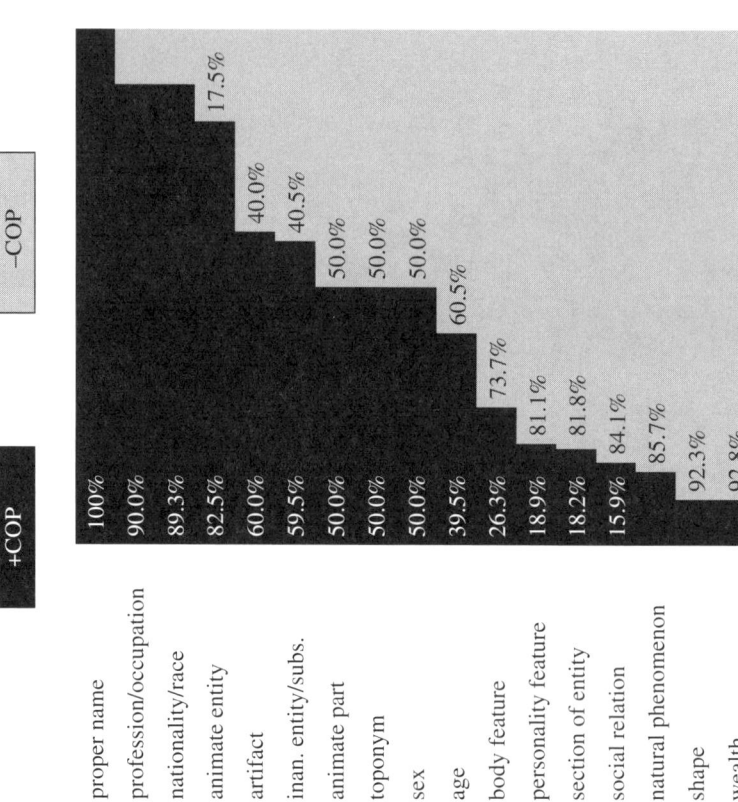

	+COP		−COP
proper name	100%		
profession/occupation	90.0%		
nationality/race	89.3%		
animate entity	82.5%		17.5%
artifact	60.0%		40.0%
inan. entity/subs.	59.5%		40.5%
animate part	50.0%		50.0%
toponym	50.0%		50.0%
sex	50.0%		50.0%
age	39.5%		60.5%
body feature	26.3%		73.7%
personality feature	18.9%		81.1%
section of entity	18.2%		81.8%
social relation	15.9%		84.1%
natural phenomenon			85.7%
shape			92.3%
wealth			92.8%

action	100%
bodily state/exper.	100%
carries substance	100%
change of state	100%
consistency	100%
dimension	100%
emotion	100%
evaluation	100%
location/position	100%
mental property	100%
motion	100%
quantity	100%
smell/taste	100%
social behavior	100%
sound	100%
speech	100%
speed	100%
temperature	100%
transitive	100%
visual property/state	100%
weather	100%

Mandarin

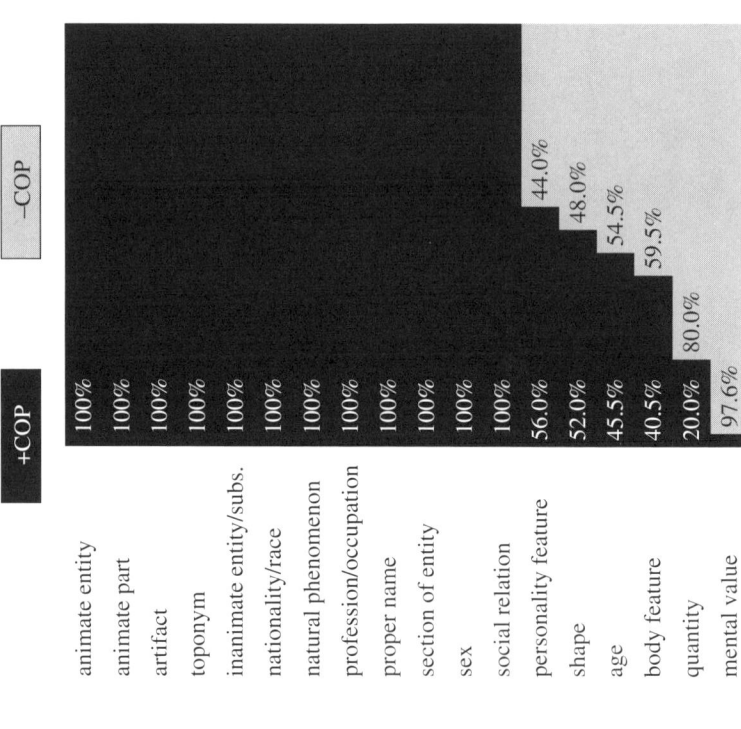

Category	Percentage
action	100%
bodily state/exper.	100%
carries substance	100%
change of state	100%
consistency	100%
dimension	100%
emotion	100%
evaluation	100%
emotional response	100%
location/position	100%
mental property	100%
mental process	100%
motion	100%
smell/taste	100%
social behavior	100%
sound	100%
speech	100%
speed	100%
temperature	100%
transitive	100%
visual property/state	100%
weather	100%

Spanish

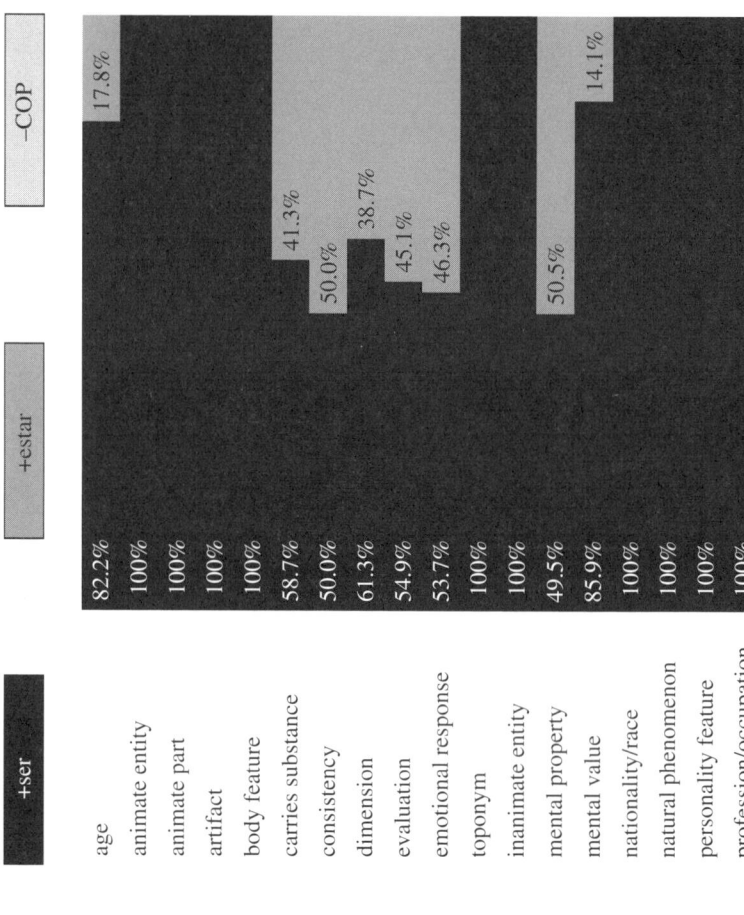

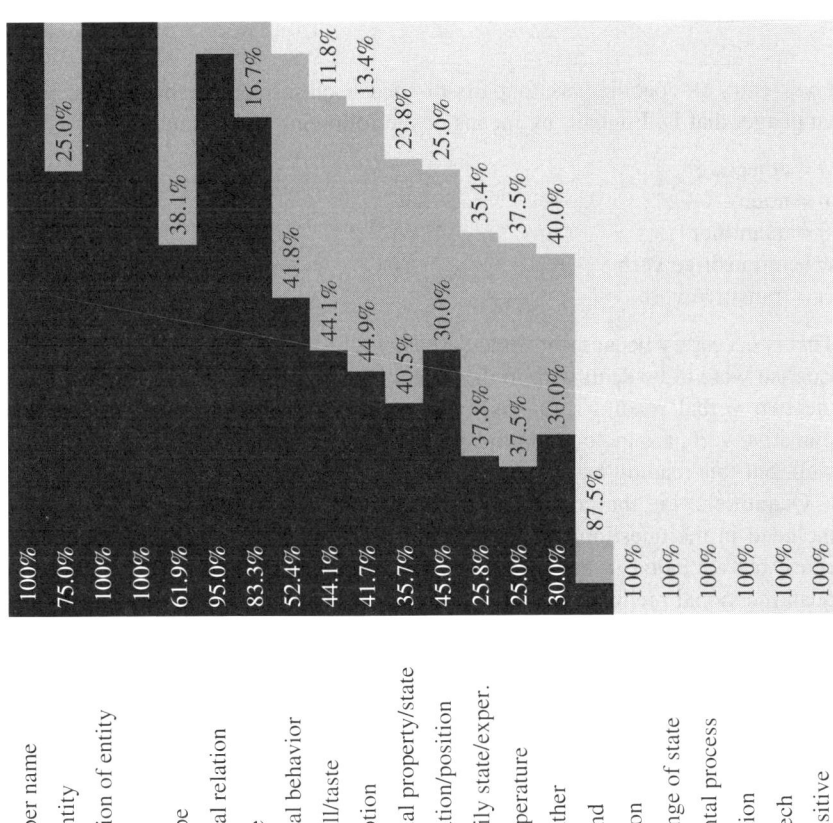

proper name	100%	
quantity	75.0%	25.0%
section of entity	100%	
sex	100%	
shape	61.9%	38.1%
social relation	95.0%	
time	83.3%	16.7%
social behavior	52.4%	41.8%	11.8%
smell/taste	44.1%	44.1%	13.4%
emotion	41.7%	44.9%	
visual property/state	35.7%	40.5%	23.8%
location/position	45.0%	30.0%	25.0%
bodily state/exper.	25.8%	37.8%	35.4%
temperature	25.0%	37.5%	37.5%
weather	30.0%	30.0%	40.0%
sound	87.5%		
action	100%	
change of state	100%	
mental process	100%	
motion	100%	
speech	100%	
transitive	100%	

Appendix D
Questionnaire

Each entry is specified as to parts-of-speech class membership in the meta-language, that is, English, by means of the following abbreviations:

a = adjective
n = noun
q = quantifier
vi = intransitive verb
vt = transitive verb

This is necessary because in some cases not all the meanings of a lexical root in English were to be dealt with in the object language. For instance, for *bend* only the two verbal readings, that is, *bend* as an intransitive verb and *bend* as a transitive verb, are included in the questionnaire. *Bend* has a nominal reading as well, but this reading has been excluded from the list of basic vocabulary.

Quantifiers, i.e. the concepts 'all', 'few', 'many', 'much', and 'some' were included in the questionnaire in order to obtain data on quantificational predicates, but excluded in the final analyses of the language-specific data because quantificational predicates form a predicate class of their own according to what is said in §2.1.4. Thus, the surveys and statistical analyses focus solely on lexemes that can be used to form ascriptive predicates.

ache	*vi*	American	*a*	ask	*vt*
acidic	*a*	American	*n*	asleep	*a*
actor	*n*	angry	*a*	attack	*vt*
admire	*vt*	angular	*a*	aunt	*n*
adult	*n*	animal	*n*	Australia	*n*
afraid	*a*	appear	*vi*	awake	*a*
aggressive	*a*	apple	*n*	axe	*n*
air	*n*	area	*n*	baby	*n*
alike	*a*	arm	*n*	back	*n*
alive	*a*	arrive	*vi*	bad	*a*
all	*q*	arrogant	*a*	bag	*n*
allow	*vt*	arrow	*n*	ball	*n*
alone	*a*	artist	*n*	banana	*n*
ambitious	*a*	ashamed	*a*	bare	*a*
America	*n*	Asia	*n*	bark	*n*

bathe	*vi*	brittle	*a*	contain	*vt*
bathe	*vt*	broad	*a*	cook	*n*
beach	*n*	brown	*a*	cook	*vi*
bean	*n*	build	*vt*	cook	*vt*
bear	*n*	burn	*vi*	cool	*a*
beat	*vi*	burn	*vt*	copper	*n*
beat	*vt*	burst	*vi*	corner	*n*
beautiful	*a*	bury	*vt*	cough	*vi*
bed	*n*	buy	*vt*	count	*vt*
beggar	*n*	call	*vi*	courageous	*a*
believe	*vt*	calm	*a*	cousin	*n*
bend	*vi*	car	*n*	cover	*vt*
bend	*vt*	carry	*vt*	coward	*n*
bent	*a*	cat	*n*	crazy	*a*
berry	*n*	cautious	*a*	cripple	*n*
big	*a*	cave	*n*	crisp	*a*
birch	*n*	central	*a*	croak	*vi*
bird	*n*	chair	*n*	crooked	*a*
bite	*vt*	change	*vi*	cross	*n*
bitter	*a*	change	*vt*	cross-breed	*n*
black	*a*	chase	*vt*	crow	*n*
blind	*a*	cheap	*a*	cruel	*a*
blink	*vi*	cheat	*vt*	crush	*vt*
blond	*a*	child	*n*	cry	*vi*
blood	*n*	Chinese	*a*	cube	*n*
blue	*a*	Chinese	*n*	cubic	*a*
boat	*n*	choleric	*a*	cure	*vt*
body	*n*	circle	*n*	cut	*vt*
boil	*vi*	circular	*a*	dance	*vi*
boil	*vt*	clay	*n*	dangerous	*a*
bone	*n*	clean	*a*	dark	*a*
book	*n*	clear	*a*	daughter	*n*
borrow	*vt*	clever	*a*	dead	*a*
bottom	*n*	cliff	*n*	deceive	*vt*
bowl	*n*	climb	*vt*	deep	*a*
boy	*n*	close	*vi*	deer	*n*
branch	*n*	close	*vt*	demand	*vt*
brass	*n*	coin	*n*	dent	*n*
break	*vi*	cold	*a*	desert	*n*
break	*vt*	collect	*vt*	desire	*vt*
bridge	*n*	color-blind	*a*	despise	*vt*
bright	*a*	come	*vi*	destroy	*vt*
bring	*vt*	cone	*n*	die	*vi*

differ	*vi*	examine	*vt*	god	*n*
different	*a*	excellent	*a*	gold	*n*
difficult	*a*	exist	*vi*	good	*a*
dig	*vt*	expensive	*a*	gorgeous	*a*
dirty	*a*	explode	*vi*	grandchild	*n*
discover	*vt*	eye	*n*	grandfather	*n*
disk	*n*	face	*n*	grandmother	*n*
dizzy	*a*	fall	*vi*	grass	*n*
do	*vt*	farmer	*n*	gray	*a*
doctor	*n*	fat	*a*	grease	*n*
dog	*n*	father	*n*	greasy	*a*
door	*n*	fear	*vt*	greedy	*a*
dot	*n*	feel	*vt*	green	*a*
doubt	*vt*	female	*a*	grind	*vt*
dream	*n*	few	*q*	groan	*vi*
dream	*vi*	find	*vt*	grow	*vi*
dress	*n*	fire	*n*	growl	*vi*
drink	*vt*	fish	*n*	gun	*n*
drop	*vt*	flash	*vi*	hair	*n*
dry	*a*	flat	*a*	hand	*n*
dull	*a*	flow	*vi*	hang	*vi*
dust	*n*	fly	*vi*	happy	*a*
eagle	*n*	foot	*n*	hard	*a*
ear	*n*	forget	*vt*	hate	*vt*
earth	*n*	France	*n*	have	*vt*
easy	*a*	free	*a*	haze	*n*
eat	*vt*	French	*a*	head	*n*
edge	*n*	Frenchman	*n*	healthy	*a*
egg	*n*	friend	*n*	hear	*vt*
elastic	*a*	full	*a*	heart	*n*
empty	*a*	funny	*a*	heavy	*a*
end	*n*	furious	*a*	help	*vt*
end	*vi*	gas	*n*	hollow	*a*
end	*vt*	German	*a*	holy	*a*
enemy	*n*	German	*n*	horse	*n*
England	*n*	Germany	*n*	hot	*a*
English	*a*	girl	*n*	house	*n*
Englishman	*n*	give	*vt*	howl	*vi*
enough	*a*	glad	*a*	hum	*vi*
equal	*a*	glitter	*vi*	hungry	*a*
escape	*vi*	glow	*vi*	hurt	*vt*
Europe	*n*	glutton	*n*	husband	*n*
exact	*a*	go	*vi*	ice	*n*

idiot	*n*	many	*q*	pine	*n*
insect	*n*	marry	*vt*	pity	*vt*
intelligent	*a*	melt	*vi*	play	*vi*
iron	*n*	middle	*n*	pleasant	*a*
island	*n*	miser	*n*	potato	*n*
Italian	*a*	mix	*vt*	powder	*n*
Italian	*n*	money	*n*	powerful	*a*
Italy	*n*	moon	*n*	praise	*vt*
itch	*vi*	mother	*n*	pregnant	*a*
jealous	*a*	mountain	*n*	protect	*vt*
juice	*n*	mouse	*n*	proud	*a*
jump	*vi*	mouth	*n*	pull	*vt*
kill	*vt*	move	*vi*	punish	*vt*
kiss	*vt*	move	*vt*	pure	*a*
knife	*n*	much	*q*	purr	*vi*
know	*vt*	mushroom	*n*	push	*vt*
lack	*vt*	narrow	*a*	put	*vt*
lake	*n*	need	*vt*	quick	*a*
laugh	*vi*	nervous	*a*	quiet	*a*
lazy	*a*	new	*a*	quiver	*vi*
lead	*vt*	nice	*a*	rabbit	*n*
leaf	*n*	nose	*n*	rain	*n*
leave	*vi*	oak	*n*	rain	*vi*
leave	*vt*	oil	*n*	raise	*vt*
left-handed	*a*	old	*a*	rare	*a*
leg	*n*	onion	*n*	rattle	*vi*
less	*q*	open	*a*	raw	*a*
lie (prevaricate)	*vi*	open	*vi*	read	*vt*
lie (recline)	*vi*	open	*vt*	real	*a*
light	*n*	optimist	*n*	receive	*vt*
like	*vt*	optimistic	*a*	recognize	*vt*
line	*n*	ordinary	*a*	red	*a*
liquid	*a*	orphan	*n*	regret	*vt*
live	*vi*	oval	*a*	remember	*vt*
lonely	*a*	owl	*n*	resemble	*vt*
long	*a*	own	*vt*	resent	*vt*
loud	*a*	paint	*n*	right (*vs.* wrong)	*a*
love	*vt*	paint	*vt*	right-handed	*a*
low	*a*	part	*n*	ring	*n*
lump	*n*	pass	*vi*	ring	*vi*
make	*vt*	peel	*vt*	ripe	*a*
male	*a*	perfect	*a*	rise	*vi*
man	*n*	perspire	*vi*	river	*n*

road	*n*	sing	*vi*	stiff	*a*
roast	*vt*	sister	*n*	stingy	*a*
roll	*vi*	sit	*vi*	stink	*vi*
rope	*n*	sky	*n*	stir	*vt*
rot	*vi*	slash	*vt*	stone	*n*
rough	*a*	sleep	*vi*	stop	*vi*
round	*a*	slim	*a*	storm	*n*
rub	*vt*	slip	*vi*	straight	*a*
rubber	*n*	slow	*a*	strong	*a*
run	*vi*	small	*a*	stubborn	*a*
sad	*a*	smart	*a*	stupid	*a*
salt	*n*	smell	*vi*	suffer	*vi*
same	*a*	smell	*vt*	sugar	*n*
sand	*n*	smoke	*n*	sun	*n*
save	*vt*	smooth	*a*	swallow	*vt*
say	*a*	snake	*n*	sweet	*a*
scare	*vt*	sneeze	*vi*	swell	*vi*
scratch	*vt*	snow	*n*	swim	*vi*
scream	*vi*	soft	*a*	tail	*n*
sea	*n*	solid	*a*	take	*vt*
secret	*a*	some	*q*	talk	*vi*
see	*vt*	son	*n*	tall	*a*
seek	*vt*	song	*n*	tame	*a*
select	*vt*	sore	*a*	tear	*vt*
selfish	*a*	sorry	*a*	tell	*vt*
sell	*vt*	sour	*a*	tender	*a*
send	*vt*	spank	*vt*	terrible	*a*
serious	*a*	spark	*n*	thick	*a*
sew	*vt*	speak	*vi*	thin	*a*
shake	*vt*	sphere	*n*	think	*vt*
sharp	*a*	spider	*n*	thirsty	*a*
shatter	*vt*	spill	*vt*	thistle	*n*
shoe	*n*	spin	*vi*	throw	*vt*
short	*a*	split	*vt*	thunder	*n*
show	*vt*	spotted	*a*	tip	*n*
shrink	*vi*	square	*a*	tired	*a*
shy	*a*	square	*n*	tooth	*n*
sick	*a*	squeeze	*vt*	top	*n*
side	*n*	stand	*vi*	touch	*vt*
silver	*n*	star	*n*	tough	*a*
similar	*a*	start	*vi*	town	*n*
simple	*a*	stay	*vi*	toy	*n*
sincere	*a*	steal	*vt*	trader	*n*

tree	*n*	wake up	*vt*	wild	*a*
triangle	*n*	walk	*vi*	willow	*n*
triangular	*a*	want	*vt*	win	*vt*
trout	*n*	warm	*a*	wind	*n*
true	*a*	warn	*vt*	wipe	*vt*
trust	*vt*	wash	*vt*	wise	*a*
turn	*vi*	watch	*vt*	wish	*vt*
turn	*vt*	water	*n*	woman	*n*
twist	*vt*	wave	*vt*	wood	*n*
ugly	*a*	weak	*a*	wool	*n*
understand	*vt*	wealthy	*a*	work	*vi*
use	*vt*	weapon	*n*	worm	*n*
vain	*a*	wear	*vt*	worry	*vi*
valuable	*a*	wet	*a*	worth	*a*
vanish	*vi*	wheel	*n*	write	*vt*
vicious	*a*	whisper	*vi*	wrong	*a*
villain	*n*	whistle	*vi*	yawn	*vi*
visit	*vt*	white	*a*	yell	*vi*
wait	*vi*	wide	*a*	yellow	*a*
wake up	*vi*	wife	*n*	young	*a*

Appendix E
The semantic structure of the lexical samples

Burmese

CLASS	VALENCE	TRANSIENCE	DYNAMICITY	EXAMPLES	$+$ COP	$-$ COP	TOTAL
A	0	−	−	prototypical nominals ('house', 'dog'); nominals designating sex ('woman'); age nominals denoting permanent membership in age group ('old man'); nominals referring to bodily or mental disposition ('glutton', 'genius')	169	0	169
B	1	−	−	body features; adjectivals denoting nationality ('French'); personality features ('smart'); body features ('color-blind'); relational nouns including body parts and terms of relationship; age adjectivals denoting permanent membership in age group ('old')	16	11	27
C	0	+/−	−	occupations/professions ('teacher'); nominals for shape ('triangle')	19	0	19
D	1	+/−	−	prototypical adjectivals ('big', 'good', 'red'); positionals ('to sit', 'to stand') and other statives ('to stink')	2	104	106

CLASS	VALENCE	TRANSIENCE	DYNAMICITY	EXAMPLES	+ COP	− COP	TOTAL
E	1	+/−	+/−	'to stand/rise'	0	1	1
F	1	+/−	+	'to glitter'	0	1	1
G	2	+/−	−	emotional/mental acts or states ('to love', 'to know'); concepts denoting possession ('to have'); concepts denoting resemblance ('to resemble')	0	15	15
H	2	+/−	+/−	'to cover (either temporarily or permanently)'	0	1	1
I	2	+/−	+	'to understand'	0	1	1
K	0	+	+	meteorological events ('to rain')	0	1	1
L	1	+	−	bodily/mental states ('tired', 'angry')	0	24	24
N	1	+	+	prototypical intransitive verbals ('to go')	0	56	56
O	2	+	−	transitive transient non-dynamic events ('to hold')	0	11	11
Q	2	+	+	prototypical transitive verbals ('to buy')	0	94	94

Cantonese

CLASS	VALENCE	TRANSIENCE	DYNAMICITY	EXAMPLES	+ COP	− COP	TOTAL
A	0	−	−	prototypical nominals ('house', 'dog'); nominals designating sex ('woman'); age nominals denoting permanent membership in age group ('old man'); nominals referring to bodily or mental disposition ('glutton', 'genius')	147	0	147
B	1	−	−	body features; adjectivals denoting nationality ('French'); personality features ('smart'); body features ('color-blind'); relational nouns including body parts and terms of relationship; age adjectivals denoting permanent membership in age group ('old')	27	28	55
C	0	+/−	−	occupations/professions ('teacher'); nominals for shape ('triangle')	25	0	25
D	1	+/−	−	prototypical adjectivals ('big', 'good', 'red'); positionals ('to sit', 'to stand') and other statives ('to stink')	19	96	115
F	1	+/−	+	'to flow'; 'to glitter'	0	2	2
G	2	+/−	−	emotional/mental acts or states ('to love', 'to know'); concepts denoting possession ('to have'); concepts denoting resemblance ('to resemble')	0	18	18

CLASS	VALENCE	TRANSIENCE	DYNAMICITY	EXAMPLES	+ COP	− COP	TOTAL
I	2	+/−	+	'to cover (either temporarily or permanently)'; 'to scare (either temporarily or permanently'; 'to understand'	0	3	3
K	0	+	+	meteorological events ('to rain')	0	1	1
L	1	+	−	bodily/mental states ('tired', 'angry')	0	21	21
N	1	+	+	prototypical intransitive verbals ('to go')	0	59	59
O	2	+	−	transitive transient non-dynamic events ('to hold')	0	8	8
Q	2	+	+	prototypical transitive verbals ('to buy')	0	90	90

German

CLASS	VALENCE	TRANSIENCE	DYNAMICITY	EXAMPLES	+ COP	− COP	TOTAL
A	0	−	−	prototypical nominals ('house', 'dog'); nominals designating sex ('woman'); age nominals denoting permanent membership in age group ('old man'); nominals referring to bodily or mental disposition ('glutton', 'genius')	167	0	167
B	1	−	−	body features; adjectivals denoting nationality ('French'); personality features ('smart'); body features ('color-blind'); relational nouns including body parts and terms of relationship; age adjectivals denoting permanent membership in age group ('old')	32	0	32
C	0	+/−	−	occupations/professions ('teacher'); nominals for shape ('triangle')	29	0	29
D	1	+/−	−	prototypical adjectivals ('big', 'good', 'red'); positionals ('to sit', 'to stand') and other statives ('to stink')	145	13	158
F	1	+/−	+	'to flow'; 'to glitter'	0	2	2
G	2	+/−	−	emotional/mental acts or states ('to love', 'to know'); concepts denoting possession ('to have'); concepts denoting resemblance ('to resemble')	1	15	16

CLASS	VALENCE	TRANSIENCE	DYNAMICITY	EXAMPLES	+ COP	− COP	TOTAL
H	2	+/−	+/−	'to cover (either temporarily or permanently)'	0	1	1
I	2	+/−	+	'to scare (either temporarily or permanently)'; 'to understand'	0	2	2
K	0	+	+	meteorological events ('to rain')	0	1	1
L	1	+	−	bodily/mental states ('tired', 'angry')	13	11	24
N	1	+	+	prototypical intransitive verbals ('to go')	0	79	79
O	2	+	−	transitive transient non-dynamic events ('to hold')	0	9	9
P	2	+	+/−	'to carry/wear'	0	1	1
Q	2	+	+	prototypical transitive verbals ('to buy')	0	90	90

Hungarian

CLASS	VALENCE	TRANSIENCE	DYNAMICITY	EXAMPLES	+ COP	− COP	TOTAL
A	0	−	−	prototypical nominals ('house', 'dog'); nominals designating sex ('woman'); age nominals denoting permanent membership in age group ('old man'); nominals referring to bodily or mental disposition ('glutton', 'genius')	174	0	174
B	1	−	−	body features; adjectivals denoting nationality ('French'); personality features ('smart'); body features ('color-blind'); relational nouns including body parts and terms of relationship; age adjectivals denoting permanent membership in age group ('old')	50	0	50
C	0	+/−	−	occupations/professions ('teacher'); nominals for shape ('triangle')	25	0	25
D	1	+/−	−	prototypical adjectivals ('big', 'good', 'red'); positionals ('to sit', 'to stand') and other statives ('to stink')	132	10	142
F	1	+/−	+	'to flow'; 'to glitter'	0	2	2
G	2	+/−	−	emotional/mental acts or states ('to love', 'to know'); concepts denoting possession ('to have'); concepts denoting resemblance ('to resemble')	1	14	15
I	2	+/−	+	'to understand'	0	1	1

CLASS	VALENCE	TRANSIENCE	DYNAMICITY	EXAMPLES	+ COP	− COP	TOTAL
L	1	+	−	bodily/mental states ('tired', 'angry')	8	15	23
N	1	+	+	prototypical intransitive verbals ('to go')	0	96	96
O	2	+	−	transitive transient non-dynamic events ('to hold')	0	5	5
P	2	+	+/−	'to carry/wear'	0	1	1
Q	2	+	+	prototypical transitive verbals ('to buy')	0	102	102

Indonesian

CLASS	VALENCE	TRANSIENCE	DYNAMICITY	EXAMPLES	+ COP	− COP	TOTAL
A	0	−	−	prototypical nominals ('house', 'dog'); nominals designating sex ('woman'); age nominals denoting permanent membership in age group ('old man'); nominals referring to bodily or mental disposition ('glutton', 'genius')	181	0	181
B	1	−	−	body features; adjectivals denoting nationality ('French'); personality features ('smart'); body features ('color-blind'); relational nouns including body parts and terms of relationship; age adjectivals denoting permanent membership in age group ('old')	20	55	75
C	0	+/−	−	occupations/professions ('teacher'); nominals for shape ('triangle')	31	0	31
D	1	+/−	−	prototypical adjectivals ('big', 'good', 'red'); positionals ('to sit', 'to stand') and other statives ('to stink')	3	176	179
E	1	+/−	+/−	'to bend (*itr.*)/to be bent'; 'to act courageously/ to be courageous'; 'to ripen/to be ripe'	0	3	3
F	1	+/−	+	'to flow'; 'to glitter'	0	2	2
G	2	+/−	−	emotional/mental acts or states ('to love', 'to know'); concepts denoting possession ('to have'); concepts denoting resemblance ('to resemble')	0	22	22

CLASS	VALENCE	TRANSIENCE	DYNAMICITY	EXAMPLES	+ COP	− COP	TOTAL
H	2	+/−	+/−	'to cover (either temporarily or permanently)'	0	1	1
I	2	+/−	+	'to understand'	0	1	1
K	0	+	+	meteorological events ('to rain')	0	1	1
L	1	+	−	bodily/mental states ('tired', 'angry')	0	30	30
M	1	+	+/−	'to break (itr.)/to be broken'; 'to burn (itr.)/to be burnt'; 'to come/to be there'; 'to quiver/to be nervous'; 'to wake up/to be awake'	0	5	5
N	1	+	+	prototypical intransitive verbals ('to go')	0	99	99
O	2	+	−	transitive transient non-dynamic events ('to hold')	0	1	1
Q	2	+	+	prototypical transitive verbals ('to buy')	0	121	121

Japanese

CLASS	VALENCE	TRANSIENCE	DYNAMICITY	EXAMPLES	+ COP	− COP	TOTAL
A	0	−	−	prototypical nominals ('house', 'dog'); nominals designating sex ('woman'); age nominals denoting permanent membership in age group ('old man'); nominals referring to bodily or mental disposition ('glutton', 'genius')	212	0	212
B	1	−	−	body features; adjectivals denoting nationality ('French'); personality features ('smart'); body features ('color-blind'); relational nouns including body parts and terms of relationship; age adjectivals denoting permanent membership in age group ('old')	92	18	110
C	0	+/−	−	occupations/professions ('teacher'); nominals for shape ('triangle')	39	0	39
D	1	+/−	−	prototypical adjectivals ('big', 'good', 'red'); positionals ('to sit', 'to stand') and other statives ('to stink')	95	97	192
E	1	+/−	+/−	'to fall in love/to be in love'; 'to sit down/to sit'; 'to get up/to stand'	0	3	3
F	1	+/−	+	'to act aggressively'; 'to flow'; 'to glitter'	0	3	3

CLASS	VALENCE	TRANSIENCE	DYNAMICITY	EXAMPLES	+ COP	− COP	TOTAL
G	2	+/−	−	emotional/mental acts or states ('to love', 'to know'); concepts denoting possession ('to have'); concepts denoting resemblance ('to resemble')	2	24	26
H	2	+/−	+/−	'to seek/to desire'	0	1	1
I	2	+/−	+	'to understand' (2 lexemes)	0	2	2
L	1	+	−	bodily/mental states ('tired', 'angry')	9	22	31
M	1	+	+/−	'to get angry/to be angry/to get furious/to be furious'; 'to get shy/to be shy'; 'to fall asleep/to sleep' (2 lexemes)	0	4	4
N	1	+	+	prototypical intransitive verbals ('to go')	0	79	79
O	2	+	−	transitive transient non-dynamic events ('to hold')	0	12	12
Q	2	+	+	prototypical transitive verbals ('to buy')	0	140	140

Lakota

CLASS	VALENCE	TRANSIENCE	DYNAMICITY	EXAMPLES	+ COP	− COP	TOTAL
A	0	−	−	prototypical nominals ('house', 'dog'); nominals designating sex ('woman'); age nominals denoting permanent membership in age group ('old man'); nominals referring to bodily or mental disposition ('glutton', 'genius')	193	0	193
B	1	−	−	body features; adjectivals denoting nationality ('French'); personality features ('smart'); body features ('color-blind'); relational nouns including body parts and terms of relationship; age adjectivals denoting permanent membership in age group ('old')	10	17	27
C	0	+/−	−	occupations/professions ('teacher'); nominals for shape ('triangle')	20	0	20
D	1	+/−	−	prototypical adjectivals ('big', 'good', 'red'); positionals ('to sit', 'to stand') and other statives ('to stink')	0	143	143
E	1	+/−	+/−	'to curl up/to be curled up'; 'to get a bump or bumps/to have a bump or bumps'; 'to get up/to stand'; 'to joke/to be funny'; 'to misbehave (like a child)/to be disobedient/to be excited'; 'to slow	0	9	9

CLASS	VALENCE	TRANSIENCE	DYNAMICITY	EXAMPLES	+ COP	− COP	TOTAL
				down/to be slow/to be weak'; 'to sparkle/to be bright'; 'to unwind by itself/to be unwound'; 'to wiggle/to be crooked'			
G	2	+/−	−	emotional/mental acts or states ('to love', 'to know'); concepts denoting possession ('to have'); concepts denoting resemblance ('to resemble')	0	17	17
H	2	+/−	+/−	'to brag about/to be proud of'; 'to lose/to be without/to have lost'; 'to take care of/to respect'	0	3	3
I	2	+/−	+	'to understand'	0	1	1
J	0	+	−	'to be cold (weather)'	0	1	1
K	0	+	+	meteorological events ('to rain')	0	4	4
L	1	+	−	bodily/mental states ('tired', 'angry')	0	42	42
M	1	+	+/−	'to crack by itself/to have dry skin'; 'to die/to be close to dying'; 'to disappear/to disintegrate/to be gone'; 'to get up/to wake up/ to be awake'; 'to have the fits/to hallucinate/to be wild/to be crazy/to be frantic'; 'to lose one's orientation/ to be lost/to have lost one's orientation'; 'to peel by itself/to be chipped/to be with the surface peeled off'; 'to recover/to be well'	0	8	8
N	1	+	+	prototypical intransitive verbals ('to go')	0	120	120
O	2	+	−	transitive transient non-dynamic events ('to hold')	0	18	18
Q	2	+	+	prototypical transitive verbals ('to buy')	0	215	215

Swahili

CLASS	VALENCE	TRANSIENCE	DYNAMICITY	EXAMPLES	+ COP	− COP	TOTAL
A	0	−	−	prototypical nominals ('house', 'dog'); nominals designating sex ('woman'); age nominals denoting permanent membership in age group ('old man'); nominals referring to bodily or mental disposition ('glutton', 'genius')	164	0	164
B	1	−	−	body features; adjectivals denoting nationality ('French'); personality features ('smart'); body features ('color-blind'); relational nouns including body parts and terms of relationship; age adjectivals denoting permanent membership in age group ('old')	45	1	46
C	0	+/−	−	occupations/professions ('teacher'); nominals for shape ('triangle')	24	0	24
D	1	+/−	−	prototypical adjectivals ('big', 'good', 'red'); positionals ('to sit', 'to stand') and other statives ('to stink')	94	14	108
F	1	+/−	+	'to flow/pass by'; 'to glitter/blink'	0	2	2
G	2	+/−	−	emotional/mental acts or states ('to love', 'to know'); concepts denoting possession ('to have'); concepts denoting resemblance ('to resemble')	1	14	15
H	2	+/−	+/−	'to know/understand'	0	1	1

CLASS	VALENCE	TRANSIENCE	DYNAMICITY	EXAMPLES	+ COP	− COP	TOTAL
I	2	+/−	+	'to understand'	0	1	1
K	0	+	+	meteorological events ('to rain')	0	1	1
L	1	+	−	bodily/mental states ('tired', 'angry')	6	14	20
N	1	+	+	prototypical intransitive verbals ('to go')	0	75	75
O	2	+	−	transitive transient non-dynamic events ('to hold')	0	2	2
Q	2	+	+	prototypical transitive verbals ('to buy')	0	91	91

Thai

CLASS	VALENCE	TRANSIENCE	DYNAMICITY	EXAMPLES	+ COP	− COP	TOTAL
A	0	−	−	prototypical nominals ('house', 'dog'); nominals designating sex ('woman'); age nominals denoting permanent membership in age group ('old man'); nominals referring to bodily or mental disposition ('glutton', 'genius')	153	0	153
B	1	−	−	body features; adjectivals denoting nationality ('French'); personality features ('smart'); body features ('color-blind'); relational nouns including body parts and terms of relationship; age adjectivals denoting permanent membership in age group ('old')	26	33	59
C	0	+/−	−	occupations/professions ('teacher'); nominals for shape ('triangle')	24	0	24
D	1	+/−	−	prototypical adjectivals ('big', 'good', 'red'); positionals ('to sit', 'to stand') and other statives ('to stink')	21	125	146
E	1	+/−	+/−	'to act sad/to be sad'; 'to die/to be dead'	0	2	2
F	1	+/−	+	'to flow'; 'to act in a crazy way (sporadically or permanently)'	0	2	2
G	2	+/−	−	emotional/mental acts or states ('to love', 'to know'); concepts denoting possession ('to have'); concepts denoting resemblance ('to resemble')	0	18	18
H	2	+/−	+/−	'to act in a jealous way towards/to be jealous of'	0	1	1

CLASS	VALENCE	TRANSIENCE	DYNAMICITY	EXAMPLES	+ COP	− COP	TOTAL
I	2	+/−	+	'to understand'	0	1	1
K	0	+	+	meteorological events ('to rain')	0	1	1
L	1	+	−	bodily/mental states ('tired', 'angry')	0	19	19
M	1	+	+/−	'to act crazy/to be crazy'	0	1	1
N	1	+	+	prototypical intransitive verbals ('to go')	0	81	81
O	2	+	−	transitive transient non-dynamic events ('to hold')	0	6	6
Q	2	+	+	prototypical transitive verbals ('to buy')	0	93	93

Turkish

CLASS	VALENCE	TRANSIENCE	DYNAMICITY	EXAMPLES	+/− COP	− COP	TOTAL
A	0	−	−	prototypical nominals ('house', 'dog'); nominals designating sex ('woman'); age nominals denoting permanent membership in age group ('old man'); nominals referring to bodily or mental disposition ('glutton', 'genius')	154	0	154
B	1	−	−	body features; adjectivals denoting nationality ('French'); personality features ('smart'); body features ('color-blind'); relational nouns including body parts and terms of relationship; age adjectivals denoting permanent membership in age group ('old')	76	1	77
C	0	+/−	−	occupations/professions ('teacher'); nominals for shape ('triangle')	18	0	18
D	1	+/−	−	prototypical adjectivals ('big', 'good', 'red'); positionals ('to sit', 'to stand') and other statives ('to stink')	118	15	133
F	1	+/−	+	'to flow'	0	1	1
G	2	+/−	−	emotional/mental acts or states ('to love', 'to know'); concepts denoting possession ('to have'); concepts denoting resemblance ('to resemble')	0	13	13
I	2	+/−	+	'to understand'	0	1	1

CLASS	VALENCE	TRANSIENCE	DYNAMICITY	EXAMPLES	+/− COP	− COP	TOTAL
L	1	+	−	bodily/mental states ('tired', 'angry')	0	21	21
N	2	+	−	prototypical intransitive verbals ('to go')	0	3	3
O	1	+	+	transitive transient non-dynamic events ('to hold')	0	74	74
Q	2	+	+	prototypical transitive verbals ('to buy')	0	89	89

Appendix F
Copula use and semantic similarity space

The following bar charts are based on the raw distributional figures reproduced in the tables given in appendix E. As for the graphic representation chosen, semantic classes are arranged in the horizontal axis of the diagrams according to their distance to class A, or the nominal prototype, in semantic similarity space. Class A constitutes the leftmost position in the axis. The greater the distance of a given lexical class from class A in semantic similarity space, the further to the right it will be located. In some language-specific space diagrams, however, mixed classes are found which are equidistant from class A. Since the specific structure of the bar charts used for graphic representation of the data is such that a single position in the axis cannot be occupied by more than one class, separate diagrams are established in such cases. The Lakota data are not dealt with in what follows because, obviously, comparing the internal composition of language-specific mixed classes presupposes the existence of at least two mixed classes. In Lakota, only a single mixed class could be identified.

Burmese

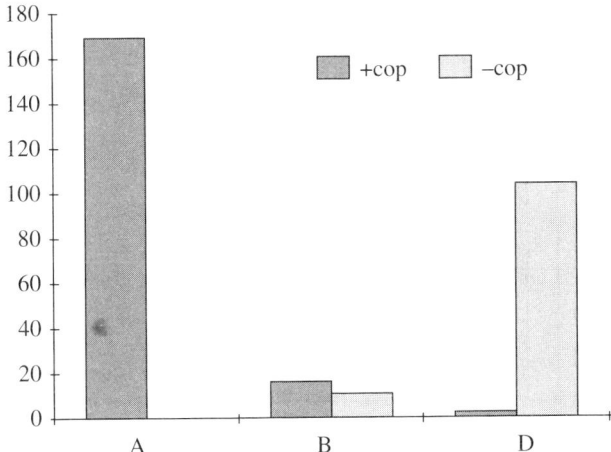

Cantonese

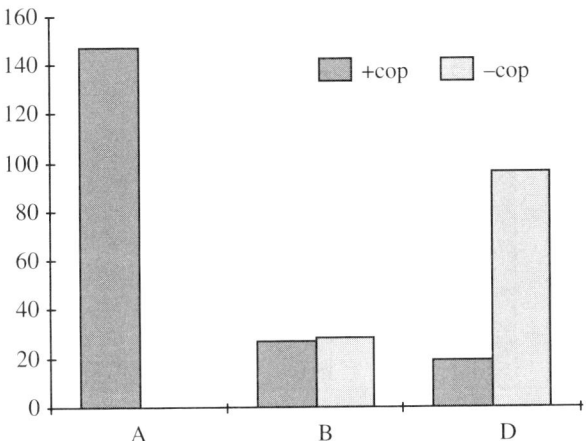

German (A)

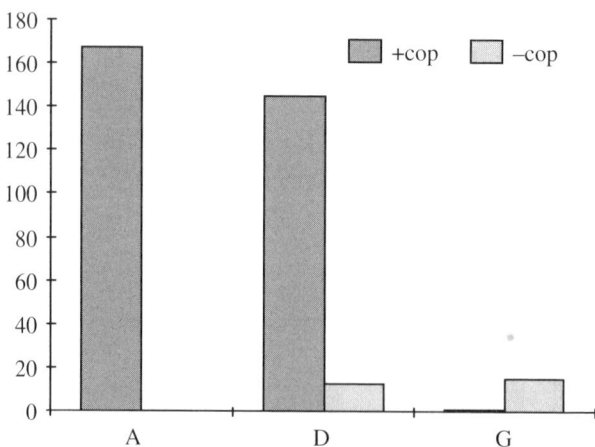

German (B)

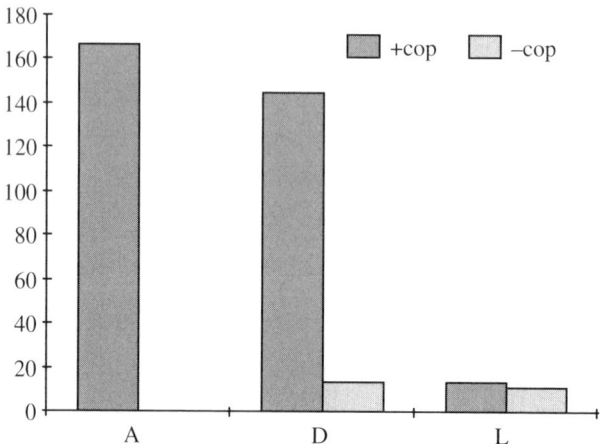

Hungarian (A)

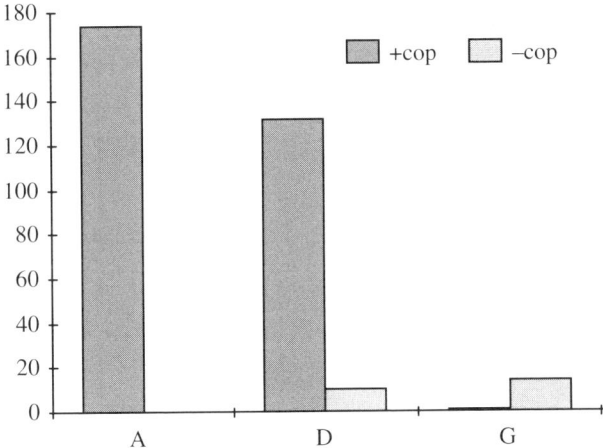

Hungarian (B)

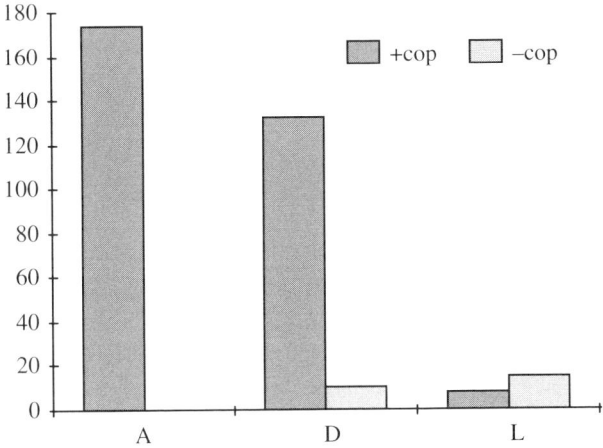

Indonesian

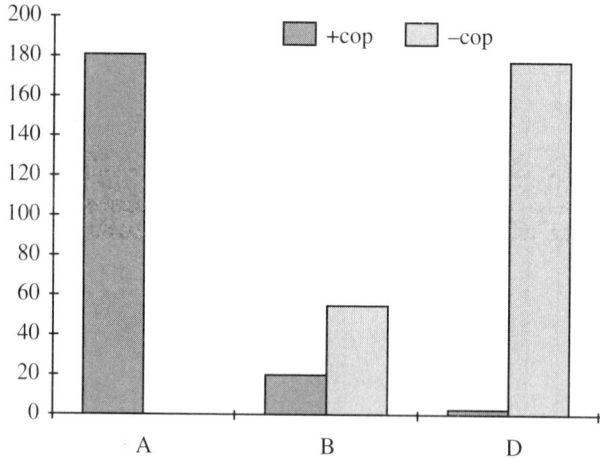

Japanese (A)

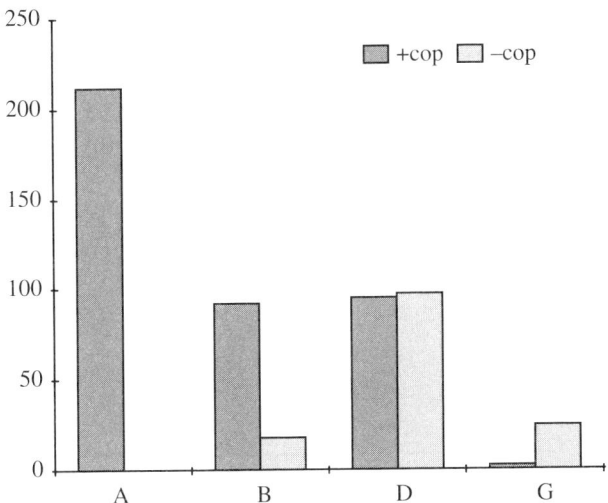

Japanese (B)

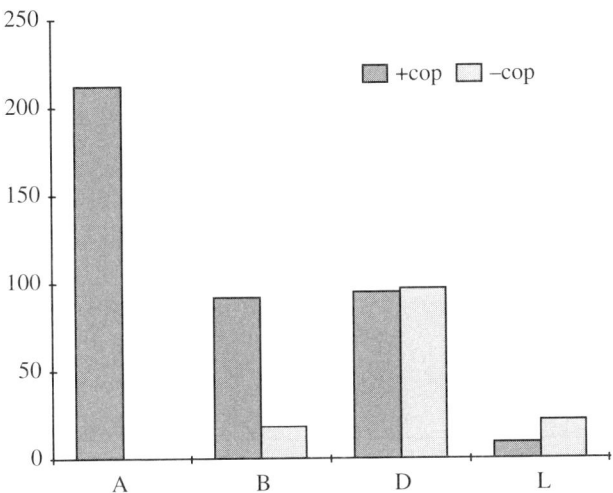

Swahili (A)

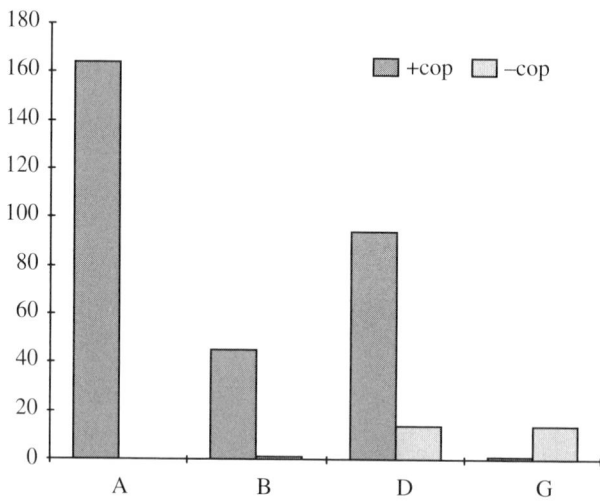

Swahili (B)

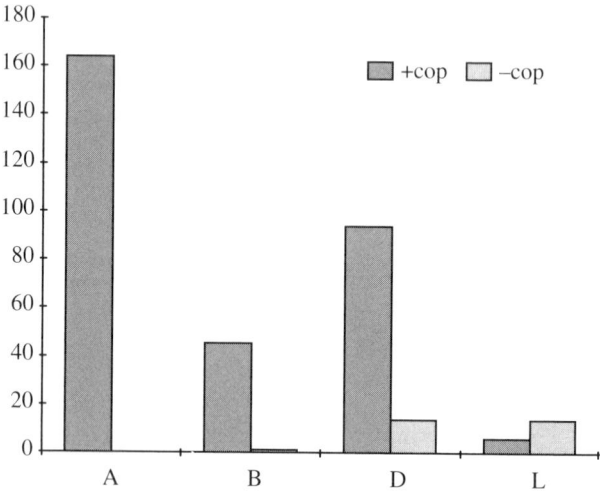

Thai

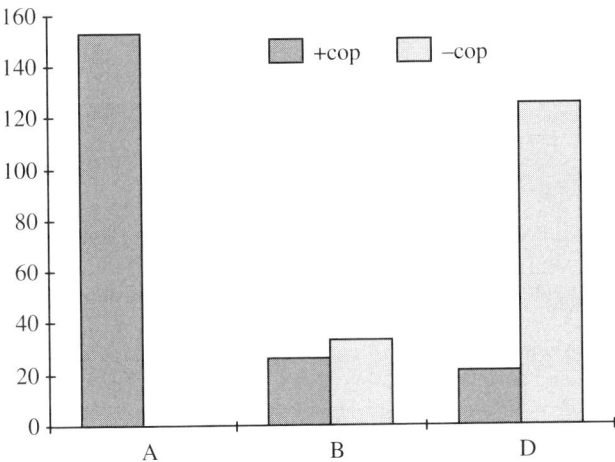

Turkish

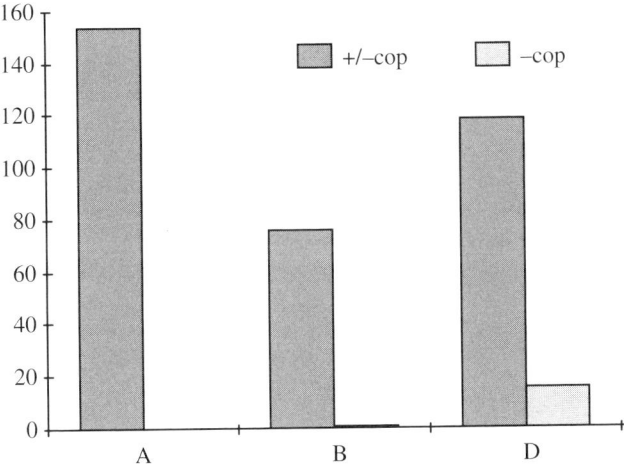

References

Adelaar, W. F. H. (1977). *Tarma Quechua. Grammar, Texts, Dictionary*. Lisse: De Ridder.

Aissen, J. (1987). *Tzotzil Clause Structure*. Dordrecht etc.: Reidel.

Andrade, M. J. (1955). *A Grammar of Modern Yucatec*. Chicago: University of Chicago Library.

Andrews, R. J. (1975). *Introduction to Classical Nahuatl*. Austin, London: University of Texas Press.

Anward, J., Moravcsik, E., and Stassen, L. (1997). 'Parts of speech: a challenge for typology', *Linguistic Typology* 1: 167–83.

Arends, J. (1986). 'Genesis and development of the equative copula in Sranan' in P. C. Muysken and N. Smith (eds.), *Substrata vs. Universals in Creole Genesis*, 103–27. Amsterdam, Philadelphia: Benjamins.

Armstrong, S. L., Gleitman, L. R., and Gleitman, H. (1983). 'What some concepts might not be', *Cognition* 13: 263–308.

Asher, R. E. (1982). *Tamil*. Amsterdam: North-Holland.

——and Kumari, T. C. (1997). *Malayalam*. London: Routledge.

Ashton, E. O. (1944). *Swahili Grammar*. London etc.: Longmans, Green & Co.

Austin, P. (1981). *A Grammar of Diyari, South Australia*. Cambridge etc.: Cambridge University Press.

Barsalou, L. W. and Hale, C. R. (1993). 'Components of conceptual representation: from feature lists to recursive frames' in Van Mechelen *et al.* (eds.), *Categories and Concepts. Theoretical Views and Inductive Data Analysis*, 97–144. London etc.: Academic Press.

Bauer, W. (1993). *Maori*. London, New York: Routledge.

Bell, C. R. V. (1953). *The Somali Language*. London etc.: Longmans, Green & Co.

Benveniste, É. (1946). 'Relations de personne dans le verbe', *BSL* 43: 1–12.

Berger, H. (1998). *Die Burushaski-Sprache von Hunza und Nager*. Wiesbaden: Harrassowitz.

Bhat, D. N. S. (1994). *The Adjectival Category*. Amsterdam, Philadelphia: Benjamins.

——and Ningomba, M. S. (1997). *Manipuri Grammar*. Munich, Newcastle: Lincom Europa.

Bhatia, T. K. (1993). *Punjabi. A Cognitive-Descriptive Grammar*. London, New York: Routledge.

Blair, R. W. and Vermont-Salas, R. (1965/1967). *Spoken Yucatec Maya*. Chicago: University of Chicago, Department of Anthropology.

Bloomfield, L. (1933[2]). *Language*. New York: Holt.

Boas, F. and Deloria, E. (1941). *Dakota Grammar*. Washington, DC: Government Printing Office.

Bolinger, D. (1967). 'Adjectives in English: attribution and predication', *Lingua* 18: 1–34.

Borg, A. and Azzopardi-Alexander, M. (1997). *Maltese*. London, New York: Routledge.

Bouda, K. (1933). *Das Transitive und das Intransitive Verbum des Baskischen*. Amsterdam: Noord-Hollandsche Uitgebers Maatschappei.

Breedveld, J. O. (1995). *Form and Meaning in Fulfulde. A Morphonological Study of Maasinankoore*. Leiden: Research School CNWS.

Bruce, L. (1984). *The Alamblak Language of Papua New Guinea (East Sepik)*. Canberra: Australian National University.

Buechel, E. (1939). *A Grammar of Lakota, the Language of the Teton Sioux Indians*. St. Louis etc.: John S. Swift.

Buechel, E. (1970). *Lakota-English Dictionary*. Pine Ridge, SD: Red Cloud Indian School.

Butt, J. and Benjamin, C. (1988). *A New Reference Grammar of Modern Spanish*. London etc.: Arnold.

Bybee, J. L. and Moder, C. L. (1983). 'Morphological classes as natural categories', *Language* 59: 251–70.

Campión, A. (1884). *Gramática de los Cuatro Dialectos Literarios de la Lengua Euskara*. Bilbao: La gran enciclopedia Vasca.

Carlin, E. (1993). *The So Language*. Köln: Insitut für Afrikanistik.

Chang, S. (1996). *Korean*. Amsterdam, Philadelphia: Benjamins.

Childs, G. T. (1995). *A Grammar of Kisi. A Southern Atlantic Language*. Berlin, New York: Mouton de Gruyter.

Churchward, M. C. (1940). *Rotuman Grammar and Dictionary*. Sydney: AMS.

Churchward, S. (1926). *A New Samoan Grammar*. Samoa: Spectator Publishing.

Closs, E. (1967). 'Some copula constructions in Swahili', *Journal of African Linguistics* 6: 105–31.

Colarusso, J. (1992). *A Grammar of the Kabardian Language*. Calgary: University of Calgary Press.

Cole, D. T. (1955). *An Introduction to Tswana Grammar*. London etc.: Longmans, Green & Co.

Coleman, L. and Kay, D. (1981). 'Prototype semantics: The English word "lie" ', *Language* 57: 26–44.

Comrie, B. (1976). *Aspect*. Cambridge: Cambridge University Press.

Craig, C. (1977). *The Structure of Jacaltec*. Austin, London: University of Texas Press.

Crazzolara, J. P. (1933). *Outlines of a Nuer Grammar*. Wien: Mechitharisten-Buchdruckerei.

——(1938). *A Study of the Acooli Language*. London etc.: Oxford University Press.

——(1960). *A Study of the Logbara (Ma'di) Language. Grammar and Vocabulary*. London etc.: Oxford University Press.

Creider, C. A. and Tapsubei Creider, J. (1993). *A Grammar of Nandi*. Hamburg: Buske.

Croft, W. (1991). *Syntactic Categories and Grammatical Relations*. Chicago, London: University of Chicago Press.

——(1995). 'Autonomy and functionalist linguistics', *Language* 71: 490–532.

——(1999). 'Some contributions of typology to cognitive linguistics' in T. Janssen and G. Redeker (eds.), *Cognitive Linguistics: Foundations, Scope, and Methodology*, 61–93. Berlin, New York: Mouton de Gruyter.

——(2001). *Radical Construction Grammar. Syntactic Theory in Typological Perspective*. Oxford etc.: Oxford University Press.

Cruse, D. A. (1973). 'Some thoughts on agentivity', *Journal of Linguistics* 9: 11–23.

Crystal, D. (1980). *A First Dictionary of Linguistics and Phonetics*. London: Deutsch.

Davies, J. (1981). *Kobon*. Amsterdam: North-Holland.

Dayley, J. P. (1985). *Tzutujil Grammar*. Berkeley etc.: University of California Press.

DeLancey, S. (1984). 'Notes on agentivity and causation', *Studies in Language* 8: 181–213.

Dench, A. (1991). 'Panyjima' in R. M. W. Dixon and B. J. Blake (eds.), *The Handbook of Australian Languages*, vol. 4, 125–244. Amsterdam: Benjamins.

——(1995). *Martuthunira. A Language of the Pilbara Region of Western Australia*. Canberra: The Australian National University.

Derbyshire, D. C. (1979). *Hixkaryana*. Amsterdam: North-Holland.

Dettmer, H. A. (1989). *Ainu-Grammatik*. Wiesbaden: Harrassowitz.

Dixon, R. M. W. (1972). *The Dyirbal Language of North Queensland*. Cambridge: Cambridge University Press.

——(1977a). *A Grammar of Yidiɲ*. London etc.: Cambridge University Press.

——(1977b). 'Where have all the adjectives gone?', *Studies in Language* 1: 19–80.

——(1988). *A Grammar of Boumaa Fijian*. Chicago, London: University of Chicago Press.

Dougherty, J. W. D. (1983). *West Futuna-Aniwa: An Introduction to a Polynesian Outlier Language*. Berkeley etc.: University of California Press.

Du Feu, V. (1996). *Rapanui*. London, New York: Routledge.

Durie, M. (1985). *A Grammar of Acehnese on the Basis of a Dialect of North Aceh*. Dordrecht, Cinnaminson: Foris.

Ebert, K. (1997). *A Grammar of Athpare*. Munich, Newcastle: Lincom Europa.

Eisenberg, P. (1986). *Grundriss der Deutschen Grammatik*. Stuttgart: Metzler.

England, N. C. (1983). *A Grammar of Mam, a Mayan Language*. Austin: University of Texas Press.

Evans, N. (1995). *A Grammar of Kayardild*. Berlin, New York: Mouton de Gruyter.

Everett, D. L. and Kern, B. (1997). *Wari'. The Pacaas Novos Language of Western Brazil*. London, New York: Routledge.

Faraclas, N. G. (1996). *Nigerian Pidgin*. London, New York: Routledge.

Feldman, H. (1986). *A Grammar of Awtuw*. Canberra: Australian National University.

Fillmore, C. J. (1986). 'Pragmatically controlled zero anaphora', *BLS* 12: 95–107.

Foley, W. (1991). *The Yimas Language of New Guinea*. Stanford: Stanford University Press.

Frajzyngier, Z. (1986). 'From preposition to copula', *BLS* 12: 371–86.

——(1989). *A Grammar of Pero*. Berlin: Reimer.

Frantz, D. G. (1991). *Blackfoot Grammar*. Toronto etc.: University of Toronto Press.

Galloway, B. D. (1993). *A Grammar of Upriver Halkomelem*. Berkeley etc.: University of California Press.

Gary, J. O. and Gamal-Eldin, S. (1982). *Cairene Egyptian Colloquial Arabic*. Amsterdam: North-Holland.

Geeraerts, D. (1988). 'Where does prototypicality come from?' in B. Rudzka-Ostyn (ed.), 207–29.

Geerdts, D. B. (1988). *Object and Absolutive in Halkomelem Salish*. New York, London: Garland.

Givón, T. (1979). *On Understanding Grammar*. New York etc.: Academic Press.

——(1984). *Syntax. A Functional-Typological Introduction*. Amsterdam, Philadelphia: Benjamins.

—— (1986). 'Prototypes: Between Plato and Wittgenstein' in C. Craig (ed.), *Noun Classes and Categorization*, 77–102. Amsterdam, Philadelphia: Benjamins.

——(1991). 'Markedness in grammar: distributional, communicative and cognitive correlates of syntactic structure', *Studies in Language* 15: 335–70.

——(1995). *Functionalism and Grammar*. Amsterdam, Philadelphia: Benjamins.

Glinert, L. (1989). *The Grammar of Modern Hebrew*. Cambridge: Cambridge University Press.

Greenberg, J. (1966). *Universals of Language with Particular Reference to Feature Hierarchies*. The Hague: Mouton.

Greene, L. A. (1999). *A Grammar of Belizean Creole*. New York etc.: Peter Lang.

Haiman, J. (1980). *Hua: A Papuan Language of the Eastern Highlands of New Guinea*. Amsterdam, Philadelphia: Benjamins.

Halliday, M. A. K. (1994). *An Introduction to Functional Grammar*. London etc.: Arnold.

Hamel, P. J. (1994). *A Grammar and Lexicon of Loniu, Papua New Guinea*. Canberra: Australian National University.

Hampton, J. (1993). 'Prototype models of concept representation', in Van Mechelen *et al.* (eds.), 67–95.

——(1998). 'Similarity-based categorization and fuzziness of natural categories', *Cognition* 65: 137–65.

Harms, P. L. (1994). *Epena Pedee Syntax*. Arlington: Summer Institute of Linguistics & University of Texas Press.

Harrison, S. P. and Albert, S. Y. (1976). *Mokilese Reference Grammar*. Honolulu: The University Press of Hawaii.

Hashimoto, A. Y. (1969). 'The verb "to be" in Modern Chinese' in J. W. M. Verhaar (ed.), *The Verb 'be' and its Synonyms*, vol. 9, 72–111, Dordrecht: Reidel.

Haspelmath, M. (1993). *A Grammar of Lezgian*. Berlin, New York: Mouton de Gruyter.

Haviland, J. (1979). 'Guugu Yimidhirr' in R. M. W. Dixon and B. J. Blake (eds.), *The Handbook of Australian Languages*, vol. 1, 27–180. Amsterdam, Philadelphia: Benjamins.

Hayward, D. (1984). *The Arbore Language: A First Investigation*. Hamburg: Buske.

Heath, J. (1999). *A Grammar of Koyra Chiini. The Songhay of Timbuktu*. Berlin, New York: Mouton de Gruyter.

Heidolph, K. E. *et al.* (1981). *Grundzüge einer Deutschen Grammatik*. Berlin: Akademie Verlag.

Heine, B. (1993). *Auxiliaries. Cognitive Forces and Grammaticalization*. New York, Oxford: Oxford University Press.

——, Claudi U. and Hünnemeyer, F. (1991). *Grammaticalization. A Conceptual Framework*. Chicago, London: University of Chicago Press.

Hengeveld, K. (1986). 'Copular verbs in a functional grammar of Spanish', *Linguistics* 24: 393–420.

——(1990). 'A functional analysis of copula constructions in Mandarin Chinese', *Studies in Language* 14: 291–323.

——(1992). *Non-verbal Predication*. Berlin, New York: Mouton de Gruyter.

Hercus, L. A. (1994). *A Grammar of the Arabana-Wangkangurru Language, Lake Eyre Basin, South Australia*. Canberra: The Australian National University.

Hewitt, B. G. (1979). *Abkhaz*. Amsterdam: North-Holland.

Hilders, J. H. and Lawrence, J. C. D. (1956). *An Introduction to the Ateso Language*. Nairobi etc.: The Eagle Press.

Hinds, J. (1988). *Japanese*. London, New York: Routledge.

Hoddinott, W. G. and Kofod, F. M. (1988). *The Ngankikurungkurr Language (Daly River Area, Northern Territory)*. Canberra: The Australian National University.

Hoffmann, C. (1963). *A Grammar of the Margi Language*. London: Oxford University Press.

Hollenbach, B. E. (1992). 'A syntactic sketch of Copala Trique' in H. C. Bradley and B. E. Hollenbach (eds.), *Studies in the Syntax of Mixtecan Languages*, vol. 4, 173–431. Arlington: Summer Institute of Linguistics & University of Texas.

Hopper, P. J. and Thompson, S. A. (1980). 'Transitivity in grammar and discourse', *Language* 56: 251–99.

——and Thompson, S. A. (1984). 'The discourse basis for lexical categories in universal grammar', *Language* 60: 703–52.

——and——(1985). 'The iconicity of the universal categories "noun" and "verb" ' in J. Haiman (ed.), *Iconicity in Syntax*, 151–83. Amsterdam, Philadelphia: Benjamins.

——and Traugott, E. C. (1993). *Grammaticalization*. Cambridge: Cambridge University Press.

Howeidy, A. (1953). *Concise Hausa Grammar*. Wheatley, Oxford: Ronald.

Huttar, G. L. and Huttar, M. L. (1994). *Ndyuka*. London, New York: Routledge.

Jakobson, R. (1971). *Selected Writings*. The Hague: Mouton.

Jansky, H. (1986[11]). *Lehrbuch der Türkischen Sprache*. Wiesbaden: Harrassowitz.

Jensen, J. T. (1977). *Yapese Reference Grammar*. Honolulu: The University Press of Hawaii.

Jespersen, O. (1924). *The Philosophy of Grammar*. London: Allen & Unwin.

Jones, W. and Jones, P. (1991). *Barasano Syntax*. Arlington: Summer Institute of Linguistics & University of Texas.

Josephs, L. S. (1975). *Palauan Reference Grammar*. Honolulu: The University Press of Hawaii.

Junger, J. (1981). 'Copula constructions in Modern Hebrew' in T. Hoekstra, H. Van der Hulst, and M. Moortgart (eds.), *Perspectives on Functional Grammar*, 117–34. Dordrecht: Foris.

Kastenholz, R. (1998). *Grundkurs Bambara (Manding) mit Texten*. Köln: Köppe.

Keenan, E. (1976). 'Towards a universal definition of subject' in C. Li (ed.), *Subject and Topic*, 303–33. New York: Academic Press.

Keesing, R. M. (1985). *Kwaio Grammar*. Canberra: The Australian National University.

Kenesei, I., Vago, R. M. and Fenyvesi, A. (1998). *Hungarian*. London, New York: Routledge.

Khim, A. (1994). *Kriyol Syntax. The Portuguese-based Creole Language of Guinea-Bissau*. Amsterdam, Philadelphia: Benjamins.

Kimball, G. D. (1991). *Koasati Grammar*. Lincoln, London: University of Nebraska Press.

Klamer, M. (1994). *Kambera. A Language of Eastern Indonesia*. Den Haag: Holland Institute of Generative Linguistics.

Kohnen, B. (1933). *Shilluk Grammar*. Verona: Missioni Africane.

Kornfilt, J. (1997). *Turkish*. London, New York: Routledge.

Koshal, S. (1979). *Ladakhi Grammar*. Delhi etc.: Motilal Banarsidass.

Kouwenberg, S. (1994). *Berbice Dutch Creole*. Berlin, New York: Mouton de Gruyter.

Kraft, C. H. and Kraft, M. G. (1973). *Introductory Hausa*. Berkeley etc.: University of California Press.

Krishnamurti, B. and Gwynn, J. P. L. (1985). *A Grammar of Modern Telugu*. Delhi etc.: Oxford University Press.

Kuipers, A. H. (1967). *The Squamish Language*. The Hague: Mouton.

Kuno, S. and Wongkhomthong, P. (1981). 'Characterizational and identificational sentences in Thai', *Studies in Language* 5: 65–109.

Kutsch Lojenga, C. (1994). *Ngiti. A Central-Sudanic Language of Zaire*. Köln: Köppe.

Lakoff, G. (1973). 'Hedges: A study in meaning criteria and the logic of fuzzy concepts', *Journal of Philosophical Logic* 2: 458–508.

——(1977). 'Linguistic gestalts', *CLS* 13: 236–87.

——(1987). *Women, Fire and Dangerous Things: What Categories Reveal about the Mind*. Chicago: University of Chicago Press.

——and Johnson, M. (1980). *Metaphors We Live By*. Chicago: University of Chicago Press.

——and——(1999). *Philosophy in the Flesh*. New York: Basic Books.

Langacker, R. (1987). 'Nouns and verbs', *Language* 63: 53–94.

——(1988). 'The nature of grammatical valence' in B. Rudzka-Ostyn (ed.), 91–125.

Lee, H. H. B. (1989). *Korean Grammar*. Oxford: Oxford University Press.

Lehtinen, M. (1963). *Basic Course in Finnish*. Bloomington, Indiana: Indiana University Press.

Lewis, G. L. (1967). *Turkish Grammar*. Oxford: Clarendon.

Li, C. (ed.) (1977). *Mechanisms of Syntactic Change*. Austin, London: University of Texas Press.

——and Thompson, S. A. (1977). 'A mechanism for the development of copula morphemes' in C. Li (ed.), 419–43.

——and——(1981). *Mandarin Chinese. A Functional Reference Grammar*. Berkeley etc.: University of California Press.

Lichtenberk, F. (1983). *A Grammar of Manam*. Honolulu: University of Hawaii Press.

Long, R., Koita, M., and Konaré, M. (1970/71). *Basic Bambara*. Bloomington, Indiana: Indiana University.

Lyons, J. (1968). *Introduction to Theoretical Linguistics*. Cambridge etc.: Cambridge University Press.

——(1977). *Semantics*. Cambridge etc.: Cambridge University Press.

Macaulay, M. (1996). *A Grammar of Chalcatongo Mixtec*. Berkeley etc.: University of California Press.

Macdonald, R. R. and Darjowidjojo, S. (1967). *A Students' Reference Grammar of Modern Formal Indonesian*. Washington, DC.: Georgetown University Press.

MacKay, C. (1999). *A Grammar of Misantla Totonac*. Salt Lake City: University of Utah Press.

Mahootian, S. (1997). *Persian*. London: Routledge.

Martin, S. E. (1975). *A Reference Grammar of Japanese*. New Haven: Yale University Press.

Matthews, P. H. (1981). *Syntax*. Cambridge etc.: Cambridge University Press.

Matthews, S. and Yip, V. (1994). *Cantonese: A Comprehensive Grammar*. London, New York: Routledge.

McGregor, R. S. (1977). *Outline of Hindi Grammar*. Delhi: Oxford University Press.

McGregor, W. (1990). *A Functional Grammar of Gooniyandi*. Amsterdam, Philadelphia: Benjamins.

Mervis, C. G. and Rosch, E. (1981). 'Categorization of natural objects', *Annual Review of Psychology* 32: 89–115.

Migeod, F. W. H. (1914). *A Grammar of the Hausa Language*. London: Kegan Paul.

Miller, M. (1999). *Desano Grammar*. Dallas: Summer Institute of Linguistics & University of Texas at Arlington.

Misra, B. G. (ed.) (1979). *Ladakhi Grammar*. Delhi etc.: Motilal Banarsidass.

Morphy, F. (1983). 'Djapu, a Yolngu dialect' in R. M. W. Dixon and B. J. Blake (eds.), *The Handbook of Australian Languages*, vol. 3, 1–188. Amsterdam: Benjamins.

Morse, N. L. and Maxwell, M. B. (1999). *Cubeo Grammar*. Dallas: Summer Institute of Linguistics & University of Texas Press.

Mosel, U. and Hovdhaugen, E. (1992). *Samoan Reference Grammar*. Oslo: Scandinavian University Press.

Mous, M. (1993). *A Grammar of Iraqw*. Hamburg: Buske.

Munro, P. (1976). *Mojave Syntax*. New York, London: Garland.

——(1977). 'From existential to copula: the history of Yuman BE' in C. Li (ed.), 445–90.

——(ed.) (1990). *Kawaiisu. A Grammar and Dictionary with Texts*. Berkeley etc.: University of California Press.

Newman, P. (2000). *The Hausa Language. An Encyclopedic Reference Grammar*. New Haven, London: Yale University Press.

Noonan, M. (1992). *A Grammar of Lango*. Berlin, New York: Mouton de Gruyter.

Nordlinger, R. (1998). *A Grammar of Wambaya, Northern Territory (Australia)*. Canberra: The Australian National University.

Noss, R. B. (1964). *Thai Reference Grammar*. Washington, DC: Foreign Service Institute.

Oinas, F. J. (1966). *Basic Course in Estonian*. Bloomington, Indiana: Indiana University Press.

Okell, J. (1969). *A Reference Grammar of Colloquial Burmese*. London: Oxford University Press.

Parker, G. J. (1969). *Ayacucho Quechua Grammar and Dictionary*. The Hague, Paris: Mouton.

Popjes, J. and Popjes, J. (1986). 'Canela-Krahô' in D. C. Derbyshire and G. K. Pullum (eds.), *Handbook of Amazonian Languages*, vol. 1, 128–99. Berlin, New York: Mouton de Gruyter.

Poppe, N. (1954). *Grammar of Written Mongolian*. Wiesbaden: Harrassowitz.

——(1960). *Buriat Grammar*. The Hague: Mouton.

——(1970). *Mongolian Language Handbook*. Washington, DC: Center for Applied Linguistics.

Porroche Ballesteros, M. (1988). *Ser, Estar y Verbos de Cambio*. Madrid: Arco/Libros.

Pulkina, I. M. (1978). *A Short Russian Reference Grammar*. Moscow: Russian Language Publ.

Pustet, R. (1989). *Die Morphosyntax des 'Adjektivs' im Sprachvergleich*. Frankfurt a. M. etc.: Lang.

——(2000). 'How arbitrary is lexical categorization? Verbs vs. adjectives', *Linguistic Typology* 4: 175–212.

——(2001). 'Copula and time-stability' in A. Cienki, B. J. Luka, and M. B. Smith (eds.), *Conceptual and Discourse Factors in Linguistic Structure*, 185–96. Stanford, CA: CSLI Publications.

——(forthcoming). *Lakota Texts*. Lincoln, London: University of Nebraska Press.

Quirk, R. *et al.* (1972). *A Grammar of Contemporary English*. London: Longman.

Refsing, K. (1986). *The Ainu Language*. Aarhus: Aarhus University Press.

Rehg, K. L. (1981). *Ponapean Reference Grammar*. Honolulu: The University Press of Hawaii.

Renck, G. L. (1975). *A Grammar of Yagaria*. Canberra: Australian National University.

Rennison, J. R. (1997). *Koromfe*. London: Routledge.

Robinson, C. H. (1953⁵). *Hausa Grammar*. London: Routledge & Kegan Paul.

Rosch, E. (1973a). 'Natural categories', *Cognitive Psychology* 4: 328–50.

——(1973b). 'On the internal structure of perceptual and semantic categories' in T. E. Moore (ed.), *Cognitive Development and the Acquisition of Language*, 111–44. New York: Academic Press.

——(1975a). 'Universals and cultural specifics in human categorization' in R. W. Brislin, S. Bochner, and W. J. Lonner (eds.), *Cross-cultural Perspectives on Learning*, 177–206. New York: Wiley.

——(1975b). 'Cognitive representations of semantic categories', *Journal of Experimental Psychology: General* 104: 192–233.

——(1978). 'Principles of categorization' in E. Rosch and B. B. Lloyd (eds.), *Cognition and Categorization*, 27–48. Hillsdale, NJ: Erlbaum.

——, Gray, W. D., Johnson, D. M., and Boyes-Braem, P. (1976). 'Basic objects in natural categories', *Cognitive Psychology* 8: 382–439.

——and Mervis, C. B. (1975). 'Family resemblances: Studies in the internal structure of categories', *Cognitive Psychology* 7: 573–605.

Rudzka-Ostyn, B. (ed.) (1988). *Topics in Cognitive Linguistics*. Amsterdam, Philadelphia: Benjamins.

Ruhlen, M. (1987). *A Guide to the World's Languages*. London: Arnold.

Saeed, J. I. (1987). *Somali Reference Grammar*. Wheaton, Maryland: Dunwoody Press.

Saltarelli, M. (1988). *Basque*. London, New York: Routledge.

Samarin, W. J. (1966). *The Gbeya Language. Grammar, Texts, and Vocabularies*. Berkeley, Los Angeles: University of California Press.

Sapir, E. (1921²). *Language*. New York: Harcourt, Brace & Co.

Saul, J. E. and Freiberger Wilson, N. (1980). *Nung Grammar*. Arlington: Summer Institute of Linguistics & University of Texas.

Saussure, F. de (1916). *Cours de Linguistique Générale*. Paris: Payot.

Schachter, P. (1985). 'Parts-of-speech systems' in T. Shopen (ed.), *Language Typology and Syntactic Description*, vol. 1, 3–61. Cambridge etc.: Cambridge University Press.

——and Otanes, F. (1972). *Tagalog Reference Grammar*. Berkeley etc.: University of California Press.

Schiffman, H. F. (1983). *A Reference Grammar of Spoken Kannada*. Seattle, London: University of Washington Press.

——(1999). *A Reference Grammar of Spoken Tamil*. New York: Cambridge University Press.

Schön, J. F. (1862). *Grammar of the Hausa Language*. London: Church Missionary House.

Seiler, W. (1985). *Imonda, a Papuan Language*. Canberra: Australian National University.

Senft, G. (1986). *Kilivila. The Language of the Trobriand Islanders*. Berlin etc.: Mouton de Gruyter.

Shibatani, M. (1985). 'Passives and related constructions: a prototype analysis', *Language* 61: 821–48.

——(1990). *The Languages of Japan*. Cambridge etc.: Cambridge University Press.

Sischo, W. R. (1979). 'Michoacán Nahual' in R. Langacker (ed.), *Modern Aztec Grammatical Sketches*, 308–80. Arlington: Summer Institute of Linguistics & University of Texas.

Sjoberg, A. F. (1963). *Uzbek Structural Grammar*. The Hague: Mouton.

Smith, E. W. (1907). *A Handbook of the Ila Language*. Ridgewood, New Jersey: The Gregg Press.

Snapp, A., Anderson, J., and Anderson, J. (1982). 'Northern Paiute' in R. Langacker (ed.), *Uto-Aztecan Grammatical Sketches*, 1–92. Arlington: Summer Institute of Linguistics & University of Texas.

Sneddon, J. N. (1996). *Indonesian: A Comprehensive Grammar*. London, New York: Routledge.

Sohn, H. (1976). *Woleaian Reference Grammar*. Honolulu: The University Press of Hawaii.

Spagnolo, L. M. (1933). *Bari Grammar*. Verona: Missioni Africane.

Sridhar, S. N. (1990). *Kannada*. London, New York: Routledge.

Stassen, L. (1994). 'Typology versus mythology: the case of the zero copula', *Nordic Journal of Linguistics* 17: 105–26.

——(1997). *Intransitive Predication*. Oxford: Clarendon.

Strom, C. (1992). *Retuarã Syntax*. Arlington: Summer Institute of Linguistics & University of Texas.

Sulkala, H. and Karjalainen, M. (1992). *Finnish*. London, New York: Routledge.

Talmy, L. (1988). 'Force dynamics in language and cognition', *Cognitive Science* 12: 49–100.

Taylor, F. W. (1959). *A Practical Hausa Grammar*. Oxford: Clarendon.

Thompson, L. C. (1987). *A Vietnamese Reference Grammar*. Honolulu: University of Hawaii Press.

Thompson, S. A. (1988). 'A discourse approach to the cross-linguistic category "adjective"' in J. A. Hawkins (ed.), *Explaining Language Universals*, 167–85. Oxford, New York: Blackwell.

Tomič, O. M. (ed.) (1989). *Markedness in Synchrony and Diachrony*. Berlin, New York: Mouton de Gruyter.

Topping, D. M. (1973). *Chamorro Reference Grammar*. Honolulu: The University Press of Hawaii.

Tosco, M. (1997). *Af Tunni. Grammar, Texts, and Glossary of a Southern Somali Dialect*. Köln: Köppe.

Tovar, A. (1957). *The Basque Language*. Philadelphia: University of Pennsylvania Press.

Traugott, E. C. and Heine, B. (eds.) (1991). *Approaches to Grammaticalization*. Amsterdam, Philadelphia: Benjamins.

Trubetzkoy, N. S. (1939). *Grundzüge der Phonologie*. Prague: Cercle Linguistique de Prague.

Tucker, A. N. (1993). *A Grammar of Kenya Luo (Dholuo)*. Köln: Köppe.

——and Mpaayei, O. T. (1955). *A Maasai Grammar*. London: Longmans, Green & Co.

Tversky, A. (1977). 'Features of similarity', *Psychological Review* 84: 327–52.

Umandi (1976). *Gramatica Vasca*. Tolosa: ESET.

Van Driem, G. (1987). *A Grammar of Limbu*. Berlin etc.: Mouton de Gruyter.

——(1993). *A Grammar of Dumi*. Berlin etc.: Mouton de Gruyter.

Van Mechelen, I., Hampton, J., Michalski, R. S., and Theuns, P. (eds.) (1993). *Categories and Concepts. Theoretical Views and Inductive Data Analysis*. London etc.: Academic Press.

Verhaar, J. W. M. (1995). *Toward a Reference Grammar of Tok Pisin*. Honolulu: University of Hawaii Press.

Vogel, P. M. and Comrie, B. (eds.) (2000). *Approaches to the Typology of Word Classes*. Berlin, New York: Mouton de Gruyter.

Ward, I. C. (1952). *An Introduction to the Yoruba Language*. Cambridge: Heffer.

Welmers, W. E. (1973). *African Language Structures*. Berkeley etc.: University of California Press.

Wetzer, H. (1996). *The Typology of Adjectival Predication*. Berlin, New York: Mouton de Gruyter.

Whorf, B. L. (1950). 'An American Indian model of the universe', *International Journal of American Linguistics* 16: 67–72.

Wierzbicka, A. (1986). 'What's in a noun? (Or: how do nouns differ in meaning from adjectives?)', *Studies in Language* 10: 353–89.

——(1990). 'Prototypes save: On the uses and abuses of the notion of "prototype" in linguistics and related fields' in S. L. Tsohatzidis (ed.), *Meanings and Prototypes: Studies in Linguistic Categorization*, 347–67. London: Routledge.

——(1995). 'Adjectives vs. verbs: the iconicity of part-of-speech membership' in M. E. Landsberg (ed.), *Syntactic Iconicity and Linguistic Freezes*, 223–45. Berlin, New York: Mouton de Gruyter.

Wittgenstein, L. (1918). *Tractatus Logico Philosophicus*. New York: The Humanities Press.

Woollams, G. (1996). *A Grammar of Karo Batak, Sumatra*. Canberra: The Australian National University.

Yallop, C. (1977). *Alyawarra. An Aboriginal Language of Central Australia*. Canberra: Australian Institute of Aboriginal Studies.

Young, F. W. (1987). *Multidimensional Scaling: History, Theory, and Applications*. Hillsdale, NJ: Erlbaum.

Young, R. W. and Morgan, W. (1987). *The Navajo Language. A Grammar and Colloquial Dictionary*. Albuquerque: University of New Mexico Press.

Zepeda, O. (1988). *A Papago Grammar*. Tucson, Arizona: University of Arizona Press.

Zipf, G. K. (1935). *The Psychobiology of Language*. Boston: Houghton Mifflin.

Zwicky, A. M. (1993). 'Heads, bases and functors' in G. G. Corbett, N. M. Fraser, and S. McGlashan (eds.), *Heads in Grammatical Theory*, 291–333. Cambridge etc.: Cambridge University Press.

Zylstra, C. F. (1991). 'A syntactic sketch of Alacatlatzala Mixtec' in H. C. Bradley and B. E. Hollenbach (eds.), *Studies in the Syntax of Mixtecan Languages*, vol. 3, 1–177. Arlington: Summer Institute of Linguistics & University of Texas.

Index